Silhouetted against the late-night sun, a lone U.S. soldier walks guard along a barbed-wire barricade protecting the harbor at Camp Laugarnec, Iceland. Iceland was one of countless outposts where Allied troops manned support bases or fought bitter campaigns on the fringes of the major combat zones.

# WAR IN THE OUTPOSTS

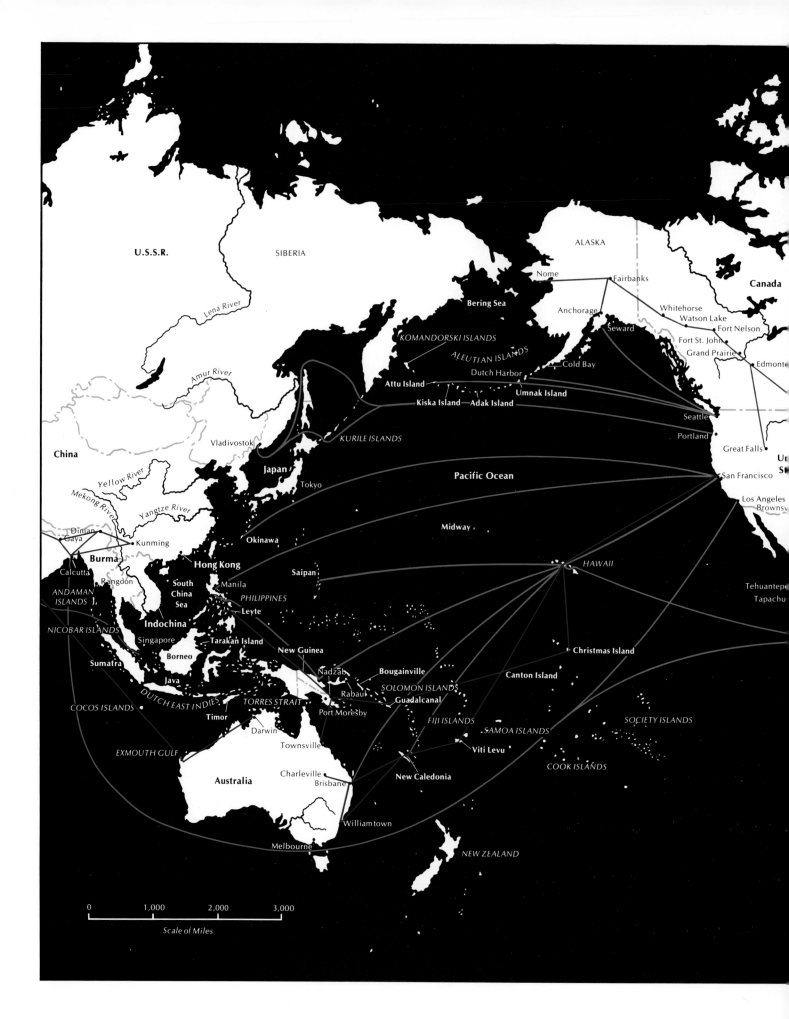

Greenland

Spitzbergen

Longyear City
Barentsburg

Little Koldewey Island

Shannon Island
Sandodden Sabine Island
Eskimonaes

Scoresbysund Jan Mayen
*SCORESBY SOUND*

Tromso
Murmansk

Iceland

Archangel

Bluie West 8

U.S.S.R.

Reykjavik
Trondheim

Ivigtut Bluie West 1

*Volga River*

*SHETLAND ISLANDS*

Prestwick
Liverpool
Antwerp
Moscow

Goose Bay

NEWFOUNDLAND
Gander
Berlin
Minneapolis
St. John's London
Stephenville *ENGLISH CHANNEL* Paris
Dorval Odessa
Vichy
Boston Presque Isle Marseilles
New York *Greece*
*Mississippi River* *AZORES*
Hampton Roads Lisbon Naples Habbaniya Teheran
Charleston *Sicily* *Crete* Lydda New Delhi
Orleans Casablanca *Mediterranean Sea* Cairo Basra Khurramshahr
Bermuda Suez Jodhpur
West Palm Beach Karachi Agra
Tampico Miami *SUEZ CANAL* *PERSIAN* India
Veracruz Nassau El Fasher *Nile River* *GULF* Bombay
Puerto Rico El Geneina Aden
*Atlantic Ocean* Dakar Fort-Lamy Khartoum Asmara *GULF OF ADEN* Bangalore
*Caribbean Sea* Kano El Obeid Socotra Trincomalee
*Niger River* Maiduguri Colombo
Panama Trinidad Freetown Lagos *Africa* Ceylon
Managua Monrovia Accra *MALDIVE ISLANDS*
Takoradi *Congo River*
*Amazon River* Belém Leopoldville Addu Atoll
Natal
Diego Garcia
Ascension Island
South
America Mombasa

St. Helena Mauritius

Madagascar

*Indian Ocean*

Durban
Cape Town

*CAPE OF GOOD HOPE*

The supply lines used by the Allies in World War II were chosen to
avoid major combat zones and territories conquered by the Axis powers.
Sea-lanes (blue), following chains of support bases, curved around
Africa to Egypt, the Middle East, India and Burma; circled Scandinavia
to Soviet ports; and veered across the Pacific to Siberia, New Zealand
and Australia. Air cargo routes (red) zigzagged to islands and
across safe land areas where airstrips were built for refueling stops.

3

*Other Publications:*
THE EPIC OF FLIGHT
THE GOOD COOK
THE SEAFARERS
THE ENCYCLOPEDIA OF COLLECTIBLES
THE GREAT CITIES
HOME REPAIR AND IMPROVEMENT
THE WORLD'S WILD PLACES
THE TIME-LIFE LIBRARY OF BOATING
HUMAN BEHAVIOR
THE ART OF SEWING
THE OLD WEST
THE EMERGENCE OF MAN
THE AMERICAN WILDERNESS
THE TIME-LIFE ENCYCLOPEDIA OF GARDENING
LIFE LIBRARY OF PHOTOGRAPHY
THIS FABULOUS CENTURY
FOODS OF THE WORLD
TIME-LIFE LIBRARY OF AMERICA
TIME-LIFE LIBRARY OF ART
GREAT AGES OF MAN
LIFE SCIENCE LIBRARY
THE LIFE HISTORY OF THE UNITED STATES
TIME READING PROGRAM
LIFE NATURE LIBRARY
LIFE WORLD LIBRARY
FAMILY LIBRARY:
   HOW THINGS WORK IN YOUR HOME
   THE TIME-LIFE BOOK OF THE FAMILY CAR
   THE TIME-LIFE FAMILY LEGAL GUIDE
   THE TIME-LIFE BOOK OF FAMILY FINANCE

*Previous World War II Volumes:*
Prelude to War
Blitzkrieg
The Battle of Britain
The Rising Sun
The Battle of the Atlantic
Russia Besieged
The War in the Desert
The Home Front: U.S.A.
China-Burma-India
Island Fighting
The Italian Campaign
Partisans and Guerrillas
The Second Front
Liberation
Return to the Philippines
The Air War in Europe
The Resistance
The Battle of the Bulge
The Road to Tokyo
Red Army Resurgent
The Nazis
Across the Rhine
War under the Pacific

WORLD WAR II · TIME-LIFE BOOKS · ALEXANDRIA, VIRGINIA

BY SIMON RIGGE

AND THE EDITORS OF TIME-LIFE BOOKS

# WAR IN THE OUTPOSTS

Time-Life Books Inc.
is a wholly owned subsidiary of
**TIME INCORPORATED**

Founder: Henry R. Luce 1898-1967

Editor-in-Chief: Henry Anatole Grunwald
Chairman of the Board: Andrew Heiskell
President: James R. Shepley
Editorial Director: Ralph Graves
Vice Chairman: Arthur Temple

**TIME-LIFE BOOKS INC.**

Managing Editor: Jerry Korn
Executive Editor: David Maness
Assistant Managing Editors: Dale M. Brown
(planning), George Constable, George G. Daniels
(acting), Martin Mann, John Paul Porter
Art Director: Tom Suzuki
Chief of Research: David L. Harrison
Director of Photography: Robert G. Mason
Assistant Art Director: Arnold C. Holeywell
Assistant Chief of Research: Carolyn L. Sackett
Assistant Director of Photography: Dolores A. Littles

Chairman: Joan D. Manley
President: John D. McSweeney
Executive Vice Presidents: Carl G. Jaeger,
John Steven Maxwell, David J. Walsh
Vice Presidents: George Artandi (comptroller);
Stephen L. Bair (legal counsel); Peter G. Barnes;
Nicholas Benton (public relations); John L. Canova;
Beatrice T. Dobie (personnel); Carol Flaumenhaft
(consumer affairs); Nicholas J. C. Ingleton (Asia);
James L. Mercer (Europe/South Pacific);
Herbert Sorkin (production); Paul R. Stewart
(marketing)

**WORLD WAR II**

Editorial Staff for War in the Outposts
Editor: Gerald Simons
Designer/Picture Editor: Raymond Ripper
Chief Researcher: Charles S. Clark
Picture Editor: Clara Nicolai
Text Editors: Bobbie Conlan, Brian McGinn,
Robert Menaker, Mark M. Steele, Henry Woodhead
Staff Writers: Donald Davison Cantlay,
Peter Kaufman, Glenn Martin McNatt, John Newton
Researchers: Kristin Baker, LaVerle Berry,
Loretta Britten, Jane Freundel, Cronin Buck Sleeper,
Reiko Uyeshima, Betty Hughes Weatherly,
Jayne T. Wise, Paula York
Art Assistants: Mary L. Orr, Susan K. White
Editorial Assistant: Connie Strawbridge

Special Contributors
Champ Clark, Keith Wheeler (text)

Editorial Production
Production Editor: Douglas B. Graham
Operations Manager: Gennaro C. Esposito,
Gordon E. Buck (assistant)
Assistant Production Editor: Feliciano Madrid
Quality Control: Robert L. Young (director),
James J. Cox (assistant), Daniel J. McSweeney,
Michael G. Wight (associates)
Art Coordinator: Anne B. Landry
Copy Staff: Susan B. Galloway (chief), Allan Fallow,
Victoria Lee, Barbara F. Quarmby, Celia Beattie
Picture Department: Alvin L. Ferrell

Correspondents: Elisabeth Kraemer (Bonn); Margot
Hapgood, Dorothy Bacon, Lesley Coleman (London);
Susan Jonas, Lucy T. Voulgaris (New York); Maria
Vincenza Aloisi, Josephine du Brusle (Paris); Ann
Natanson (Rome). Valuable assistance was also
provided by: Wibo van de Linde (Amsterdam);
Katrina Van Duyn (Copenhagen); Bing Wong (Hong
Kong); Judy Aspinall, Karin B. Pearce (London); John
Dunn (Melbourne); Carolyn T. Chubet, Miriam Hsia,
Christina Lieberman (New York); John Scott (Ottawa);
M. T. Hirschkoff (Paris); Mimi Murphy (Rome);
Susumu Naoi, Katsuko Yamazaki (Tokyo).

The Author: SIMON RIGGE is a writer and editor based
in London. He was executive editor of the eight-
volume History of the 20th Century, published in
Great Britain and on the European continent. He also
served as deputy editor of the Time-Life Books series
The World's Wild Places and as series editor of The
Great Cities. He has written numerous articles on
military and general history.

The Consultants: COLONEL JOHN R. ELTING, USA (Ret.),
is a military historian and author of The Battle of
Bunker's Hill, The Battles of Saratoga and Military
History and Atlas of the Napoleonic Wars. He edited
Military Uniforms in America: The Era of the Ameri-
can Revolution, 1755-1795 and Military Uniforms in
America: Years of Growth, 1796-1851, and was asso-
ciate editor of The West Point Atlas of American Wars.

HENRY H. ADAMS is a retired Navy captain who served
aboard the destroyer U.S.S. Owen in the major campaigns of the central Pacific. After his service in World
War II he was a professor at the U.S. Naval Academy
in Annapolis, Maryland, and was later head of the
English Department at Illinois State University. His
books include 1942: The Year That Doomed the Axis,
Years of Deadly Peril, Years of Expectation, Years to
Victory and Harry Hopkins: A Biography.

NORMAN R. BENNETT, Professor of History at Boston
University, has lived and taught in several nations of
eastern Africa. He has served as President of the African Studies Association and is editor of the International Journal of African Historical Studies. His books
include Studies in East African History and Africa and
Europe from Roman Times to the Present.

JOSEPH J. MALONE, President of the consulting firm
Middle East Research Associates, Inc. in Washington,
D.C., has lived and taught in Iran and the Arab world
periodically since 1952. Formerly Chairman of the
History Department at the American University in
Beirut and Director of Middle Eastern Studies at the
National War College, he served as an analyst at the
U.S. Army's Intelligence and Special Weapons School
in Germany. His books include The Arab Lands of
Western Asia and Britain and Iraq: Involvement in an
Ottoman Pashalic.

**Library of Congress Cataloguing in Publication Data**
Rigge, Simon.
    War in the Outposts.

    (World War II; v. 24)
    Bibliography: p.
    Includes index.
    1. World War, 1939-1945—Campaigns.
I. Time-Life Books.    II. Title.    III. Series.
D743.R54      940.54'1      80-8532
ISBN 0-8094-3381-8
ISBN 0-8094-3380-X (lib. bdg.)
ISBN 0-8094-3379-6 (retail ed.)

For information about any Time-Life book, please write:

Reader Information
Time-Life Books
541 North Fairbanks Court
Chicago, Illinois 60611

# CONTENTS

# MANNING THE ATLANTIC FRONT

On balmy Bermuda, American troops are inspected by the British governor in November of 1941. This base placed U.S. forces 600 miles out in the Atlantic.

# AN AGGRESSIVE DEFENSE OF THE AMERICAS

When the United States declared war on the Axis powers in December 1941, one of its few military assets was a picket line of strategic bases in the Atlantic. These bases greatly enhanced the range of U.S. naval and air patrols, and they grew more important as Germany broadened its U-boat war. The Army troops manning the outposts had little to do but sit and wait, yet their presence forestalled any German attempt to advance westward from occupied Europe.

The architect of the U.S. Atlantic defense system was President Franklin D. Roosevelt, who pressed his base-building plans despite stiff opposition at home. His first effort, begun on September 6, 1939 (three days after the start of World War II), was to strengthen the three weak U.S. bases in the Atlantic: the naval enclave in Cuba's Guantá-namo Bay, a radio and hydrographic station on Puerto Rico, and the Panama Canal, which was—said its commander—''vulnerable to attack at any time.'' F.D.R. also created a ''neutrality patrol'' to sweep a 300-mile-wide belt of coastal waters reaching from northern Canada to South America.

Then in September 1940, Roosevelt scored a major defensive triumph. He arranged a pact with Britain that gave the United States 99-year leases to build and maintain bases on the Bahamas, Jamaica, St. Lucia, Antigua, Trinidad and British Guiana. In return, the hard-pressed Royal Navy got 50 overage destroyers of a type that the States had been selling for scrap at $5,000 each. It was, said F.D.R., ''the most important action for American defense since the 1803 Louisiana Purchase.'' The British, in dire need of warships, were so pleased that Prime Minister Winston Churchill threw in Newfoundland and Bermuda as a bonus.

The Lend-Lease agreement alarmed many conservative Americans; the *New York Daily News* declared, ''The United States has one foot in the war and the other on a banana peel.'' But Roosevelt made even bolder arrangements for bases in Danish Greenland and Iceland. He explained that his strategy was to move in before the enemy did: ''If you hold your fire until you see the whites of his eyes, you will never know what hit you.''

*The United States advanced its prewar Atlantic defenses in three stages: expanding old bases (red dots), leasing British bases (gray squares), acquiring outposts (black crosses) in Brazil and in Danish territories.*

Delivering a Lend-Lease destroyer at Halifax, Nova Scotia, American sailors explain the peculiarities of a 4-inch gun to the ship's Royal Navy crewmen.

*Warships of the U.S. fleet fill the Canal Zone's crowded Balboa Harbor during the Navy's annual springtime maneuvers.*

*Old Navy biplanes line McCalla Hill Field, one of two Naval airfields under construction at Guantánamo Bay in 1940.*

*In the shade of a stone archway, a U.S. soldier stands guard atop the steep ramp entrance to 17th Century Fort San Cristobal in San Juan, Puerto Rico.*

# NEW MUSCLE FOR OLD BASES

With Roosevelt's encouragement, the U.S. Congress in June of 1939 appropriated $50 million to strengthen the defenses of the Panama Canal and outlying bases.

In Panama, the Navy built new depots and barracks, enlarged its submarine base, and modernized air and radio stations.

The Army planted antiaircraft guns and batteries of searchlights in clearings in the jungles and increased its Panama troop strength from 12,000 to 28,000. The influx of GIs so far outstripped the construction of barracks that for a time the men were quartered in the hangars of a local airfield.

To guard the canal's eastern Caribbean approaches, the Army cleared a cow pasture at the northwestern tip of Puerto Rico and within two months built the Point Bo-

rinquen air base for nine long-range B-17s. The Navy constructed another Puerto Rican airfield on a drained portion of the San Juan harbor.

And at Cuba's Guantánamo Bay, four new installations were built in 1940: two airfields, a fuel depot and facilities for 2,000 Marines.

By December 1941, U.S. defenses in the Panama Canal Zone and the Caribbean were manned by 58,000 troops.

*Monitoring signals from a radio direction finder, two soldiers based on Newfoundland track ships and planes traveling along the Atlantic convoy route.*

# YANKEE GARRISONS IN BRITISH COLONIES

Immediately after Roosevelt concluded his 1940 destroyer deal with Great Britain, Army and Navy planners sent American contractors to build airstrips, docks and barracks in the eight British territories. In several colonies, the inhabitants had never before seen such hectic activity. The Bermudians, who had banned automobiles to preserve the tranquillity of their islands, reconciled themselves sadly to the great American trucks that rumbled persistently along their narrow roads with supplies for an airfield and a naval base.

Even before the new facilities were finished, the garrisons began arriving. In late January, 1941, a thousand U.S. soldiers landed at St. John's, Newfoundland. They were the first U.S. troops to set foot on foreign soil in World War II.

By autumn 1941, all eight bases were operational. U.S. air and sea patrols from Newfoundland protected Lend-Lease convoys part of the way to Britain and the north Soviet ports of Murmansk and Archangel. Patrols based at Trinidad, British Guiana and Bermuda guarded the freighters bringing oil and bauxite (to be refined into aluminum) from South America to Baltimore, Philadelphia and New York. Only five Allied merchant ships were sunk off the North American coast before the United States entered the War.

Camouflaged by clumps of palm fronds, a Bermuda ammunition magazine is patrolled by a lone guard from the U.S. naval station.

Army engineers on Trinidad survey a section of tropical forest while beginning construction on one of the island's three U.S. airfields.

At Brazil's Bahia airport on the route to Africa, local workers plant grass with hoes to cut down on dust between newly completed runways. Hand tools were employed in order to spare the time and expense of shipping earth-moving equipment from the United States.

# EASTWARD TO ICELAND, SOUTHWARD TO BRAZIL

In the summer of 1941, the United States advanced its line of bases far across the Atlantic and also established a military presence on the coast of Brazil. At a dozen Brazilian locations, Pan American Airways, supervised by the U.S. Army Corps of Engineers, constructed or improved airstrips from which American-built transports and bombers could be flown across the South Atlantic to British forces in North Africa. In the middle of September, nine U.S. warships began operating from the Brazilian ports of Recife and Bahia, patrolling the Atlantic far to the south.

In the North Atlantic, U.S. forces were sent to garrison Danish Greenland and Iceland. From bases built there, American planes patrolled the nearby convoy routes, escorting merchantmen and warning them of U-boat sightings. Edging closer to war, Roosevelt ordered the U.S. escorts to fire back if attacked. "Convoys mean shooting," he said, "and shooting means war."

U.S. Army troops in Iceland huddle in their tents, half-buried by wind-whipped snowdrifts. The subarctic winter was so fierce that the Army commander recommended limiting a tour of duty so that no one would have to endure two winters. But the suggestion was dropped when the United States joined the War.

# 1

**Monsieur Feline declines to fight**
**Flank campaigns to thwart Axis expansion**
**Middle East subversion by German "tourists"**
**A medieval base in the Arabian Sea**
**A plague of wideawakes**
**The small war for Island X**
**Hunting down will-o'-the-wisp German trawlers**
**The race to occupy Spitzbergen**
**A never-ending struggle against "polar madness"**
**Slaughter on the Barentsburg ice sheet**
**Two mighty battleships to bombard a weather station**

Five British soldiers, together with a handful of local porters and paddlers, spent three days in September of 1942 trekking south from the recently captured port of Tamatave on the east coast of Madagascar. They traveled part of the way in dugout canoes through gloomy mangrove swamps, batting at mosquitoes and warily steering clear of crocodiles.

Finally the little party arrived at the town of Vatomandry, headquarters of a large administrative district, where the enemy was waiting—in the person of a Vichy French *chef de district* named Feline. Monsieur Feline had been warned of the British approach by the Malagasy grapevine and had dressed for the encounter in his best gold-braided uniform.

"You have, of course, some soldiers?" Feline asked the British leader.

The Englishman was amused. He realized that Feline, like several of Madagascar's Vichy officials before him, was trying to avoid a fight yet preserve his honor; the usual charade was to pretend that even a feeble foe was an overwhelming force.

"Yes," he replied. "We have some soldiers."

"Naturally they are armed?"

"Naturally."

"Automatic weapons, I presume?"

"Tommy guns."

Within minutes, the British were enjoying drinks with the district chief, and a cable was on its way to Feline's government: VATOMANDRY OCCUPIED AT 1600 HOURS BY BRITISH FORCES ARMED WITH AUTOMATIC WEAPONS AND SUPPORTED BY ARTILLERY. FURTHER COMMUNICATION IMPOSSIBLE. FELINE.

The British soldiers did not blame Feline for declining to shed blood over his outpost; their first reaction was that the place was hardly worth winning. But one of the Englishmen, sitting on the hotel veranda that night, perceived a real significance in their victory.

"We had added an area of several hundred square miles to the British zone of occupation," he mused. "We had achieved a minute fragment of history."

Madagascar and scores of remote outposts like it had taken on strategic importance, for the war that began in Europe in September 1939 had by now become the first truly worldwide conflict. Every major nation and dozens of small ones had been drawn into the struggle on either side. From

# WARFARE AT WORLD'S END

the pack ice of the Arctic to the peaceful shores of South America to the uninhabited atolls of the Pacific, every stretch of land and sea was a potential combat zone.

In this global struggle, the territorial ambitions of the aggressors quickly established the major theaters. By December 1941, Hitler's Wehrmacht stood at the gates of Moscow; the Germans had engulfed most of Europe and spilled over into North Africa. By the next summer, the Japanese, already the conquerors of much of China and still ravenous for raw materials, had swept across most of the southwest Pacific, through Southeast Asia and into the eastern reaches of the Indian Ocean. The decisive land battles of the War were won or lost in these theaters, which encompassed less than 10 per cent of the world's land surface.

The location of the primary combat zones inexorably shaped the conduct of the War throughout the rest of the world. A basic Allied strategy, originated by the British, called for defending the flanks of the major theaters to prevent further Axis expansion. As a result, many outpost campaigns—holding operations, preemptive strikes and local counterattacks—were mounted in the Middle East, on the islands guarding the approaches to India and Australia, even on the Aleutian Islands extending west from Alaska's coast. In turn, the colossal task of supporting both the major combat zones and the flank campaigns spread a globe-girdling network of small intermediary outposts—air and naval bases, staging areas and weather stations.

By far the most important flank campaigns took place in the oil-rich Middle East, at the juncture of three continents and as many major theaters. In the spring of 1941, with German forces driving into the Balkans and attacking across the Libyan Desert toward Egypt, Prime Minister Winston Churchill feared that Iraq and Vichy French Syria would fall to what he called "petty air forces, tourists and local revolts." The tourists were German fifth columnists who arrived wearing sports jackets and carrying identical suitcases, thus providing a forewarning of Hitler's intentions. Since German take-overs in Iraq and Syria might have forced the British to abandon Egypt, the Suez Canal and Palestine, Churchill decided that it was better to strike first than to be forced to evict an entrenched enemy.

Even after those two campaigns were fought and won, the Allies' troubles in the Middle East were not over. To nip more German subversion in the bud, and to deliver Lend-Lease war matériel to the Soviet Union through the Persian Corridor, the Allies made Iran another target for invasion. And eight months later, the British invaded Madagascar to deny its ports to Japanese submarines that were preying on Allied supply ships en route to Iran.

By striking first in the Middle East, the Allies avoided the fate that befell their troops deep in the southwest Pacific and on the islands athwart seaways into the Indian Ocean. There, Allied forces had to fight their flank campaigns twice: first to contain or delay the advancing Japanese, then to reclaim lost territories. The Australians' defense of Timor and, three years later, their reconquest of Borneo, were classic examples of each stage—and as savage as the better-known battles of the main American island-hopping campaigns to the north.

The flank campaigns differed in detail, but common threads ran through them all. Most of the campaigns were struggles for the colonies or former colonies of Great Britain, France, the Netherlands, Belgium and neutral Portugal. Thus many were marked by those familiar figures of empire, the governor general, the high commissioner and the district chief; by disputes between deposed rulers, client kings and the Allies themselves; and by the deployment of colonial levies—conscripted empire troops led by European officers.

"Where European warfare dealt in armies," wrote John Bagot Glubb, the commander of Trans-Jordan's Arab Legion in the Iraq-Syria campaign, "we handled companies." Moreover, the small forces engaged in flank campaigns ordinarily fought with few weapons and obsolete equipment—all that was left after the Allies had outfitted their huge armies in the major theaters. Many small units made a virtue of their lack of equipment; they fought as guerrillas, unencumbered by heavy weapons. Some companies were elite units expressly trained for irregular operations.

In the aggregate, hundreds of thousands of Allied men took part in the flank campaigns as combat troops or garrison soldiers, and hundreds of thousands more manned the support outposts. Most of the men found their assignments dull and trivial compared with the great battles being fought on Saipan and the beaches of Normandy. Typically, a British subaltern stationed in Palestine lamented the "feeling of futility at being out of it, a spectator in this safe and sun-kissed country while the civilized world, our world, is being rocked to its foundations."

And yet duty in the outposts returned a kind of austere satisfaction to those men who, like the British soldier musing on the veranda in Tamatave on Madagascar, realized that their sideshow often had a considerable impact on the course of the War. Small, grotesquely ill-equipped units pinned down and sometimes defeated much larger enemy forces that might have swung the balance in major battles elsewhere. A few resolute men, in the right outpost at the right time, played more important roles than did whole divisions in monstrous European battles, where soldiers died by the tens of thousands and sometimes succeeded only in establishing which army could better afford the sacrifice.

The support bases were remote by design, proliferating along roundabout sea and air routes to avoid the perils of the major combat zones. But maintaining the distant fronts taxed to the limit the resources of Great Britain and the United States, maritime powers that, with each extension of the War, had to tie up more ships on long voyages and safeguard their passage to far-flung theaters.

Britain was in a particularly difficult position. When Italy entered the War in June 1940, the Mediterranean became a war zone closed to most convoys, and ships bound for Suez, India and beyond had to make a 12,000-mile detour around Africa. The distance from England to Bombay was thus doubled and the distance to Suez was quadrupled.

During 1942 and 1943, Great Britain had more than twice as many troops overseas as the United States, and the British committed more dry-cargo tonnage to the needs of their armed forces than did the Americans (8.5 million versus six million tons). At the same time Britain had to provide shipping to import food and raw materials, whereas the United States imported no food and fewer raw materials.

The Axis domination of the Mediterranean gave new importance to sea routes through the South Atlantic and around Africa—routes that had lain unfurrowed since the opening of the Suez Canal in 1869. Islands that had faded into semioblivion began to appear in Allied war reports. St. Helena, where Napoleon ended his days in British captivity, was used as a British naval base in the South Atlantic. Hostilities even spread to the Antarctic, where armed German merchant cruisers captured Anglo-Norwegian whalers.

On many faraway islands, airstrips were cleared, from which patrol planes covered focal areas and extended surveillances into the empty reaches of the oceans. Repair shops, docks and refueling stations were constructed, from which naval units escorted troopships and supply convoys. On the route through the South Atlantic and the Indian Ocean to Durban, Mombasa, Aden, Bombay, Ceylon and Burma, depots, listening posts and communications centers were built on such little-known Indian Ocean islands as Mauritius, Addu Atoll and Diego Garcia, the Cocos Islands southwest of Sumatra—and Socotra in the Arabian Sea.

Perhaps Socotra was the least known of these remote islands. When the first handful of Allied personnel was ordered there in April 1942, few of the men had any idea where or even what it was; one man thought it was a ship. It was in fact an island 72 miles long, strategically situated at the entrance to the Gulf of Aden; it had been a dependency

*President Franklin D. Roosevelt, wearing a black arm band to mourn his mother's death, shares center stage with British Prime Minister Winston Churchill at a White House press conference on December 23, 1941. The two leaders spent the week working on plans for Anglo-American cooperation, including the establishment of the ABDA (American-British-Dutch-Australian) Command to defend outposts in the southwest Pacific.*

of the British Empire since 1886. The exposed island was difficult to visit owing to its lack of harbors, its abundance of dangerous reefs and desiccating southwest winds, which blew so strongly half the year that no sailing craft could approach from the African mainland. Fishermen could not put out in their dhows to fish, supplies of maize from East Africa stopped, the wadies filled with sand, wells dried up and the grass withered and turned brown. In 1943, about 10 per cent of the Bedouin hill people died of famine, and many who survived by stealing goats had their hands chopped off by the local sultan's executioner.

The sultan, honoring Socotra's 19th Century agreements with Britain, allowed the British to build an airstrip on his medieval island, which was cut off from the modern world without roads, electricity, sanitation or even a doctor. Dribs and drabs of Allied personnel came and went: Royal Air Force pilots and ground crews, detachments of levies from Britain's Aden Protectorate, officers and men of the Royal Netherlands Naval Air Force, companies of Somaliland Scouts, colonial troops from French West Africa and a battalion of the 1st Punjabi Regiment from India.

The first British arrivals lived in caves, then in sandbag huts on the stony northern coastal plain, overlooked by the jagged spires of the central Haggier mountain range. By 1943 the European presence on the island still numbered only a dozen or so RAF men who lived at the edge of the airstrip in a single hut with a corrugated iron roof held down with wire guys. A mile or two away was encamped a detachment of Aden Protectorate levies, commanded by a British officer and two or three British noncoms who messed with the RAF. In May of that year, four Royal Navy radiomen arrived in an Arab coaster and waded to the beach with their equipment and personal kits. Their job was to listen for distress signals from cargo vessels torpedoed by enemy submarines and then transmit the ships' coordinates to Aden so that aircraft could be sent out on rescue missions and on search and destroy operations.

At first, no aircraft were regularly stationed on Socotra, and sometimes two weeks went by without a plane landing there. But on September 27, 1943, two PBY Catalinas with Dutch crews arrived from Mombasa to make their base on the island. "A momentous day!" wrote one of the Royal Navy radiomen in his diary; the new arrivals had more than

doubled the size of the European garrison. The Dutch airmen had a shock when they saw the barren plain and the bell tents in which they would live, but they soon settled in and got on well with the British. Later, Wellington bombers and other aircraft detached from Aden used the airstrip; from time to time, Socotra almost bustled.

The men on the island led a free and easy life, wearing shorts and sandals and doing what they pleased in their off-duty hours. Some visited the tiny capital of Hadibu, with its white flat-roofed houses set among palm trees beyond a rugged spur of the mountains. A few became explorers, trekking off on private missions of archeology or anthropology or searching out such botanical oddities as myrrh and frankincense trees, Adenium trees, cucumber trees, and dragon's-blood trees shaped like umbrellas blown inside out. Most of the men passed the time playing football and cricket on the airstrip, from which they occasionally had to drive away stray camels, and swimming out into the tepid bay from a nearby sandy beach. Their diet of tinned bacon and chapatties (Indian flat bread), corned beef and hard biscuits became monotonous, but it was bearable for the six to 10 months that most of the troops spent on the island.

Small excitements were epic events on Socotra. Ten airmen were killed in various mishaps and buried on Cemetery Hill west of the airfield. Occasionally, survivors from torpedoed merchant ships staggered ashore from lifeboats. Two dhows machine-gunned by a Japanese submarine drifted to the island full of dead and dying men; the survivors were too shocked and weak to jettison the bodies. One of Socotra's Wellington bombers damaged a U-boat with depth charges, forcing it to be scuttled on the coast of British Somaliland, where the 59 survivors were captured by a naval party and a detachment of the Somaliland Camel Corps.

It was hardly inspiring duty. Yet the distress calls picked up on Socotra saved many lives, and the air escorts that flew from Socotra helped to fend off submarines waiting to ambush India- and Burma-bound convoys. These were jobs that needed doing—a useful part of the worldwide war—and the jobs were done.

By itself, sea transportation was not enough. Fast troop transports from Britain sailing around the Cape took from six to 10 weeks to reach the Middle East. Freighters took much longer, and though their pace was good enough for the steady movement of most supplies, it was too slow for the many emergencies that arose in wartime. The lack of critically needed spare parts, radar equipment or other high-technology gear could spell disaster at the battlefronts.

As a consequence, military airlines were established to transport high-priority supplies, key personnel and combat planes to Allied outposts all over the world. The British were pioneers in this aerial enterprise, but the Americans carried it to its ultimate development. The U.S. Air Transport Command (pages 154-167), a branch of the Army Air Forces, employed 200,000 men at its peak and operated more than 3,000 aircraft over half a dozen major routes and scores of feeder lines.

The ATC's first route, across the South Atlantic, was set up in June 1941 and was operated until October of the following year by civilian contractors, chiefly Pan American Airways. In those early days, only four-engined bombers and twin-engined aircraft fitted with extra fuel tanks could fly the South Atlantic nonstop, and then only via the shortest route from the coast of Brazil to the coast of West Africa. Planes setting out from West Palm Beach, Florida, where the route began, made a series of hops down through the Caribbean and along the coast of South America, touching down in Puerto Rico, Trinidad, British Guiana and Belém, at the mouth of the Amazon River, before reaching Natal on the easternmost bulge of the Brazilian coastline.

But in April 1942, a new base of great strategic importance was opened on Ascension Island, a barren flyspeck in the mid-Atlantic. This base made it possible for unmodified medium and light bombers and even some fighter planes to land for refueling and make the transatlantic trip in two stages. The pilots who flew the route memorialized the 34-square-mile island with a ditty: "If I don't hit Ascension, / My wife will get a pension." In practice, however, the pilots found the island with little or no trouble, homing in on a powerful radio beam.

The British had annexed the arid volcanic island in 1815 and later turned it into a coaling station for the Royal Navy. When the Americans arrived to build the air base, it contained a British cable station and a population of 165, the maximum that could be supported by the water supply, and among the facilities that had to be provided was a water-distillation plant. The runway, hastily blasted out of solid rock, was left with a disconcerting hump in the middle, which pilots could not avoid without overrunning the airstrip. And there were other disadvantages. The base was labeled Wideawake Field after the large colony of wideawake terns that habitually nested on the rocky area at one end of the runway, where they posed a hazard to planes landing or taking off. At the approach of a plane, the terns rose in panic from their nests, and the dense feathery cloud in front of the aircraft threatened to break its windscreen, clog its engines and air scoops or dent the leading edges of its wings and tail. In short the pilots were always in imminent danger of plowing into the runway or ditching in the Atlantic.

The birds were unsuccessfully attacked with smoke candles and dynamite. When the Americans announced that they were bringing in more "cats"—Caterpillar tractors—for construction projects, the announcement inspired a mistaken tale: Phalanxes of house cats were said to have been imported to eat the terns—but were themselves pounced on and eaten by the island's booby birds, a larger and more powerful species. Several responsible publications reported the wild yarn as fact.

The tern hazard continued until someone thought to call in an ornithologist from the American Museum of Natural History. The terns' eggs should be removed to another location, he advised, and then the birds would not return. The Army proved him right, though it impatiently destroyed 40,000 eggs in the process.

From Ascension Island, the planes flew on to Accra and Dakar on the west coast of Africa. There they joined the main British air reinforcement route coming from London by way of neutral Lisbon. The U.S. bombers and the British flying boats (many of them American-made PBYs) crossed the interior of the continent to avoid the Germans on the Mediterranean coast; en route the planes staged at a series of exotic bases: Lagos, Kano or Maiduguri in Nigeria, Fort-Lamy in French Equatorial Africa, and Sudanese oasis outposts such as El Geneina, El Fasher and El Obeid. The eastern end of the African leg was Khartoum or Cairo.

All aircraft heading east from Cairo flew to Iraq and Iran or to Aden, then on to Karachi, Delhi and Calcutta. The last leg was over the Hump of the Himalayas to Kunming, termi-

A Free French warship pulls alongside the quay in St. Pierre harbor to an enthusiastic welcome by a gathering of local citizens.

De Gaulle's cross-of-Lorraine flag and the French tricolor fly overhead as three St. Pierre residents return to their homes after voting.

Islanders and Free French sailors come together for the plebiscite that allied St. Pierre and Miquelon with the Free French movement.

# A DIPLOMATIC STORM OVER TWO TINY ISLANDS

In December 1941, St. Pierre and Miquelon, two tiny French possessions off the southern coast of Newfoundland, became the center of a diplomatic imbroglio that rocked the British-American alliance.

The islands were governed by Vichy, but the 4,700 inhabitants were in sympathy with General Charles de Gaulle's Free French movement. The United States did not recognize de Gaulle. The State Department, which had negotiated an agreement with Vichy establishing the neutrality of St. Pierre and Miquelon, feared that a Free French take-over of the islands would provide the Germans with a pretext for occupying and defending Vichy's possessions in North Africa and the Caribbean. Winston Churchill favored the take-over, but to placate the Americans he extracted a promise from de Gaulle not to invade the islands without Allied approval.

De Gaulle immediately broke his word and ordered four Free French warships to seize the islands. On Christmas Eve, a handful of Free French sailors ousted the islands' Vichy governor. Then, in a hastily arranged plebiscite, an overwhelming majority of the islanders endorsed de Gaulle.

U.S. Secretary of State Cordell Hull was outraged; he felt betrayed by the British, who welcomed de Gaulle's victory, and called de Gaulle a "marplot" for endangering Allied plans. Hull spent three weeks furiously urging the British to persuade de Gaulle to withdraw from the islands. His attempts succeeded only in whipping up U.S. public support for de Gaulle.

Finally, the State Department backed down. Thus, as Hull later wrote, "a matter that had threatened to become a whole chapter in history declined to a footnote."

nal of the India-China supply route 14,000 miles away from Florida. A branch line from India to Australia functioned briefly in December 1941 and early January 1942, while the Americans were building island bases for a transpacific route. But by January 15, ATC planes from the U.S. West Coast began flying the 7,800-mile run to Australia.

In 1943 a new air route was opened across the central Atlantic to North Africa by way of the Azores, where an airfield was opened under the terms of a 600-year-old alliance between Portugal and England. Other major Air Transport Command routes spanned the North Atlantic, with way stations in Iceland and Greenland. Another route provided air ferry service through Canada to Alaska, where Russian fliers picked up the planes and flew them to the Russian front via Siberia and Moscow. As the islands of the central and southwest Pacific were won back from the Japanese, the Air Transport Command knit them together with the last of its routes. All together, the routes of the Air Transport Command did more than anything else to make one war of the flank campaigns throughout the world.

Without doubt, the loneliest and harshest of all the support outposts—the places where the elements brought men to the brink of death—were the Arctic and subarctic islands where tiny bands of British, Americans, Danes, Norwegians and their common adversaries, the Germans, waged the so-called weather war. This remote and top-secret small war was fought out along a frigid frontier that stretched from eastern Greenland through Jan Mayen Island and the Sval-

bard Archipelago to the unexplored wastes of Franz Josef Land. There, and on a handful of ships with sophisticated weather gear, teams of meteorologists endured the long Arctic night under nearly insufferable conditions and studied the violent storms that brewed the next day's weather in the North Atlantic and on the European continent.

To both the British and the Germans it was obvious from the start that crucial operations by land, sea and air could be vitally influenced by weather forecasts emanating from the Arctic. And in May 1940, both sides took first steps toward penetrating the frigid wilderness. Under Major General Robert G. Sturges, who later commanded the British forces on steaming Madagascar, a party of Royal Marines landed at Reykjavik, the capital of Iceland, arrested the German consul general and destroyed enemy weather-watching stations. In the summer of 1941, the troop-short British turned the occupation of Iceland over to the United States, still neutral but busily expanding its Atlantic defenses.

At about the same time, a Luftwaffe unit designated Wetterstaffel 5 began sending weather-reconnaissance planes out of a base near Trondheim in recently occupied Norway. With a cruising range of almost 2,000 miles, German Heinkel-111s and Junkers-88s were soon probing as far as Jan Mayen Island, known to meteorologists as "the wind factory of the Atlantic"—and shortly to become a desolate battleground for the forces engaged in the weather war.

Jan Mayen, lying about 1,100 miles from the North Pole, had been discovered by the British explorer Henry Hudson in 1607, and in time became a Dutch whaling base. In

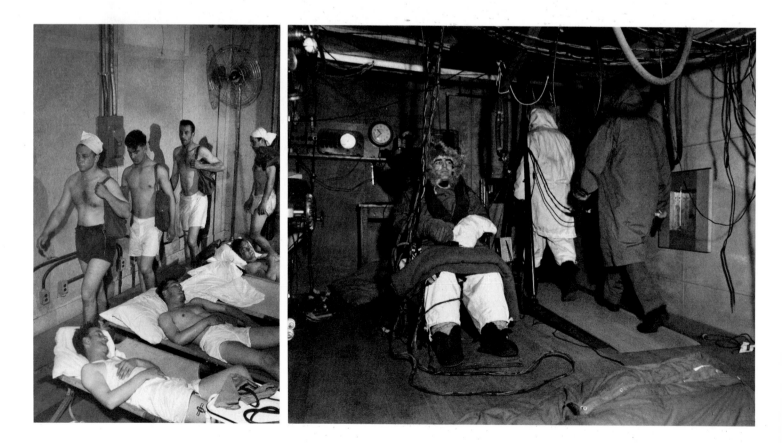

1882, during an international meteorological observance, Austria briefly maintained a weather station on the grim little island. In 1921, after a League of Nations grant of jurisdiction over Jan Mayen, Norway opened a permanent weather base, which at the start of World War II was occupied by four men.

Few bleaker places existed on earth. The island, about 30 miles long and less than two miles wide at its narrowest point, was dominated by the giant, glum Beerenberg, an 8,000-foot extinct volcano whose mile-wide crater overflowed with ice. Except for a hardy Arctic moss, Jan Mayen's jagged lava fields were devoid of vegetation; its gray volcanic sand beaches were littered with Siberian driftwood and other flotsam—raw rubber, barrels of oil and, on one wartime occasion, a container of unspoiled biscuits from a Norwegian bakery. In summer the island lay hidden in a shroud of fog broken only by shrieking gales and driving rains. In the two and a half months of winter darkness, Jan Mayen was battered by hurricane-force storms.

When Norway fell to the Germans in the spring of 1940, the four Norwegians on Jan Mayen stayed at their posts—but patriotically began beaming their weather reports to Great Britain instead of Norway. It was an act of defiance that the Germans could hardly be expected to abide indefinitely, and to forestall an enemy move, the British in October mounted an expedition to reinforce and supply Jan Mayen, which they code-named Island X.

Cautiously approaching Jan Mayen's forbidding coast, the crew of the Norwegian gunboat *Fridtjof Nansen,* which had escaped to England when the Germans invaded Norway in April 1940, was greeted by a rare and pleasing sight: The waters around the island were for once ice-free and reasonably calm. But then, with a scream of ripping metal, the *Fridtjof Nansen* shuddered to a dead stop, aground on one of the numerous uncharted lava reefs that girdled Jan Mayen. Her hull terribly gashed, the gunboat listed, and at the order to abandon ship the 68 crewmen scrambled for the lifeboats. Even as they pulled at the oars to clear the wreck, the *Fridtjof Nansen* went under.

Remarkably, all hands were still alive, and they soon joined the four Norwegians ashore. But the British expedition commander, prompted by the loss of the gunboat, decided to abandon Jan Mayen until the following spring and

radioed for a rescue ship. Within a few days a ship arrived. The four Norwegians were evacuated with their would-be reinforcements after demolishing the weather station to prevent it from falling into German hands. Jan Mayen lay temporarily uninhabited as the polar night closed in.

The island, however, remained a hunting ground. On November 16 a patrolling British destroyer picked up on radar a German trawler laboring toward Jan Mayen from the south. The trawler was carrying a team of weathermen to be put ashore on the island, and as the destroyer bore down, the German captain sped recklessly toward Jan Mayen. The trawler crashed onto the rocks just offshore. Most of the men struggled through the roaring surf and reached shore, where they were captured by a landing party from the destroyer. Two Germans were found floating face down in the icy shallows. Given the scale of the weather war, the German losses—a few dozen weathermen and crewmen in all—were extremely high.

The Allies returned to Jan Mayen on March 10, when the Norwegian ship *Veslekari,* escorted by the patrol boat *Honningsvaag,* edged up to the island's wide belt of ocean ice. The snow on the ice sheet was so soft and deep that Huskies could not move the sledges, and the cargo had to be manhandled across the broad stretch of ice by weathermen on skis. Within a few hours 12 Norwegians were huddled inside an old hunter's hut. This time the Allies meant to stay.

The team's radio transmissions soon betrayed its presence to the enemy, and thereafter, whenever the weather permitted, German planes from Norway bombed and strafed Jan Mayen. They did little damage: The Norwegians' Huskies heard the approaching planes long before the men, and the dogs' yelps served as an efficient air-raid warning system. Men and dogs took cover in the lava rocks until the Luftwaffe pilots decided to go home.

By summer, two more ships had arrived with supplies, reinforcements and even antiaircraft guns. Island X now had a garrison of a few dozen weathermen and soldiers. The meteorologists transmitted their brief, coded reports to Britain at three-hour intervals—and braced themselves for winter's onslaught. For protection against gale-force winds, they stacked bags of powdered lava high against the walls of the headquarters hut, the radio shack, the bunk huts and storage

*The U.S. Army's medical laboratory at Fort Knox tests the adaptability of soldiers to climatic extremes in special chambers that could duplicate any weather condition. Soldiers carrying 20-pound packs (far left) slog along a treadmill in a room that was heated to 120° F. in an experiment to determine the exact amount of salt and water a man needed to work effectively in the desert or in the tropics. At left, in a room chilled to sub-zero temperatures to simulate Arctic conditions, volunteers test cold-weather gear to measure the efficiency of the insulation.*

sheds. They strung taut life lines between the buildings. When the high winds came howling in, the men took their lives in their hands every time they ventured outdoors. To travel from one building to the next, they crawled through the snow, hauling themselves hand over hand along the life line. They were always exhausted by the journey between the headquarters hut and the radio shack— 300 yards. In one tempest, a sledge dog chained to a heavy stake was blown away, never to be seen again.

German planes occasionally braved lesser storms. One crashed into the Beerenberg. Another went down near the Allied camp; the weathermen retrieved the bodies of six enemy airmen and buried them in cairns marked with driftwood crosses. By the end of 1941 the air raids stopped— and not just because of the weather. The Germans had given up hope of evicting the Allies from Jan Mayen.

The struggle for Island X was a microcosm of the weather war: In the course of 1941, superior Allied forces were ev-

erywhere gaining the upper hand, crowding the Germans out of their northern weather stations. The Germans were increasingly forced to rely on mobile weather stations— trawlers with sophisticated meteorological equipment. To counter this threat, the Royal Navy dispatched three cruisers and four destroyers to sweep the northern seas.

In May the cruiser *Edinburgh* found and sank the 1,200-ton weather trawler *München*. A month later the cruiser *Nigeria* and three destroyers made radar contact with the weather ship *Lauenburg* as she lay hidden in dense fog off Jan Mayen. So swiftly did the British warships sweep in through the darkness that they captured intact all the enemy's weather-recording equipment and, more important, a top-secret Enigma coding machine.

Other German trawlers, most notably the will-o'-the-wisp *Sachsen,* kept up their Arctic journeys, transmitting sporadically. But their difficulties increased in the summer of 1941, when the United States occupied bases in Danish Green-

land. The U.S. Coast Guard began a memorable patrol on Greenland (*pages 34-47*), taking a toll of German trawlers and making the northeastern coast of the enormous island too dangerous for German weather teams.

The most bitterly contested struggle of the weather war began in August of 1941 about 500 miles northeast of Jan Mayen and 600 miles from the North Pole. The place was the Svalbard Archipelago—nine major islands consisting of more than 24,000 square miles of land area.

The island group was discovered by 13th Century Norsemen, then forgotten and rediscovered by a 16th Century merchant adventurer seeking a short passage to China. In June 1596, the Dutch explorer Willem Barents made landfall on an unknown island where crewmen killed a polar bear—hence the name Bear Island. Barents later sighted the archipelago's largest island, whose twin peaks reminded him of the ears of a spitz dog. Barents named the island Spitzbergen. Before long, British, French and even Basque hunters invaded the Svalbards in quest of fur-bearing seals, ivory-tusked walruses and, later, whales for their oil.

In the early 20th Century, whaling in the Svalbard Archipelago gave way to another industry: coal. The coal was first mined on a significant scale by an American named Longyear, who founded Longyear City—or Longyearbyen in Norwegian—on Spitzbergen's west coast. In 1916, Longyear's holdings were sold to Norwegian interests; four years later, the League of Nations awarded Norway sovereignty over the entire archipelago. At the beginning of World War II, Spitzbergen was inhabited primarily by miners—about 1,000 Norwegians and 2,000 Soviet workers running a coal-mine concession.

The miners dwelt in a climatic anomaly: From the north and east the Svalbards were flogged by fierce Arctic storms; from the south and west they were warmed by a branch of the Gulf Stream. In winter the banshee winds howled and the archipelago was encased in ice; in summer there blossomed yellow poppies, purple sorrel and white mountain avens. Concealed in the conflicts of the Svalbard climate lay many of the secrets of European weather.

Obviously, as with Jan Mayen and Greenland, possession of the islands—or at least the denial of the islands to the enemy—was to the clear advantage of either antagonist in

the War. In the race for the most useful island, Spitzbergen, the British moved first.

According to their original plan, Canadian troops were to land on Spitzbergen in 1940 and permanently occupy the island. But winter was fast approaching and Allied resources were stretched thin. It was decided to make do with a raiding party that would destroy the existing weather stations, put the coal-mining facilities out of commission, evacuate the Russian and Norwegian workers and then withdraw until spring.

At 7 o'clock on the misty morning of August 25, 1941, the former luxury liner *Empress of Canada,* accompanied by two Royal Navy cruisers and three destroyers, slid silently into Green Harbor, a bay lying inside the great Is Fjord on Spitzbergen's west coast. There stood the Russian mining community of Barentsburg, a tumble-down town where gulls were relied upon to pick clean the garbage strewn freely about the premises.

The *Empress of Canada* disgorged a detachment of Canadian engineers, a Norwegian platoon and some troops of the Royal Army Service Corps. The first soldiers to land were taken to the settlement's Russian leader, who listened

*Wideawake terns, denizens of tiny Ascension Island, rise in a cloud as a U.S. warplane roars over the Air Transport Command's mid-Atlantic base. The birds posed a serious hazard to aircraft landing or taking off.*

*Serving on remote Socotra in the Arabian Sea, a British officer, flanked by a Bedouin guide (left) and two soldiers from Aden, pauses beside an Adenium tree during a patrol across the island's harsh granitic plain.*

# THE AERIAL WORK HORSE OF ALL THEATERS

From Greenland and Ceylon to the Aleutians and the Solomons, the PBY Catalina was a plane of all work (the one shown here is a PBY-5A model fitted with retractable tricycle landing gear for amphibious operations). Designed as a patrol bomber, the rugged twin-engined flying boat was used to protect convoys, haul gliders, carry cargo, search for enemy ships and rescue downed airmen and sailors. The PBY did all this even though it was ungainly and slow—a sitting duck for enemy fighters and antiaircraft gunners.

But what the PBY lacked in speed and maneuverability, it made up for with the greatest carrying capacity and endurance of any twin-engined aircraft used in the War. Operating as a flying boat with no runway restrictions, the Catalina could carry a load nearly equal to its own weight. And at its leisurely cruising speed, the plane was capable of remaining on patrol for as long as 30 hours when its 1,750-gallon fuel tanks had been topped. On such protracted missions, three plexiglass machine-gun blisters—one located in the nose and two aft—allowed the crew members a broad field of vision.

The remarkable range of the PBY was made possible by a number of features. The broad hull was designed to provide a measure of lift that helped the wings keep the plane in the air. The PBY's floats retracted in flight, an innovation that streamlined the wings and reduced drag. Wherever it was possible, the spars and framing members of the hull and wings were constructed of an especially lightweight aluminum alloy. The skin was also of light alloy; to save more weight in surfaces that were normally made of aluminum, the ailerons and the rear third of the wings were sheathed in cotton fabric, as were the elevators and the rudder.

When this light but sturdy airframe was married to a pair of powerful engines, there seemed to be few limitations to the magic that the PBY could perform. Indeed, in one Herculean feat, a PBY on patrol in the Philippines took 56 shipwrecked sailors on board—in addition to its flight crew of eight.

"If we could get a load into the airplane," said one crew member, "we knew the airplane could fly with it."

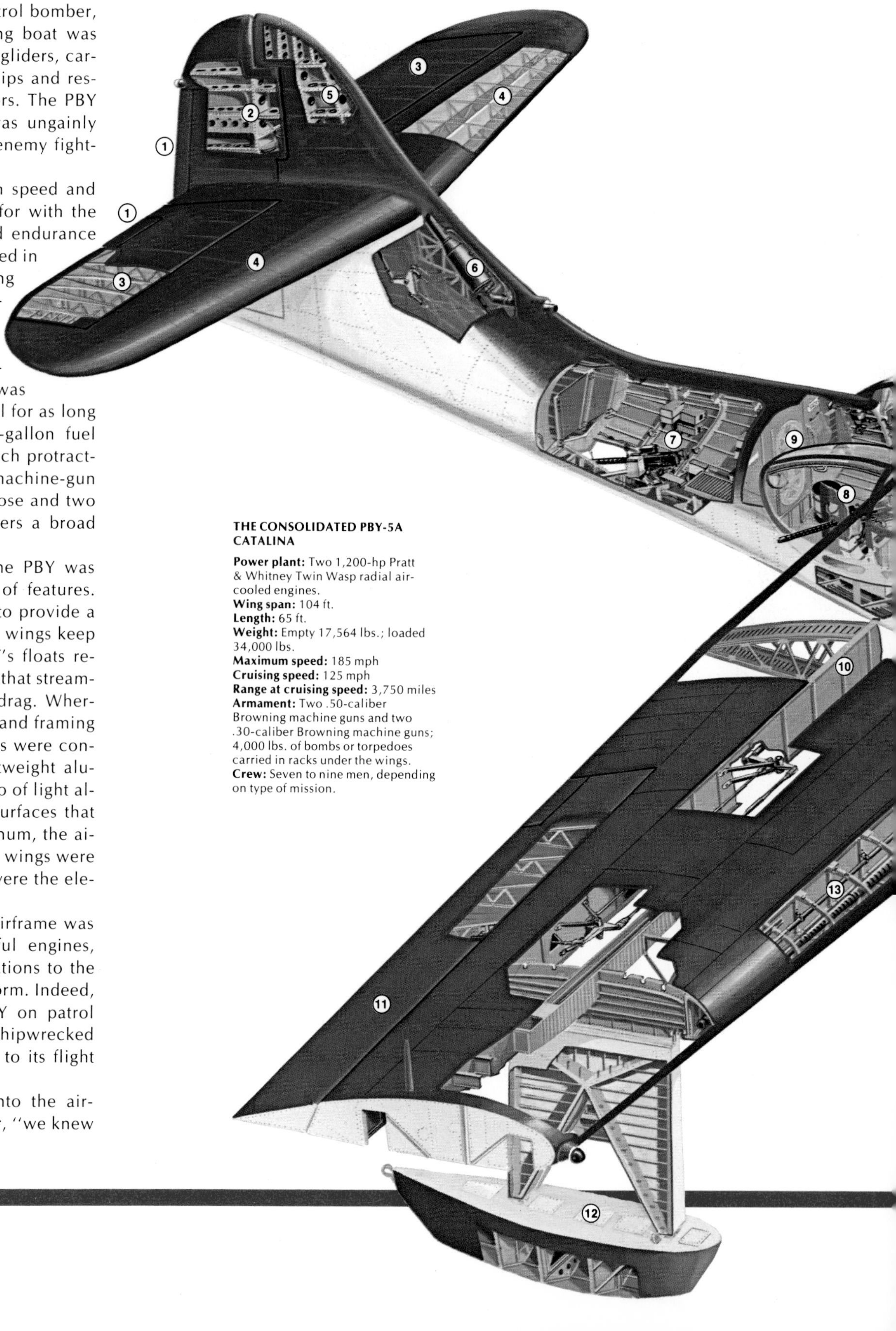

**THE CONSOLIDATED PBY-5A CATALINA**

**Power plant:** Two 1,200-hp Pratt & Whitney Twin Wasp radial air-cooled engines.
**Wing span:** 104 ft.
**Length:** 65 ft.
**Weight:** Empty 17,564 lbs.; loaded 34,000 lbs.
**Maximum speed:** 185 mph
**Cruising speed:** 125 mph
**Range at cruising speed:** 3,750 miles
**Armament:** Two .50-caliber Browning machine guns and two .30-caliber Browning machine guns; 4,000 lbs. of bombs or torpedoes carried in racks under the wings.
**Crew:** Seven to nine men, depending on type of mission.

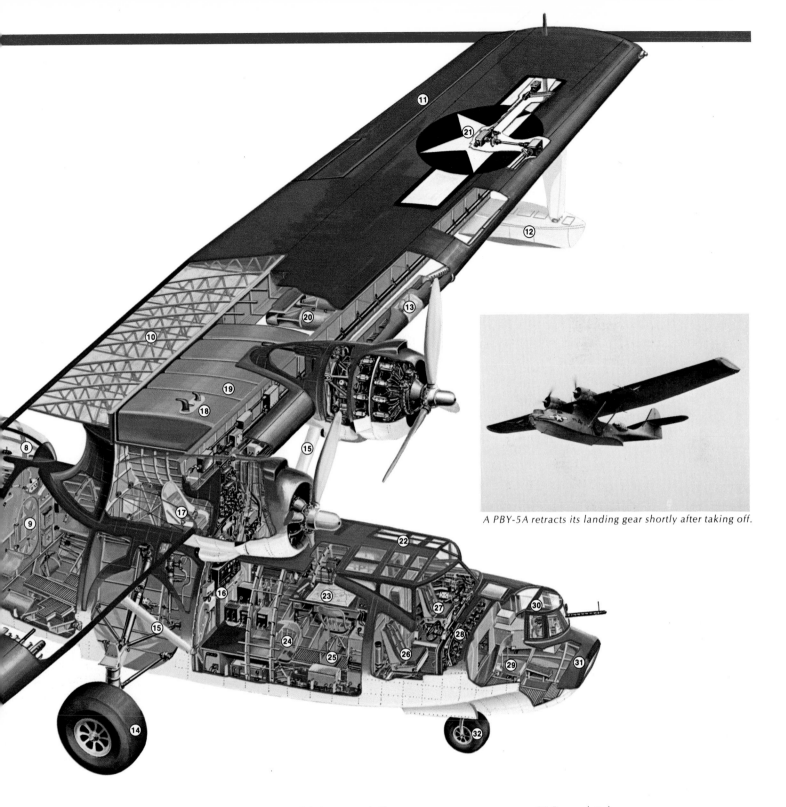

A PBY-5A retracts its landing gear shortly after taking off.

1 Metal trim tabs
2 Fabric-covered rudder
3 Fabric-covered elevators
4 Metal-skinned horizontal stabilizer
5 Fin
6 Anti-icing heater for fin and stabilizer
7 Ventral gun position
8 Blister upper-gun positions
9 Watertight hatches
10 Metal wing ribs and spars

11 Fabric-covered ailerons
12 Retractable wing floats
13 Anti-icing ducts for wings
14 Retractable main wheels
15 Wing braces
16 Main electrical panel
17 Flight engineer's station in pylon
18 Fuel-tank vents
19 Center-section fuel tanks
20 Bombs
21 Float-retraction mechanism

22 Escape hatch
23 Navigator's station
24 Radio operator's position
25 Radar operator's position
26 Copilot's position
27 Pilot's position
28 Pilot's instrument panel
29 Turret gunner's platform
30 Retractable bow-gun turret
31 Bomb/torpedo sight—viewing port
32 Retractable nose wheel

glumly as the British commander, Brigadier Arthur E. Potts, outlined plans for the immediate evacuation of the mining population.

"It will take three days," insisted the Russian.

"Embarkation will begin in an hour's time," said Potts. "Demolition will start at once."

By 6 o'clock that afternoon, the 2,000 Russians had been taken aboard ship and the *Empress of Canada* was on her way to deliver them to the Soviet port of Archangel. The demolition work at Barentsburg took longer. The mine shafts were spared for future use, but heavy mining machinery was wrecked with explosive charges. In the process, a wooden building was accidentally set afire, and the flames, racing before a strong wind, soon engulfed most of the town and spread to nearby coal dumps. The smoldering fuel cast a heavy pall of smoke that held up demolitions and lasted for many months.

On the return trip from Archangel to England, the *Empress of Canada* stopped at Barentsburg and took aboard the demolition men who had been left behind, and also the Norwegian miners, who had been brought over from Longyear City, 50 miles away. For the winter, the grim island would be left to its gulls—or so the Allies thought.

On September 25, a month to the day after the Allied raiders had landed at Barentsburg, a Junkers-52 bearing 10 German scientists and construction workers from Norway touched down on packed snow near Longyear City. By great good luck, the Germans found two tractors that the Allies had failed to destroy. They used the machines to carve out a less hazardous landing strip, to build a weather station and to erect machine-gun emplacements for its defense.

By November 11 the installation was operational, and six workmen were taken out by plane. The four scientists began sending their coded weather reports on varying frequencies so as to confuse enemy efforts at detection. They reported regularly throughout the winter.

Meanwhile, on October 15, another German weather team had gone ashore at Spitzbergen's Signehamna Bay, 90 miles north of Barentsburg. Transported from Norway with all their equipment by the supply ship *Homan* and the ubiquitous *Sachsen*, five men under Dr. Hans Knoespel, a biologist turned wartime meteorologist, quickly set up shop.

By October, when the long day became a five-month-long night, they were snugly ensconced in two huts six feet apart and connected by a tarpaulin-covered passageway. Cooking on a gas stove, warmed by a coal stove and reading by kerosene lamps, they fought an endless battle against the agonizing tedium of the Arctic winter. Recalled a German weatherman: "The most important thing for the team was to prevent 'polar madness' from breaking out, and this meant above all that everybody had to be meaningfully employed. Among the younger men, for instance, meaningful activity consisted of trying to do the work of trappers, or dealing with the many polar bears which never stopped creating difficulties for us; we killed nine."

The great white bears, which originally had drifted to the northern islands on floes broken off from the Arctic icecap, were deadly dangerous alive—and dangerous dead. In May 1944, a German weather team in Franz Josef Land, on the Arctic Circle above the Soviet Union, killed a polar bear and delighted in its fresh meat. But after a few days, all the men fell ill. A doctor, reached by radio, diagnosed trichinosis. The weathermen were evacuated by plane and their station was permanently closed down.

The Knoespel group transmitted in relative security during the winter and into the summer of 1942. When it left, it was replaced by another group, then another and another. At war's end, there were still Germans at Signehamna Bay. But their work had become fitful and ineffectual; much of the time they did not transmit out of fear of attracting the hostile attention of the Allies—who returned to Barentsburg on May 12, 1942.

The Barentsburg expedition was mounted by about 60 Norwegians, aboard their icebreaker *Isbjorn* and the seal-hunting ship *Selis*. The force arrived at the entrance to Is Fjord—only to find its way barred by several miles of thick, snow-laden ice. For nearly 24 hours the *Isbjorn* battered at the barrier, backed off and battered again, the crash of its reinforced bow against ice resounding through the Arctic stillness. The ships had pushed to within a mile or so of Barentsburg when out of the sun swooped a four-engined German Condor, its cannon booming and machine guns blazing. Most of the men abandoned ship and took to the ice pack. Three more German planes joined the assault, strafing and bombing the ships as they lay helplessly trapped in the narrow channel that the *Isbjorn* had plowed through the ice.

The *Isbjorn* soon suffered a direct bomb hit and within minutes sank into the dark water. The *Selis* caught fire. For nearly an hour, the aircraft continued to strafe the Norwegians, who had burrowed under the snow atop the ice pack. The gunners' aim was evidently thrown off by the glare of the sun on the snow; nevertheless, by the time the planes vanished over Spitzbergen's mountains, 14 Norwegians had been killed, including the commander of the expedition.

Under the second-in-command, Captain Ove Lund, the desperate survivors returned to the burning *Selis*, groped through thick smoke and, with ammunition beginning to explode all about them, struggled to save some equipment. They managed to get out with a meager haul: three rucksacks, a few rifles, a little ammunition, several skis and a damaged radio receiver. So there they were, about 40 Norwegians, marooned in one of the world's most unforgiving places, without food or working communications equipment, with not nearly enough weapons or skis to go around, and utterly ignorant as to whether or not the enemy was lurking on the island.

Grimly the Norwegians made their way to Barentsburg, still shrouded in coal smoke. There, their situation began looking up—by an iota. In a warehouse that had somehow escaped destruction in the burn-and-run raid of the previous August, the party found cases of coffee and crates of hard candy. Someone remembered that the Russian miners had kept pigs, which they had slaughtered and stored in a snowbank at the time of their enforced evacuation. The Norwegians dug in the snow until they found a frozen carcass,

then another and another. For the next two weeks, the destitute occupying force at Spitzbergen would subsist on a menu of pork, sweets and coffee.

The Norwegians were continually harassed by German aircraft, which on fair days made strafing runs with metronomic regularity at 7 a.m. and 6 p.m. The men took refuge in an abandoned mine shaft and were safe—but apprehensive about whether the enemy planes came from Norway or from somewhere on Spitzbergen. To find out, Captain Lund decided to send a patrol to reconnoiter Longyear City, which seemed the most likely spot for a German base.

Two skilled skiers, a Sergeant Knudsen and a Corporal Ostbye, were chosen to go ahead; they would be followed in 24 hours by a larger party, many of its members using skis fashioned from planks found in the ruins of Barentsburg. After a day of trekking across broad snowfields, mountains and glacial debris, Knudsen and Ostbye chanced upon a deserted hunting shack near Advent Valley, where Longyear was located. There they spent the night. Next day, with the arrival of the main group, the entire party moved out. The men were soon stopped short by a loud humming sound that seemed to come from Advent Valley. After scouting the source of the noise, Sergeant Knudsen came skiing back with the disturbing news that it evidently came from an electric generator in a building beside a crude airstrip in the valley. Equally disturbing, Knudsen had spotted machine-gun positions in the area.

The Norwegians, lacking enough weapons to risk an attack, left the area—fast.

Back at Barentsburg, the twice-a-day air attacks contin-

*Standing beside a tent fashioned from a parachute, a family of nomadic Greenland Eskimos shows off luggage and clothing salvaged from a U.S. bomber that crashed en route from Newfoundland to England. The Eskimos also sawed sledge runners out of the plane's aluminum skin and used its plexiglass windows for their permanent home.*

ued; in fact, the planes were coming from Norway, and the airstrip near Longyear City was used only to supply and reinforce the weather station there. But Lund now had a concrete worry: the possibility of attack by enemy land forces from Longyear. To deceive any German patrols as to the size of his little group, Lund kept his men on long and patternless jaunts through the snow, skiing as many as 50 miles a day to make as many tracks as possible.

Finally, on May 29, help came to the Norwegians from the air. A PBY Catalina from the Shetland Islands, 1,500 miles away, first tried to land in Is Fjord. The flying boat was frustrated by lingering ice, but it circled low, dropping food, medical supplies and weapons by parachute.

By June 7 the ice in Green Harbor had begun to break up and a Catalina was able to land in clear water. During the rest of the month, small groups of reinforcements were flown in, and by mid-July the Norwegians were ready to move against Longyear City.

The result was something of a letdown: Having armed themselves with new weapons and having made the arduous cross-country march to Advent Valley, the Norwegians found the area empty of the enemy. The Germans, informed by aerial reconnaissance of the Allied build-up, had just been evacuated by plane.

For more than a year, the Norwegians were generally unmolested at Barentsburg and Longyear City. As the months passed without incident, the two garrisons were reduced to the skeleton forces required to operate the weather stations and man some recently delivered artillery and antiaircraft guns.

But as the autumn of 1943 approached, trouble was brewing deep in the fjords of northern Norway. There the German battleships *Tirpitz* and *Scharnhorst* had been holed up for many months. The great ships, mounting 15-inch and 11-inch guns respectively, had been largely useless to Hitler, and indeed had been subjected to repeated air attacks by the British.

Now they would strike back. On the afternoon of September 7, at a conference of ships' officers aboard the *Scharn-*horst, a large-scale map of the Svalbard Archipelago was on prominent display.

An intelligence officer explained to the officers that at dawn the next day the *Tirpitz* and the *Scharnhorst* would put to sea. Pointing to two red marks on the map, he announced that the mission of the mighty warships would be ''to destroy the Norwegian force at Barentsburg and Longyear City.'' And the briefing officer added portentously: ''The Führer attaches great importance to this mission.''

It was never explained why Hitler chose to bring such overwhelming force against such pitiful targets. Perhaps the Germans believed that there was more to the Allied presence on Spitzbergen than weather stations—that the Allies were building an air-and-sea base from which to harass occupied Norway. Or perhaps it was a simple case of finding something to do for the long-idle surface ships.

Early on the morning of September 9, three German destroyers steamed into Green Harbor; the *Tirpitz* and two other destroyers lay farther off but within easy range of the battleship's awesome main batteries. At Cape Heer, a short distance from Barentsburg, a Norwegian officer watched hopelessly as a destroyer swung in and began unloading troops into boats for landings between Barentsburg and his own puny battery of light antiaircraft guns. Realizing that his position could not conceivably be held, he ordered seven of his men to head for Barentsburg while he and two others stayed behind to make a last stand at the guns.

When German soldiers appeared in the rear of the battery, the Norwegians swung the guns against them. At that moment the *Tirpitz* unloosed a salvo. The shells landed close to the battery, and one of the Norwegians fell wounded by a fragment. In the shock of the bombardment, the attacking German soldiers ducked for cover—and the two hale Norwegians, dragging their wounded comrade between them, escaped.

The *Tirpitz* next turned her guns on Barentsburg and German troops moved against the town. But many of the battleship's shells exploded in the huge heaps of ash in the coal dumps, which had finally burned out. The badly outnumbered Norwegian defenders were able to withdraw to safety on high ground behind an enormous cloud of coal ash.

The Germans had never contemplated remaining on Spitzbergen in force; the aim of their assault was simple destruction and speedy departure. At 6:30 a.m., about three and a half hours after the *Tirpitz* fired her first salvo, sirens wailed on the destroyers, the troops ashore turned back to their boats and the bombardment ceased. The little town of Barentsburg once more lay in flaming ruins.

In the meantime, the *Scharnhorst* and several destroyers had steamed on to Longyear City, where they made short work of their job. Troops quickly stormed an outlying Norwegian battery, capturing five of the 11 defenders; the others escaped. The main Norwegian force retreated inland, leaving behind six dead comrades. The *Scharnhorst's* guns leveled the settlement. By 11 a.m. the biggest battle of the weather war was over.

For the *Tirpitz* and the *Scharnhorst*—indeed, for Germany's entire surface fleet—the Arctic attack was a final aggressive act. The *Scharnhorst* was sunk off Norway's North Cape in a running battle with a British battleship task force in December 1943; the *Tirpitz* was capsized in Norway's Tromso harbor by British bombers in April 1944. As for Barentsburg and Longyear City, the Norwegians simply rebuilt them, and their weather stations were soon back on the air.

Their pay-off, and it was momentous, came in June 1944.

For General Dwight D. Eisenhower, Supreme Commander, Allied Expeditionary Force, several factors weighed in the decision to launch the cross-Channel invasion of Normandy. The Allied armada had to sail by night to conceal its size and direction; yet moonlight was needed for preceding air assaults. Prelanding bombardment of enemy shore installations required at least 40 minutes of daylight before the landings; yet the sunrise must come at a time when tides were low enough to permit U.S. forces on Omaha Beach to remove offshore obstructions. All of these preconditions would be met in the period from June 5 through 7, and would not reoccur for 28 days. Moreover, once the enormous scattered forces of planes, ships and men were set in motion, the invasion could not be aborted and rescheduled in time for the next combination of perfect conditions.

Yet even though the necessities of moonlight and sunrise and tides were met between June 5 and 7, by far the overriding consideration for traversing the treacherous English Channel was weather.

"If none of the three days should prove satisfactory from the standpoint of weather," Eisenhower wrote later, "consequences would ensue that were almost terrifying to contemplate. Secrecy would be lost. Assault troops would be unloaded and crowded back into assembly areas enclosed in barbed wire. Complicated movement tables would be scrapped. Morale would drop. If really bad weather should endure permanently, the Nazi would need nothing else to defend the Normandy coast!"

Operation *Overlord* was scheduled for June 5. But on June 4, heavy rain and gale-force winds whipped the Channel, and the prospects were for worse weather to come. The only hope was for a brief abatement in the weather before another storm rolled in. Eisenhower reluctantly postponed the invasion until June 6. The final, irrevocable decision would have to be made in the early hours of June 5.

All through the 5th, even as the Channel storm raged with undiminished fury, Allied meteorologists anxiously studied reports arriving from weather stations from the Azores on up to the edge of the earth in the distant Arctic. And at 4:15 a.m., the weathermen had good news for Eisenhower. Their observations of wind, temperature and barometric pressure indicated to Supreme Command meteorologists that the present storm would abate by the next morning and a relatively calm interlude of about 36 hours would ensue before another storm front struck.

For the Allied commander, that hole in the weather was just wide enough. In the predawn darkness of June 6, the invasion of Europe began—thanks in part to the tiny groups of weathermen who had spent their war on Greenland's eternal icecap, on storm-swept Jan Mayen and in the former mining camps on Spitzbergen.

# GREENLAND VIGIL

A Coast Guard officer surveys Greenland's barren landscape at a U.S. base near the Arctic Circle. The ship anchored in the fiord below brought mail from home.

# THE COAST GUARD'S NORTHERNMOST PATROL

In November of 1940, the government of Danish Greenland asked the United States for help in protecting the enormous island (the size of Alaska and Texas combined) from the fate that had just befallen Denmark itself: German occupation. After five months of negotiations, the United States took up the challenge because of the territory's strategic location. Meteorological stations on Greenland's east coast could forecast Western Europe's weather 24 hours in advance, and air bases on the island could be crucial in guarding Allied convoys en route to Britain with Lend-Lease supplies.

The task of patrolling Greenland's jagged coastline was assigned to the Coast Guard, long experienced in Alaskan and North Atlantic waters. During the summer of 1941, the Coast Guard formed the Greenland Patrol under a renowned Arctic veteran, Commander Edward H. "Iceberg" Smith. The patrol eventually grew to a force of 37 cutters and trawlers, which hunted German weather ships and coastal weather stations, escorted supply vessels and rescued shipwrecked sailors and downed fliers.

Greenland's 1,600-mile east coast was too long for the Coast Guard to police by itself. So Smith and the Danish governor, Eske Brun, hired some of Greenland's best Scandinavian and Eskimo hunters to patrol the northeast with dog sledges. These intrepid scouts were the Coast Guard's eyes and ears during the winter months, when the only light came from the moon, the stars and the aurora borealis.

In September 1941, the scouting reports sent the Coast Guard on a mission that produced a bizarre first for the United States. Smith, alerted by the scouts' radio report that a suspicious party had landed in a lonely fjord, hurried to the area in the cutter *Northland*. There he spotted the *Buskoe*, a Norwegian trawler displaying a telltale array of radio antennas. Coastguardsmen boarded the *Buskoe* and discovered that she was a weather ship at work for Germany. On a crewman's tip, they landed on the coast and captured three German soldiers in a radio hut. These were the first German servicemen captured by Americans—three months before the United States declared war on Germany.

*Ready for Arctic duty, the steel hull of the cutter Northland is camouflaged with blue and white paint; on the inside it was lined with cork for warmth.*

*A Grumman Duck reconnoiters the Arctic wastes for the Coast Guard. Between missions, the amphibious aircraft was stowed on the afterdeck of a cutter.*

Crewmen of a B-25 bomber await rescue by an approaching Coast Guard cutter (top center) four days after they crash-landed near the Greenland coast.

A Coast Guard lighthouse and radio-beacon station on Greenland's south coast guided the navigators of ships and planes bound for the U.S. base at Ivigtut.

*A demolition charge throws up a geyser of ice and water as the crew of a Coast Guard cutter blasts a path through thick ice off Greenland's eastern coas*

## MISSIONS OF MERCY THROUGH ARCTIC STORMS

When Allied aircraft were forced down in Greenland's blinding blizzards, the Coast Guard sent cutters, airplanes and sledge

The rescuers sometimes had to battle 170-mph winds. Cutters often had to break through miles of thick ice. The *Northland* alone saved 30 downed fliers.

One of the boldest rescue efforts was made by Lieutenant John A. Pritchard Jr., pilot of the *Northland's* plane, in Novem-

from a downed bomber; though the icy terrain was too rough for a wheels-down landing, he brought his Duck down using its pontoons as snow skis. Pritchard evacuated two injured men to the *Northland* then returned for another. But en route back to the cutter, his plane crashed in a

## A DEADLY GAME OF HIDE-AND-SEEK

From September of 1941 until war's end, the Sledge Patrol—15 Danes, Norwegians and Eskimos led by a former bookseller named Ib Poulsen—prowled a 500-mile stretch of lonely coast in northeast Green-and, looking for German weather stations.

Singly or by twos and threes, Poulsen's men went off on two-month missions with only rifles, tents, reindeer-hide sleeping bags and camp stoves.

Time and again, the sledge teams forced groups of German weathermen to pack up and move to escape capture. Striking back in March 1943, a German weather unit at Sabine Island attacked and burned down the patrol's headquarters at Eskimonaes.

Poulsen escaped under cover of darkness.

Coast Guard cutters soon arrived with supplies for a new station, and Poulsen's scouts resumed their work. They radioed valuable weather data to U.S. bases every six hours. And thanks largely to their re-ports of enemy activity, the Coast Guard eventually was able to locate the four peri-patetic German weather stations in Green-land and put them out of business.

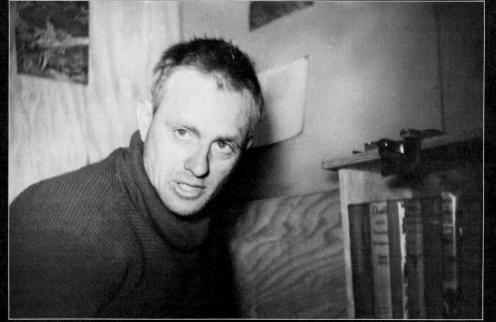

The Sledge Patrol's Sergeant Peter Nielsen, haggard after a solitary patrol in the dead of Greenland's three-month polar night, makes his report back at base in December 1944.

Setting out on patrol over an icebound inlet, a team of Eskimo dogs pulls a loaded sledge carrying Lieutenant Kurt Olson. The settlement in the background is Sandodden, the Sledge Patrol's home base in northeastern Greenland.

A wooden cross marks the sod-and-stone grave of Eli Knudsen, a Sledge Patrol member killed by a German weather group in March of 1943. Knudsen was the patrol's only fatality during its four years of hazardous work.

*Landing from the cutter Northland, a party of Coastguardsmen and soldiers run through the snow toward a German weather station on Sabine Island.*

*Coastguardsmen and U.S. troops take custody of a German parachute container on Sabine Island.*

# QUICK VICTORY ON LITTLE KOLDEWEY

The cutter *Eastwind*, with Lieutenant (jg.) Alden E. Lewis commanding a landing force, made a lucky strike in October of 1944, after the Coast Guard had failed in two attempts to capture German weather teams. Spotting a suspicious pile of building materials on Little Koldewey, a remote island off northeastern Greenland, Lewis led his commando-trained men ashore under cover of darkness.

The men found a rude camp and called on the occupants to surrender. Twelve sullen Germans emerged *(right)*. One German lighted a match—and a Coastguardsman swiftly snuffed it out. The German had intended to set fire to a kerosene-soaked bag of documents, which yielded five German codes and ciphers.

Lewis and his men did not know it, but they had captured the last German weather team in Greenland. The loss of this group so discouraged the Germans that they never sent another team.

Coastguardsmen on Shannon Island inspect a cleverly hidden German radio shack, abandoned just before their July 1944 raid.

# A PRIZE CATCH FOR A NEW CUTTER

The Coast Guard skippers had no desire to sink the German trawlers that were operating as weather stations off eastern Greenland. They wanted to capture the ships along with their advanced electronic gear and the codes used by German weather teams to send meteorological information back to Germany.

But the Germans were determined to prevent the trawlers from falling into the hands of the Allies. In 1942 and 1943, the Germans scuttled two vessels, the *Sachsen* and the *Coburg,* that had become trapped in the winter ice. In 1944, the *Northland* cornered the German trawler *Kehdingen* after a 70-mile, seven-hour chase through treacherous ice floes. But before the Coastguardsmen were able to board the *Keh-*dingen, the Germans destroyed the ship.

The Coast Guard got another chance on October 15, when the *Eastwind's* scout plane spotted the German trawler *Externsteine* caught in the ice 10 miles off the east coast of Greenland. The *Eastwind,* under Captain Charles W. Thomas, arrived at the spot late at night. Her gunners lighted up the sky with flares and fired three near misses at the trawler. The German skipper signaled "I give up."

Thomas warned the Germans that he would rake the trawler with machine-gun fire if they attempted to scuttle the ship. For added insurance, the boarding party kept the German captain, executive officer and chief engineer on the ship after removing the rest of the crew. It proved to be a wise precaution. The nervous chief engineer soon revealed and helped to dismantle five time-fused demolition charges affixed to the *Externsteine's* hull.

*Crushed by the ice off Shannon*

*Surrendering to the Coast Guard, 28 German crewmen and weather personnel from the scuttled Kehdingen approach the Northland in motorized lifeboats.*

*Island and set ablaze by members of her crew, the German weather ship Coburg is inspected by a landing party from the Northland (background) in July 1944.*

*The captured Externsteine, her bow and bridge camouflaged with sheets, gets under way with a crew from the Eastwind.*

A boarding party from the cutter Eastwind hoists the Stars and Stripes on the captured German trawler Externsteine. The trawler was later christened Eastbreeze and sailed to Boston with a prize Coast Guard crew.

The Eastwind's crew unloads supplies for the Sandodden Sledge Patrol station. The supplies, including food, ammunition and radio equipment, were captured at the German weather station on Little Koldewey.

# 2

**Churchill at odds with his Middle East commander**
**The fierce warriors known as "Glubb's Girls"**
**A crisis caused by an Iraqi coup d'état**
**The RAF delivers a "most excellent pasting"**
**Sudden attacks by Luftwaffe planes**
**Three-pronged assault on Syria**
**A "very messy" scene at Mezzé**
**Enemy troops become civilians in underwear**
**Last battles among the banana groves**
**An epilogue of Churchillian rhetoric**

In early April of 1941, Prime Minister Churchill concluded that Iraq and Syria were slipping into the German camp and that only British military intervention in both countries could prevent serious damage to the Allied cause. He cabled a call for action to the Cairo headquarters of Britain's commander in chief in the Middle East, General Sir Archibald Wavell. To Churchill's growing impatience, Wavell demurred and delayed.

During the next few weeks, Churchill repeatedly warned Wavell of the dangers on his vulnerable eastern flank. Iraq, rich in oil that Britain could ill afford to lose, was a hotbed of anti-British sentiment, and radical nationalists were known to be intriguing with Axis agents. If Iraq went over to the Germans, it was likely to be followed by neutral Iran to the east, and the British command in India would have a new set of problems on its hands.

In Syria, a French mandate since 1920, the administrators remained obedient to France's German-sponsored Vichy government, and they were expected to make local airfields available to the Luftwaffe. This would put enemy bombers within striking range of the Suez Canal and British shipping to India and the Far East. It would also give the Luftwaffe an excellent chance to win control of the air over the entire Middle East. These risks, Churchill reiterated, were totally unacceptable and must be removed at once.

Wavell was well aware of the dangers, yet he still hung back. His forces, he said, were already overextended in major areas, and he simply could not spare troops for military sideshows. In the Libyan Desert, Wavell's divisions had been rocked back on their heels by General Erwin Rommel's Afrika Korps, and they would be hard put to stop the Germans from invading Egypt. The expeditionary force he had sent to defend Greece in early March was being driven south by invading German armies (at the end of April, four fifths of the British command would be saved by a mini-Dunkirk). Furthermore, British intelligence reported that 10,000 German airborne troops were being assembled for another attack, probably aimed at Crete.

Wavell ventured his opinion on other points. He advised Churchill that military moves would have dire political consequences in the Arab world and that the Iraq situation should be resolved by negotiation.

Churchill was in a quandary. He was tempted to sack

# CAMPAIGNS ON A SHOESTRING

Wavell but respected him too much for that. The general was a distinguished commander whose career dated back to the Boer War in 1901. He had served with gallantry in World War I and had lost an eye in the fighting in Flanders. Wavell was also a Middle East expert of sorts. He had mastered the techniques of desert warfare in Britain's Palestine mandate, and had commanded the occupation forces there in 1937 and 1938, a difficult period of Arab-Jewish riots. His interest in Middle Eastern affairs was so keen that he had taken the time to learn the language of Britain's longtime rival for influence there—the Soviet Union.

Churchill kept Wavell in his post and made excuses for him: The general was weary and overwrought. But Churchill got his way nonetheless. And his way meant, as one of his generals later said, "war on a shoestring."

It was a very thin shoestring at that. The British could count on little aid in the campaigns to take control of Iraq and Syria. Free French units were available in Palestine and in North Africa, and General Charles de Gaulle was eager to use them in an invasion of Syria; but the combat capabilities of the Free French had been suspect ever since their poor performance in a joint attempt with the British to capture the French West African port of Dakar in September 1940.

The only indigenous Middle Eastern force that could help was Trans-Jordan's Army—the Arab Legion and its famed Desert Patrol (pages 64-75). This unit of tough Bedouin tribesmen had been organized and trained by John Bagot Glubb, a former British Army officer, and its loyalty and ferocity were unquestioned. But the Bedouins of the Desert Patrol—facetiously called "Glubb's Girls" because of their long hair and gingham headdresses—had few modern weapons and would be relegated to the role of scouts.

These and other practical problems disturbed Churchill not at all. As ever, he pressed ahead with unshakable confidence in the course he had chosen. In the meantime, long-simmering troubles in Iraq boiled over.

The Iraq crisis was a legacy of World War I. Postwar Iraq had been a British mandate—and an extremely resentful one—for 12 years. In 1932, the League of Nations terminated the mandate at the request of Britain and granted Iraq full independence. To prepare for the British withdrawal, an Anglo-Iraqi treaty had been signed in 1930. According to the treaty, Britain retained two air bases in Iraq—one at Basra, across the river (Shatt al Arab) from Iran, the other at Habbaniya, on the Euphrates 50 miles west of Baghdad, the Iraqi capital. The British also were guaranteed the right to transport troops across Iraqi territory in peace or war.

The British left Iraq in the hands of a resolutely pro-British royal family, which alone was enough to provoke Iraqi nationalists. When World War II broke out, the nationalists were quick to take advantage of Britain's military misfortunes, making common cause with the Germans in hopes of removing the British yoke once and for all.

In January 1941, the Emir Abdul Illah, the pro-British regent for four-year-old King Feisal II, managed to oust the incumbent Prime Minister, an ardent nationalist named Rashid Ali el Gailani. But Rashid Ali was backed by four Anglophobic colonels who controlled the Iraqi Army, and together they planned a coup d'état. On April 1, they signed Abdul Illah's death certificate, and that night they dispatched troops to make good the deadly document.

Abdul Illah escaped from his palace dressed as a woman and made his way to the home of a relative. During the night he sent word of his plight to the American legation, and the next morning the American Minister's car picked him up. Hiding under a rug, he was driven to the British air base at Habbaniya. From there he was flown to Basra, and eventually took refuge in Amman, the capital of his pro-British uncle, the Emir Abdullah of Trans-Jordan. But the damage had been done.

On April 3, Rashid Ali became Prime Minister once more, declaring a "government of national defense." Publicly, he promised that Iraq would abide by the terms of the Anglo-Iraqi treaty. But secretly he stepped up his negotiations with German representatives. They told him that when the time was ripe, German military assistance would be funneled into Iraq through Syria. Berlin had only to work out the details with Vichy.

The new British Ambassador to Iraq, Sir Kinahan Cornwallis, feared the worst and warned London that the British garrisons should be reinforced. His message prompted Churchill's first request for troops from General Wavell, and Wavell's first show of reluctance. In frustration, Churchill sent an urgent appeal for troops to General Sir Claude Auchinleck, the commander in chief in India, who regarded the security of Iraq, Iran and the Persian Gulf sheikdoms as India's western shield.

Auchinleck responded by diverting units earmarked for Malaya and hurrying them to Iraq by sea. On April 17 and 18, an infantry brigade of the Indian 10th Division and some field-artillery units—about 3,000 men in all—disembarked at Basra. At the same time, 400 officers and men of the King's Own Royal Regiment were flown from India to Basra and then north to Habbaniya.

Rashid Ali complied with the Anglo-Iraqi treaty and allowed these troops to land unopposed; he hoped that his gesture would persuade the British to recognize his government. But soon he was pressured by the four colonels to inform Ambassador Cornwallis that no more British troops could land until those already in the country had passed through. Cornwallis cabled this worrisome news to London immediately. Upon receiving Cornwallis' message, Churchill replied that British troops would land regardless, and that the Ambassador need not "entangle himself by explanations" to Rashid Ali.

On April 28, Cornwallis informed the Iraqi Foreign Office that 2,000 more troops would soon arrive at Basra. Rashid Ali repeated that these troops would not be allowed to enter the country until the first contingent had left Iraqi soil. Cornwallis was alarmed by the Prime Minister's hostility and ordered the evacuation of British dependents from Baghdad.

About 230 British nationals managed to reach Habbaniya on April 29, but then the road was blocked by large numbers of Iraqi troops moving toward the RAF base. About 500 other British subjects were trapped in Baghdad and took refuge in the British and American legations. There they would remain for a month.

At dawn on April 30, Iraqi soldiers established antiaircraft and artillery positions on a 200-foot-high plateau a half mile south of the Habbaniya base. Through the morning, the Iraqi force grew steadily to a strength of 9,000. Iraqi armored cars took up positions no more than 500 yards from the runway. Habbaniya was besieged.

And Habbaniya was eminently unready to stand a siege. "It is notorious," wrote the Arab Legion's John Glubb, "that when the Germans occupy a new station, their first task is to build defenses around it, whereas the British in similar circumstances lay out cricket and football fields. The RAF cantonment of Habbaniya was no exception." In addition to the requisite playing fields, this imperial outpost had a golf course, polo ground, swimming pool, cinema, church and a boat club on nearby Lake Habbaniya. Neat bungalows with red roofs stood along avenues planted with pink-flowered oleanders. Completing the civilized colonial scene was Air House, a large white villa, richly appointed with mahogany furniture and Persian rugs and grandly occupied by Air Vice Marshal H. G. Smart, Air Officer Commanding in Iraq.

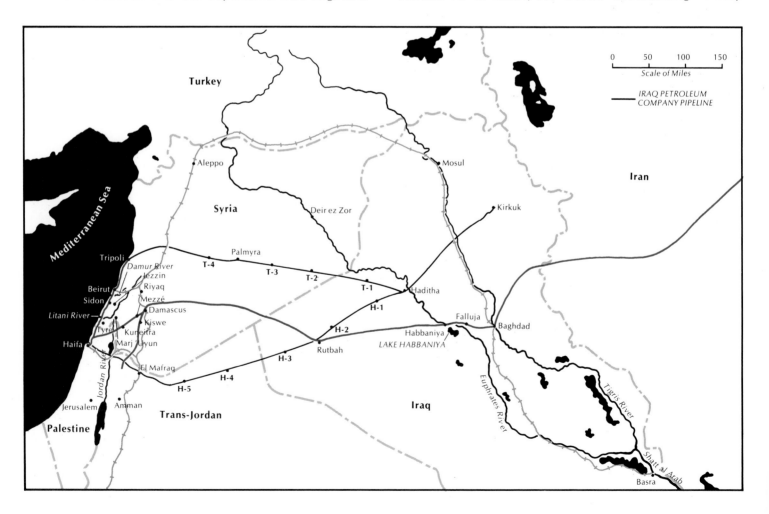

Since the start of the crisis in early April, Smart had belatedly begun turning his flight school into a combat unit: The polo ground and the golf course in the middle of the camp were sacrificed to create a dispersal area for aircraft, and his student pilots began intensive training in bombing and gunnery. But the air force at Habbaniya was less than daunting; although its 80-odd planes exceeded the Iraqi Air Force in number, they were much inferior in quality. With the exception of a solitary Blenheim bomber and nine worn-out Gladiator fighter planes, all were obsolete auxiliary aircraft—Audax and Oxford trainers, Gordon bombers and Valencia transports. These relics had been equipped with makeshift bomb racks, but their combat worthiness was dubious in the extreme.

In any case, Smart lacked enough experienced pilots to fly the planes. Almost all of the airmen at Habbaniya were students. As for the 35 instructors on the base, their combat skills were less than sharp, since they had spent most of their time there supervising student takeoffs and landings. The five squadrons that had been formed were mere skeletons. One squadron boasted 27 Oxfords but had only 15 pilots qualified to fly them. Whenever the 27 planes made a practice flight together, the squadron roster was filled out by pupils and airmen from other outfits who offered to come along for the ride.

On the ground, Habbaniya was defended by a pair of World War I field guns and 18 RAF armored cars built in the 1920s. The cantonment's normal population—aside from the airmen—numbered 9,000 British and Iraqi civilians and 1,200 local levies, armed only with rifles and World War I Lewis light machine guns. These troops were untested in combat, and it was hardly encouraging that they had been reinforced by only 400 troops from India. All things considered, the sensible course for the garrison at Habbaniya would have been to surrender.

However, Smart had no such notion, and the Iraqis, far from rushing to the attack, indulged in the usual Middle Eastern formalities that preceded violence. The Iraqi commander, under strict orders from the four colonels in Baghdad, sent two polite messages to Habbaniya's main gate declaring that the Iraqi artillery would open fire unless all flying ceased and the armored cars stayed inside the compound. Both times Smart replied that any hostile action against his planes or cars would be considered an act of war and would be met accordingly.

Thereupon Smart embarked on a risky test of Iraqi resolve. "A provocative flight was sent off to see if the Iraqis would give some excuse to start," wrote Wing Commander Peter Dudgeon. "By great good fortune they didn't, for operations would have been impossible with no one to refuel, rearm, or even start the aircraft." All hands were then fully engaged digging trenches, manning machine-gun emplacements and moving aircraft as far as possible from the enemy's artillery.

Another day passed in much the same uneventful fashion. Smart decided that if the Iraqis had not left the plateau by the next morning he would bomb them off—a decision encouraged by a directive from Churchill ordering him to strike hard if he struck at all. Smart arranged to have a squadron of Wellingtons fly up from the airfield at Basra to join in the 5 a.m. attack.

Before dawn on May 2, there was a traffic jam in the air above the small target area. "Aircraft of all types would approach unseen and flash past, causing pilots to nearly die of heart failure," wrote Dudgeon. "Camouflaged and uncamouflaged Audaxes went past at every angle, and Welling-

To secure their grip on the Middle East, the Allies planned to take over Iraq in the spring of 1941, then invade Syria. The Iraq operation called for troops from Basra and Palestine to relieve the besieged RAF base at Habbaniya, then move east and capture Baghdad, the Iraqi capital. Syria was to be wrested from the Vichy French by five invasion forces. Three columns would strike northward from Palestine and Trans-Jordan toward Beirut, Riyaq and Damascus. A fourth attack was to be launched from Palestine toward Damascus, and a fifth spearhead from Iraq would sweep across the desert to take Palmyra.

Hitler and his foreign minister, Joachim von Ribbentrop (left), receive Rashid Ali el Gailani, the ousted Prime Minister of Iraq, at the Führer's East Prussian headquarters. The Iraqi nationalist was forced to flee from Baghdad in May 1941 when invading British troops toppled his pro-Axis regime; he spent the remainder of the War in exile in Germany.

tons would sail overhead, leaving the Trainers bucketing about in their slipstreams." At precisely 5 a.m. this ragtag armada began bombing and strafing the Iraqi gun positions at low levels. The attack finally nettled the Iraqis. They responded with a severe artillery bombardment, and the undeclared war had begun.

The RAF delivered a "most excellent pasting" to the Iraqi guns, Dudgeon wrote, but the enemy's antiaircraft fire was "both intense and accurate." One old Oxford was shot down in flames, killing its instructor-pilot and the student crewmen. Several other bullet-riddled planes limped back to base with wounded men aboard.

Surprisingly, the response from the Iraqi Air Force was negligible. Some Iraqi pilots in American-built Northrop fighter-bombers attacked the compound without causing much damage, and at midday six Iraqi Gladiators strafed the camp, but most of the casualties sustained that day (13 killed and 29 wounded) were caused by shelling from the plateau. By day's end, the British had dropped more than 30 tons of bombs on the besieging army and, while they had failed to budge it from the plateau, they had prevented any attack by the Iraqi infantry.

Weighing the results of the day's fighting, Smart concluded that the garrison was in no immediate danger of falling. Therefore, his planes could expand their role to include attacks on targets farther afield. Over the next several days his squadrons bombed and strafed the Baghdad airport and other military airfields, catching the Iraqi Air Force off guard and disabling many of its planes. Despite this bludgeoning, the Iraqis persisted in their bombardment of Habbaniya, and British airmen passed the time betting on when a shell would hit the base's prominent water tower. None ever did.

Between longer missions, Smart's planes continued to punish the besiegers. Then, on the night of May 5, the King's Own Royal Regiment and a group of local levies launched a successful ground attack against the Iraqis' forward positions. By daybreak the besiegers were withdrawing from the plateau, leaving behind them large quantities of guns and ammunition.

Five miles east of Habbaniya, the retreating Iraqis encountered a column of reinforcements, and the two groups started milling around. "At about the same time," wrote Dudgeon, "every available Oxford, Audax, Gordon and Gladiator in Habbaniya was let loose." The RAF attack went on for two hours. When it was over, said Dudgeon, "the road was a solid sheet of flame for about 250 yards." The Iraqis lost about 70 vehicles, and more than 500 of their troops were killed or wounded. In addition, the British ground forces took 400 prisoners.

On May 7, Churchill wired his congratulations to Air Vice Marshal Smart: WE ARE ALL WATCHING THE GRAND FIGHT YOU ARE MAKING. KEEP IT UP. After seven days of siege, the base at Habbaniya had achieved its own rescue—but the war in Iraq was far from won.

While the fate of Smart's base was still in doubt, the Indian troops at Basra had been ordered to march 350 miles to Habbaniya, break the siege there and then attack Baghdad. But the spring flooding of the Tigris and Euphrates Rivers delayed the Indians, so the British Chiefs of Staff requisitioned substitute manpower from their reluctant commander in Cairo. On May 5, the fourth day of the battle at Habbaniya, Wavell received a stiff telegram from London flatly ordering him to send a relief force. The general was stubborn but not insubordinate. Resignedly he wired back: NICE BABY YOU HAVE HANDED ME ON MY 58TH BIRTHDAY.

To put together an expeditionary force for Iraq and to take charge of the defense of Palestine, Wavell selected General Sir Henry Maitland "Jumbo" Wilson, a tall, heavy-set, imposing man of genial temperament, who had recently commanded the ill-starred British defense of Greece. Meeting with the officers who would lead the march on Baghdad, Wilson opened the conference with a cheery warning: "More trouble, gentlemen, I am afraid."

It was big trouble. The Habbaniya Rescue Force—a name immediately contracted to Habforce—would have to carry relief supplies for the Habbaniya garrison as well as its own gear and provisions. Its several thousand men would have to cross 470 miles of desert, and once in Iraq they would face a vastly larger army—and perhaps an air attack by the Luftwaffe operating out of Syria.

The main body of Habforce consisted of an infantry battalion of the Essex Regiment and the recently mechanized 4th Cavalry Brigade. These troops were supported by an artillery battery, a unit of antitank guns and various service troops, including engineers and even a unit that specialized

*At the American legation in Baghdad, U.S. civilians take small-arms training during the British siege of the capital in May 1941. The Americans were preparing to defend the legation after it became a haven for British civilians terrified by Iraqi threats to kill them if the RAF bombed Baghdad.*

in drilling for water. Wilson added the Mechanized Regiment of Trans-Jordan's Desert Patrol, under John Glubb.

The Habforce commander, Major General George Clark, ordered Brigadier Joseph Kingstone to take a column of 2,000 men—naturally nicknamed Kingcol—to reinforce and resupply the garrison at Habbaniya and relieve the British colony in Baghdad. Kingstone was considered one of the best fighting brigadiers in the British Army, but before he could fight he would have to negotiate the treacherous desert with 500 fully loaded trucks. Glubb's Bedouins led the way in their lightly armored Ford trucks. The backbone of Kingcol was the battalion of the Essex Regiment and the 4th Cavalry Brigade's Household Cavalry Regiment—the Life Guards and Royal Horse Guards. The cavalrymen had left their mounts behind, and they looked uncharacteristically scruffy as they swatted flies and bumped along in trucks.

On May 13, a week after the siege at Habbaniya had been lifted, Kingcol crossed the Trans-Jordan frontier into Iraq and raced east along the Iraq Petroleum Company pipeline. The pipeline began in northern Iraq at Kirkuk and ran southwest to Haditha on the Euphrates, where it forked, one branch leading southwest across Iraq, through Trans-Jordan to Haifa in Palestine, the other cutting due west through Syria to the Syrian seaport of Tripoli. Pumping stations, erected at regular intervals along both pipelines, kept the oil flowing. Along the Haifa line on Kingcol's route, the stations were numbered H-1 to H-5. The stations were modern oases, with airstrips, comfortable bungalows and supplies of water, fuel and food. In between were occasional oases of the immemorial kind, including one called Rutbah.

In an effort to save Kingcol time, the Bedouins had ranged far ahead to take Rutbah, whose massive stone fort and Iraqi police garrison blocked the Baghdad road 200 miles west of Habbaniya. Glubb had been promised RAF support from a landing field at the H-4 station, so his men threw a loose picket line around the fort and sat down to wait for the planes. Eventually the RAF arrived and dropped a few bombs. A pilot then circled low and dropped a message saying that the fort had run up a white flag. "This war was too easy," Glubb wrote later. "We had not yet fired a shot."

But when Glubb and two crowded truckloads of men approached to within 200 yards of the fort, the massive gate remained closed. "The high stone walls frowned upon us in silence," Glubb wrote. "The optimistic pilot had meanwhile flown back to H-4 to spread the happy news that Rutbah was captured." Glubb sent what he called "a peevish wireless signal" to H-4 requesting further assistance; his men, armed with nothing heavier than machine guns, could hardly make a dent in the thick walls. Suddenly an Iraqi machine gun opened up from the fort, wounding a Bedouin in the hand. A desultory exchange of fire ensued.

"After two hours," Glubb reported, "a single aircraft reappeared, circled round and dropped a bomb, which missed the fort. In the afternoon another aircraft came over and again dropped a bomb, which fell harmlessly in the desert. We lay down to sleep in disgust—this was not such fun, after all."

The next day it was more of the same. That night, an Iraqi relief force arrived from the east, and Glubb fell back to H-3. There he found a company of RAF armored cars, led by a squadron leader named L. V. Cassano, which had covered 1,000 miles from the Libyan Desert in just 48 hours. Cassano's cars raced forward and engaged the Iraqi relief force, this time with more effective RAF air support.

The attack by armored cars and fighter planes prompted the Iraqis defending the fort to reassess their situation—with results that proved ironic. Early on the morning of May 11, when Cassano's armored cars were still skirmishing in the desert outside the fort, he noticed something strange about the big door of the compound. It stood ajar. Approaching gingerly, the British encountered no resistance. They entered the fort and found it empty. The Iraqis had stolen away during the night. Brigadier Kingstone arrived soon afterward to find the area firmly in British hands.

After a few days' rest, Kingcol set off eastward again on May 15 and covered 160 miles, bivouacking within 40 miles of Habbaniya. But the next day, the desert nearly defeated Kingcol. Sending the Bedouins off on a scouting trip to the north, Kingstone led the column south on a compass heading that would bring them out south of Lake Habbaniya. But they ran into such soft sand that the vehicles could make no headway. Time and again the trucks sank axle-deep in the sand and had to be dug out in heat that reached

nearly 120° F. Kingstone realized that it was pointless—indeed dangerous—to continue. He retraced his route, and after 10 terrible hours the men struggled back into their camp of the night before.

At a conference that evening, Kingstone said to Glubb, "I shall want your dusky maidens to help us find an alternative route." On May 18, the Bedouins led the column off again; the route was circuitous but mercifully firm. Later that day, however, their march was impeded again, this time by an air strike. Enemy warplanes appeared and strafed the column, causing five casualties. After the attack Kingcol set out once more, reaching Habbaniya that evening.

The most sinister aspect of the strafing was the identity of the planes. They were twin-engined Messerschmitt-110 fighter-bombers, and in spite of their Iraqi insignia they were flown by Luftwaffe pilots. The developments Churchill feared had come to pass. Hitler, on May 3, had decided belatedly to endorse Rashid Ali's new government, and the Vichyites in Syria had obligingly put their airfields and service facilities at the Germans' disposal. More than that, the Vichyites were shipping trainloads of munitions into northern Iraq from Aleppo.

By the second week in May, 28 German planes had hop-scotched from Syria to Mosul, north of Baghdad. Three days later six Me-110s shot down a hapless RAF Audax over Habbaniya, and three Heinkel-111s bombed the base "most efficiently," said Wing Commander Dudgeon. In response, London gave the RAF permission to bomb German aircraft on Syrian landing fields, and stepped up its pressure on the beleaguered Wavell to organize a force to invade Syria and prevent a German take-over there. The war on a shoestring was escalating rapidly.

On May 25, Hitler issued Directive No. 30. In it, he called the Arab nationalist movement "our natural ally against England" and declared that he would "advance developments in the Middle East by giving assistance to Iraq." The Iraqis were excited by this declaration, but they realized that the help would be meager. For on May 20, a German airborne division—the very division that had so worried Wavell—invaded Crete, severely reducing the number of planes available to help Rashid Ali. Moreover, the Führer's attention was increasingly diverted from the Middle

East by preparations for Germany's colossal invasion of the Soviet Union. On May 27, Rashid Ali bitterly told Luigi Gabbrielli, the Italian Minister in Baghdad, that Iraq was "regarded as a pawn by Germany, who does not wish to commit herself wholeheartedly."

Meanwhile, Kingcol was moving slowly—very slowly—from Habbaniya toward Baghdad. When the Iraqis had retreated from the plateau above Habbaniya, they had opened the dikes on the Euphrates, flooding much of the main road and the country on either side of it. On May 19, the day after Kingcol's arrival at the RAF base, a detachment of local troops under British officers had seized the town of Falluja, commanding a dry portion of the main road leading to Baghdad. They performed this feat by wading through the floods from Habbaniya, towing their supplies and ammunition behind them in canoes and skiffs commandeered from the RAF Boat Club on Lake Habbaniya. But before Kingcol could advance with its trucks and field guns, it had to spend three nights in exhausting labor, hauling the heavy equipment across the floodwaters to Falluja on improvised pontoon ferries—and hiding their progress each dawn from reconnoitering Messerschmitts.

By May 28, Kingcol was ready to launch a two-pronged attack on Baghdad. The main force of 750 men, under Kingstone, would head east from Falluja on the road and attack Baghdad from the west. Meanwhile, Lieut. Colonel A. H. Ferguson would lead a flanking force of 500, mainly Household Cavalry troops, on a wide sweep across the desert to the Tigris and approach the capital from the north. En route

Ferguson's men would cut the railway from Mosul, which was bringing in munitions from the Vichy French.

The main force met no Iraqi troops until it reached a fortified post about halfway to Baghdad. No sooner had Kingstone deployed his men for an attack than the Iraqi force obligingly surrendered. Kingstone learned from the captives that the Iraqi capital was in an agony of anxiety about a huge British attack; rumor had it that no fewer than 50,000 British soldiers were marching on Baghdad. To exploit the rumors, Kingstone had his Arab interpreter telephone the capital and report that the British were coming through the floods with amphibious tanks. That ruse caused great distress among the Iraqi commanders, who were already dismayed by the news that the railway to Mosul had been cut by the British flanking force.

But as the British drew to within 12 miles of the capital, they ran into more floodwaters and stiffening Iraqi resistance. Both of Kingcol's units were halted within sight of the gold domes and minarets of the Mosque of Holy al Kazinayn. To advance any farther, both columns would have to take bridges that were vulnerable to air attack. With the Iraqi garrison in and around the capital estimated at 13 battalions and five regiments of artillery, the British position was unenviable.

Fortunately for the British, the Iraqi commanders were now convinced that their position was untenable. On the night of May 30, after RAF bombers pounded an Iraqi barracks west of the city, a staff officer woke up Kingstone. "An odd sort of message has just come in," he reported. "Two

*Aiding the Allied invaders of Syria, nomadic tribesmen roll gasoline drums toward a camel caravan that will carry the fuel 140 miles from Damascus to a British base at Palmyra. Between July and October 1941, this unique supply line moved 7,200 gallons of fuel each week—logging a total of 60,000 miles.*

delegates from the Iraqi Army will appear on the Iron Bridge at two o'clock in the morning. Will we send two officers to meet them to discuss terms of armistice?"

"The answer to that is yes," said Kingstone.

It was all over in Iraq. Rashid Ali and the four colonels, despairing of significant German help and panicked by the rumors of tremendous British strength, had fled the capital on the only road left open—eastward to Iran. The Mayor of Baghdad had taken control of the city and had immediately decided to surrender it.

After an unexplained delay, two Iraqi delegates appeared on the bridge at 4 a.m. on May 31 to begin the armistice discussions. Soon afterward, as part of the surrender terms, the 500 British subjects from the British and American legations were liberated.

On June 1, the regent, Emir Abdul Illah, reentered the capital, precisely two months after he had been forced to flee for his life.

In the 30-day campaign, British casualties numbered only 100 men. Churchill's military gamble, as General Wavell was later to admit, had paid off handsomely. It was a "bold and correct decision," Wavell wrote, "which I always felt I really ought to have taken myself."

The settlement of the Iraq affair gave Wavell no surcease from the pressures in the Middle East. His primary foe, Rommel, was making alarming thrusts in a drive across North Africa toward Egypt. In mid-June, Wavell was scheduled to launch a counterattack against the Desert Fox in Libya; he would need all the forces he could muster. Nevertheless, both Churchill and de Gaulle repeatedly demanded vigorous action against Syria. If no other troops were available, Churchill declared, the Free French should undertake the invasion alone. He held Wavell responsible for making certain, by whatever means, that Germany would not take Syria by default.

As it happened, Wavell no longer disputed the argument that quick action in Syria was essential to the defense of Palestine and even Egypt. He had been shown the light by Air Marshal Arthur William Tedder, whose view in mid-May was that "two men and a boy could do *today* what it would require a division to do in a couple of months' time." But that was May, when Tedder believed Syria to be ill-prepared for a quick British thrust. It was now June and the Vichy French, having observed the British campaign in Iraq, would undoubtedly be looking to their defenses. Wavell asserted—and time would prove him right—that a major military campaign would be required. Furthermore, he refused to let de Gaulle go it alone and possibly duplicate the Free French debacle at Dakar.

ALL REPORTS FROM TRUSTWORTHY SOURCES INCLUDING ARAB AND SYRIAN AGREE THAT EFFECT OF ACTION BY FREE FRENCH ALONE LIKELY TO BE FAILURE, Wavell cabled London on May 21. YOU MUST TRUST MY JUDGMENT IN THIS MATTER OR RELIEVE ME OF MY COMMAND. Churchill was more than willing to replace Wavell, but new intelligence reports on Vichy French solidarity in Syria persuaded him to go along with his general. He and the British Chiefs of Staff endorsed Wavell's proposal that a joint invasion be launched in early June. As with the Iraq campaign, it would be commanded from Jerusalem by General Wilson.

Despite the "absolute priority" of North Africa over Syria in Britain's battle strategy, Wavell pulled the Australian 7th Division—less one brigade—from the defense of Mersa Matruh. He also diverted to the Syrian campaign the Indian 5th Brigade of the Indian 4th Division, which was on its way to Egypt after fighting successfully in Eritrea. To these he added elements of the 1st Cavalry Division in reserve in Palestine, a commando unit from Cyprus, a squadron of armored cars, and a cavalry regiment equipped with Bren carriers and obsolescent tanks. The Free French forces consisted of two mixed brigades: Foreign Legionnaires, barefoot Senegalese infantrymen, Moroccan Spahis, some battalions from French Equatorial Africa, and a few hundred Circassian cavalrymen who had fled Syria in response to de Gaulle's propaganda broadcasts and joined Free French units in Palestine.

The whole army of about six brigades would be supported by 60 RAF aircraft, as well as by warships of the Royal Navy. However, both Air Marshal Tedder and Admiral Sir Andrew Cunningham would have to remove their forces from time to time for assignments elsewhere.

Opposing the Allies was the much larger Vichy French Army of the Levant. General André de Verdilhac commanded 18 battalions of colonial and Foreign Legion infantry, 11 battalions of Syrian, Senegalese, Lebanese and Circassian levies, and 20 squadrons of North African Spahis—for a grand total of 35,000 men. The Army of the Levant also enjoyed an enormous edge in equipment, including half again as many planes as the Allies.

Wavell and Wilson planned to seize the cities and airfields of Beirut, Riyaq and Damascus in quick succession. To avoid overextending their communication lines, they intended to go no farther in the campaign's initial stages—apart from small raids. If those three cities were captured quickly, Wilson hoped, Verdilhac and Vichy High Commissioner General Henri-Fernand Dentz would admit defeat.

The three-pronged campaign would be launched simultaneously from Palestine and Trans-Jordan. Prong No. 1 on the left flank—the Australian 21st Brigade—would advance northward along the Lebanon coast road to Beirut, the seat of the Vichy government. Prong No. 2 in the center, consisting of the Australian 25th Brigade, would head through the mountains to the town of Marj 'Uyun. Beyond Marj 'Uyun the Bekaa plain offered a quick advance on Riyaq and its important airfield. Prong No. 3 on the right flank—made up of the Indian 5th Brigade—would move into Syria across broad wheatlands, bordered on the west by the Golan Heights and on the east by the mountains known as Jebel Druze, and follow the main road and the railway that ran north to Damascus.

The invasion was launched in bright moonlight at 2 a.m. on June 8, 1941, and it immediately presented the British with certain psychological difficulties. The troops had no enthusiasm for killing former allies, and instead of fighting

with intensity, they kept hoping that the Vichyites would lay down their arms. Nor did the British commanders wish to provoke the Vichyites unnecessarily; under their orders, the Australians moving along the populous coast were to wear their slouch hats—presumably as a sign of friendly interest—and refrain from donning their steel helmets unless they were fired upon.

To conciliate the Vichy French further, the RAF dropped blizzards of leaflets explaining that the British and General de Gaulle's fighting men were coming only to drive out the Germans and save Syria for France. This appeal had little effect. High Commissioner Dentz had anticipated the propaganda ploy and had seen to it that all traces of the German presence were removed. The last Luftwaffe planes and German technicians had made a timely departure 48 hours before the invasion.

In any case, the Vichy troops were of a will to fight. As they saw it, their territory was being invaded, never mind by whom, and they fought hard. Moreover, they reserved a special violence for the Free French, whom they perceived as renegades and traitors to France. Whenever Gaullist emissaries attempted to parley under a white flag, they would be greeted with contemptuous rebuffs—and occasionally with gunfire.

On the first full day of the invasion, it became obvious that the comedic aspects of the Iraq campaign would be conspicuously absent in Syria. General Wilson had pinned his greatest hopes on the coastal advance of the Australian 21st Brigade, and the Aussies captured the town of Tyre

*An Australian soldier stands by after setting fire to a damaged Vichy French fighter plane, captured during the Allied invasion of Syria in July 1941. The Vichy air force had inflicted heavy casualties on the Allied invasion troops until RAF reinforcements arrived and knocked out 55 Vichy planes they caught on the ground. The Allies later burned all captured enemy aircraft that could not be salvaged.*

with scarcely a shot fired. But thereafter, resolute Vichy defenders forced them to wear their steel helmets at all times.

Part of the Australians' problem was the terrain. They could hardly maneuver on the route they had to take—a strip 2,000 yards wide between the Mediterranean Sea and the sharply rising mountains of the Lebanon range. Small seaside towns along the route were dotted with concrete blockhouses and defended stubbornly by Algerian riflemen. Opposite, in the foothills to the east, Vichy artillery and tanks lay in wait. The Australians were supported by the guns of Admiral Cunningham's cruisers and destroyers, which shelled Vichy positions from 4,000 to 5,000 yards offshore. But the Navy gunners were considerably less effective than the Aussies had hoped.

To make matters worse, an amphibious attack on the mouth of the Litani River, intended to clear the way for the Australian advance north from Tyre, went disastrously awry. The assault force of 480 commandos from Cyprus was delayed a day by heavy surf. By the time they landed they had lost the element of surprise and took a severe beating. More than a quarter of the men, including their young colonel and most of his officers, were killed, wounded or captured.

In spite of the commando disaster, the Australian 21st managed to get across the Litani—a laborious process, since the Vichy defenders had blown up the bridge. By the middle of the week they were pushing hard for their next objective, the large town of Sidon, halfway to Beirut. But the defenders fought a skillful delaying action. For two days the Australians were held up by Vichy tanks that rumbled down from the hills and broke up their advancing columns. Not until June 15, a full week after the start of the invasion, did Sidon fall, and then only after heavy bombardment from Australian field guns and considerable help from the Royal Navy. Beirut, only 24 miles away, seemed distant indeed.

Meanwhile, there had been heavy fighting in the mountains. The Australian 25th Brigade—Prong No. 2—had succeeded in taking Marj 'Uyun, though only after a full-scale attack behind a rolling artillery barrage that inched forward 100 yards every four minutes until two miles had been covered. The defenders, covered by Spahi cavalry, retreated grudgingly and with great care, thus preventing a quick breakthrough by the Australians to the Bekaa plain.

At this point, General Wilson, eager to strengthen the drive on Beirut, put most of Prong No. 2 on the defensive and sent a mobile column off to the west to join up with the 21st along the coast. This move was sound enough in theory. But to open a route to the coast, the column had to traverse the Lebanon mountains and seize the lofty town of Jezzin. For 25 miles, the Australians moved along narrow tracks and around sharp bends, where the guns had to be unlimbered and manhandled at the edge of steep precipices. Tanks got hung up on rocks, their tracks thrashing helplessly in the air. One broken-down tank had to be pushed over a cliff to allow the rest to pass.

The Australians persevered. They took Jezzin after blasting past a roadblock and fighting their way through steeply terraced vineyards where Vichy riflemen and machine gunners lurked. But in Jezzin they stalled, their energies exhausted. It was all they could do to hold the town and keep it supplied from Marj 'Uyun, and they were of no use in the coastal advance. Thus, for all practical purposes, Prong No. 2 was out of commission, and soon afterward Riyaq was eliminated as an objective.

Prong No. 3 made good progress at first. Commanded by Brigadier W. L. Lloyd, the mixed British and Indian 5th Brigade captured four border towns with few casualties. Since the towns were in open country and difficult to defend, Vichy General Étienne Delhomme, commanding southern Syria, withdrew to a stronger position 10 miles in front of Damascus. Here the fortified town of Kiswe and a line of high hills dominated the approach from the south.

Allied plans now called for the advance of Gaullist forces, commanded in the field by General Paul-Louis Le Gentilhomme. The Free French troops crossed the Palestine border into Syria in about 200 buses. Lustily singing the "Marseillaise," they passed through the positions held by Lloyd's Indian 5th Brigade and moved forward to assault Kiswe on the road to Damascus. Lloyd evidently had orders to hold back so that the glory would belong entirely to the Free French. But little glory was forthcoming.

Le Gentilhomme launched his attack on Kiswe on the afternoon of June 11, and almost at once things started to go sour. That evening, his division commander, a Colonel Monclar of the Foreign Legion, resigned. Apparently Monclar had heard that a Vichyite Legionnaire battalion was de-fending Kiswe, and he was obeying the unwritten rule that Legionnaires do not fight Legionnaires. Following his lead, the Free French Legionnaires took little part in the attack.

After making some progress on the first day of the battle, the Free French came apart completely. They received a report that 100 Vichy armored vehicles had been seen attacking to the south, and confusion spread through·their ranks. The armored column turned out to be another Free French unit, but by then it was too late to repair the damage. Le Gentilhomme's attack was in disarray. The general himself was wounded during a Vichy air raid and was sent—protesting vigorously—to a hospital in the rear.

The next day, June 13, Brigadier Lloyd was put in overall command of the operation by Wavell and Wilson. Lloyd decided that a new assault, with extra artillery, could not be mounted until June 15. So Prong No. 3 also ground to a halt.

After a week of fighting, Beirut, Riyaq and Damascus remained in Vichy hands. The British and Free French had lost about 500 men killed, wounded and captured. But they had learned a salutary lesson: The Vichy French had to be taken in deadly earnest; they were dangerous enemies fighting for their honor as well as their country. "You thought we were yellow, didn't you?" growled a Vichyite sergeant to a journalist. "Well, we've shown you."

While the three invading columns were stuck in place, Vichy General de Verdilhac showed that he was an intelligent and daring commander. His reserves of troops and supplies were growing smaller and smaller, and it was clear that he could expect no help from Vichy, much less from Berlin. Deciding that his limited resources would best be used in an attack, Verdilhac devised his own three-pronged assault, aimed at selected points along the Allied lines of communications.

On the 15th of June, just as Brigadier Lloyd renewed his onslaught on Kiswe, Verdilhac's forces struck at Lloyd's rear and came within an ace of cutting him off completely. By that evening the Vichy French were astride Lloyd's supply line more than 20 miles behind his advance headquarters. The following day at the town of Kuneitra they surrounded the Royal Fusiliers, and after a stiff fight they forced 470 men to surrender.

But Lloyd refused to be deflected from his attack on Kiswe

*A Vichy French soldier leads a Syrian camel patrol through the ruins of the ancient city of Palmyra shortly before the Allied invasion. In May of 1941, more than 350 of these troops, led by a Vichy French colonel, switched allegiance and joined General de Gaulle's Free French Army.*

by the disturbing reports coming in from his rear. His Indian troops found the village bristling with machine guns and surrounded by an antitank ditch that was 13 feet wide and 13 feet deep. Vichy's Algerian soldiers put up a gallant defense, knocking out 10 of 12 Gaullist tanks. But the Indians, supported by Gaullist black Africans, Spahis and Circassian cavalry, worked their way through the town's defenses. In hard fighting that raged all that day and into the next in some sectors, the attackers prevailed. A captured Vichy officer complimented Lloyd on his troops' performance in combat: "What you have done is incredible. Your Indians are formidable."

By June 17, British and Australian reinforcements from Palestine had recaptured Kuneitra, and Lloyd's brigade was ready for the attack on Damascus. The Free French advanced on the main road, while the Indians swung to the left to seize Mezzé and cut the road and the railway that led west out of Damascus toward Beirut. After a fierce struggle on the night of the 18th, the Indians took possession of Mezzé. But the victory was short-lived; Vichy tanks slipped in behind the Indians and cut the road from Kuneitra.

All day the tanks hammered at Mezzé. The Vichy French also brought up artillery, and on the afternoon of the 19th, the tanks broke through on the heels of a heavy artillery bombardment. The Indians were overrun. They took refuge in a battered stone house and barricaded themselves in for one last stand.

Two days later, after the Vichy French had withdrawn, a British patrol searched the ruins of Mezzé and found no survivors. "Very messy," reported the patrol commander. It later turned out that a handful of Indians had been taken prisoner. But the Indians' disaster at Mezzé, coming on top of the Royal Fusiliers' surrender at Kuneitra, spelled the end of Lloyd's 5th Brigade as a fighting unit.

Lloyd was furious. He blamed the losses on the Free French, who had failed to make headway up the main road to Damascus. An early clash had cost the Free French heavy losses, and after that they had refused to advance until Australian machine gunners were brought up to give them additional covering fire. By the time Mezzé fell, the Free French had advanced only three miles along the main road to Damascus, and Lloyd insisted that if they had attacked with determination, they would have forced the Vichy French to slacken their pressure on Mezzé.

In spite of his considerable losses, Lloyd on June 20 launched his second night attack in two days. In a flanking movement, a detachment of recently arrived Australian troops moved through the darkness beyond Mezzé and reached the main road and railroad leading west from Damascus. Finding no enemy defenders, the Australians

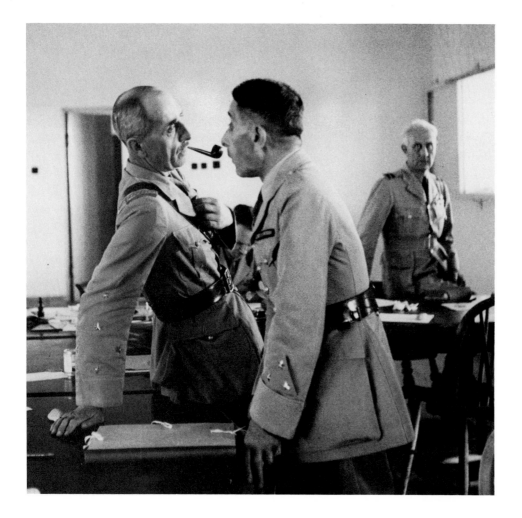

Free French General Georges Catroux (left) and Vichy General André de Verdilhac exchange heated words after the signing of the Syrian armistice on July 14, 1941. Even in defeat, the embittered Vichy forces refused to deal with Britain's Gaullist allies, so the British alone accepted the Vichy surrender.

chopped down telegraph poles and built a roadblock. As they stopped and captured vehicles, the Australians placed them across the railroad tracks to block rail traffic as well.

When the Vichy commander got word of the roadblock, he sent a small tank force out to test the enemy. The Australians succeeded in holding off the armored probe, thereby convincing the Vichyites in Damascus that they would soon be surrounded. By the morning of the 21st, six Vichy battalions abandoned the city, escaping into the mountains to the northwest. As the last of them moved out, Arab emissaries drove south to meet the approaching Free French and accompany them into Damascus. Thus the fight for the city, having begun with Allied setbacks, ended in a surprisingly easy Allied victory.

The capture of Damascus gave an immediate lift to Allied morale. Now only Beirut remained to be captured. But before the British could bask in their Damascus victory, it was eclipsed. On the very next day, June 22, came the stunning news that German armies had invaded the Soviet Union on a 1,500-mile-wide front. Syria and Damascus fell from the headlines like stones.

And so did the troubled Wavell. His desert counteroffensive, which was supposed to have knocked out Rommel's Afrika Korps, had come to nothing—in part because Wavell had felt obliged to divert some of his forces to Syria. But Churchill seized upon this failure to end his exasperating dealings with his Middle East commander. On the Prime Minister's direct orders, Wavell exchanged posts with India's commander in chief, General Auchinleck. Wavell's final contribution to the Syrian campaign was to order, as a preliminary to the assault on Beirut, a new offensive against Verdilhac's eastern flank in the Syrian desert.

Habforce—which had been split up to garrison sections of Iraq—was hastily reconstituted for an attack across the border into Syria. Major General George Clark was again placed in command, with John Glubb, the Arab Legion and Brigadier Kingstone at his side. Habforce had for its objective the oasis of Palmyra, standing amid Roman ruins at the crossroads of ancient caravan routes between the Tigris-Euphrates valley and the Mediterranean coast. On the tactical map, Palmyra lay between pumping stations T-3 and T-4 on the Iraq Petroleum Company's pipeline to Tripoli.

The French had constructed an air base much like the one at Habbaniya on the eastern approaches of the oasis. Unlike Habbaniya, the Palmyra compound was well defended by concrete pillboxes and antitank ditches. For observation posts and snipers' nests, the French used the Roman ruins and a medieval castle atop a nearby hill. But Palmyra's commandant did not intend to wait at the oasis until the British attacked, as he knew they would. He sent about 500 men—a company of Foreign Legionnaires and a corps of Bedouins with camels and half a dozen armored cars—to defend pumping stations T-2 and T-3. Thus he planned to intercept the British as they approached Palmyra from the east and fight them in depth.

Habforce, however, made its approach from two directions. Starting on the evening of June 20, a detachment of the Household Cavalry advanced westward along the pipeline toward T-2. The main force, under Kingstone, drove 150 miles north across open desert, intending to hit Palmyra by surprise. The main force advanced in three waves: first the Wiltshire Yeomanry, led by L. V. Cassano's armored cars and the Arab Legion; then the Warwickshire Yeomanry under Kingstone; and finally the Essex Regiment. According to plan, Palmyra and the small forts at T-2 and T-3 were to be captured by midday on the 21st.

But the British faced a Habbaniya in reverse: Like the Iraqis, they had more men but unsatisfactory air support, since advance bases for RAF fighters had not been built. Habforce was spotted by Vichy aircraft before its advance column reached Palmyra, and its strung-out units were vigorously bombed and strafed by low-flying Potez 63s—"a bloody good bomber," Cassano said—and De Woitine D500 fighters. Though T-2 fell quickly, the main units of Habforce did not move into position around Palmyra until June 23, and at that late date the Warwickshires were still besieging the outpost of T-3.

Days passed, and Habforce was still pinned down around its objective, bedeviled by low-level air attacks and by the blazing heat of the desert. Brigadier Kingstone collapsed and was driven to a hospital in Jerusalem. General Clark appealed repeatedly for air support, and finally, on June 28, his pleas were answered in strength. RAF planes scoured the desert skies and shot down six French America-built Martin bombers in full view of the delighted troops. "From that moment," Clark wrote, "things began to look up."

Still, the defenders in Palmyra fought on bitterly. Foreign Legionnaires drove back the Wiltshires, reducing the unit to a fighting strength of 36. But the Vichy garrison was exhausted and nearly out of food and ammunition.

At dawn on July 3, a white flag appeared above Palmyra's headquarters. The Essex Regiment marched in to take possession and found the defenders—165 men in all—gloriously drunk. Several dozen of them were German and Russian members of the Foreign Legion; as yet they were unaware of the fact that their nations were at war. T-3 surrendered the next day.

With the end of the siege of Palmyra—"that splendid affair amid the noble ruins," Churchill called it—Vichy resistance in the desert rapidly collapsed. Deir ez Zor, boasting one of the two bridges along a 500-mile stretch of the Eu-

Soaring over Jerusalem's Mount of Olives, RAF Blenheim bombers put on a show of Allied strength on July 24, 1941. This and other flybys were staged to discourage Arab nationalists from joining the Germans.

phrates, fell to the Indian 10th Division, under the command of Major General Sir William Slim, invading from northern Iraq. As Slim and his aide-de-camp drove into the town, they came across a large number of Syrian levies. "Without exception," recounted Slim, "as far as the eye could see, they were busily engaged in divesting themselves of their uniforms. Having discarded their arms and telltale uniforms, they proposed, in their somewhat scanty underclothes, to fade gently but rapidly into a civilian background." In this purpose they succeeded; the prisoners taken at Deir ez Zor were, with very few exceptions, French.

Now the Syrian campaign reached its final stage: the assault on Beirut. Although the Vichy position was hopeless, General de Verdilhac mustered all available troops for the defense of the city, together with his last few tanks and armored cars. He deployed his forces to defend strong points in a wide arc along the Damur River, extending as far as a dozen miles from Beirut.

On the night of June 29, the converging British forces opened up with all the guns they had, concentrating their fire on the Damur River line. "The most stupendous naval and aeriel bombardment starts," wrote a soldier diarist serving with the Cheshire Yeomanry, "and continues most of the night with star shells, parachute flares and a noise and concussion which shook the ground for miles around. Meanwhile the 21st Brigade advanced to the heights above the Damur. Perhaps the nastiest experience of the night was when some of the young Australians going forward cracked up under gun and machine-gun fire and came back blubbering aloud with shell shock."

Night after night, the bombardment continued, and the inhabitants of Beirut, standing in their gardens or on their rooftops, could hear the shellfire drawing closer. Day after day, the Australians worked their way toward the river, filtering through the steep ravines and over the rugged hills on Beirut's inland flank.

Early on the morning of July 6, the battle for Beirut proper began. Under a 62-gun bombardment of the Vichy positions in the hills ahead, the lead companies of the 21st Brigade crossed the Damur and headed upslope to the north. The next day, the Australian 17th Brigade, which had come up from Palestine, pressed eastward and upward for three tortuous miles, attempting to outflank the Vichyites in the

hills. Some units of the 17th later tried to break through the lush plantations along the coast west of the city, but every banana grove and orange orchard seemed to conceal a Vichy machine-gun nest.

By morning of the third day of battle, the Australians occupied positions south and east of Beirut. Both sides were exhausted, but it was now apparent to the Vichyites that their ground forces had been whittled down to a point where further resistance was merely wasteful. The RAF had almost totally wiped out the Vichy air force. So on July 8, High Commissioner Dentz called on Cornelius Engert, the American Consul General in Beirut, and handed him a note requesting negotiations with the British high command for the surrender of Syria.

In the 60 hours before the cease-fire went into effect, vainglorious commanders on both sides urged their troops to end the campaign on a victorious note. At Jezzin, Marj 'Uyun, and even out on the Euphrates River, last bursts of fighting flared up, and the survivors were still counting their dead when, at 12:01 a.m. on July 12, the 34-day war officially ended. In the final count, each side had lost more than 1,000 soldiers killed.

On July 15, Winston Churchill rose in the House of Commons and indulged in some Churchillian rhetoric. "If anyone had predicted two months ago," he declared, "when Iraq was in revolt and our people were hanging on by their eyelids at Habbaniya and our Ambassador was imprisoned in his Embassy at Baghdad, and when all Syria and Iraq began to be overrun by German tourists, and were in the hands of forces controlled indirectly but none the less powerfully by German authority—if anyone had predicted that we should already, by the middle of July, have cleaned up the whole of the Levant and have reestablished our authority there for the time being, such a prophet would have been considered most imprudent."

Churchill's self-congratulations were somewhat premature; even as he spoke, more Middle Eastern trouble was brewing in Iran. Nevertheless, the Prime Minister's daring had paid off—with an assist from the Germans. They had lacked the acumen and interest to contest seriously for Iraq and Syria. Hitler had, wrote Churchill, "cast away the opportunity of taking a great prize for little cost."

# GUARDIANS OF DESERT PEACE

Outside a fort at remote El Mafraq, Trans-Jordan, a soldier in the Arab Legion trains a fierce-looking saker falcon, the mascot of the legion's Desert Patrol.

# THE FIERCE ELITE OF THE ARAB LEGION

*Wearing the dress helmet of the Arab Legion, Major Glubb chats with the Emir Abdullah about the Desert Patrol's 1941 triumphs in Iraq and Syria.*

The Allied invasions of pro-German Iraq and Syria in 1941 hinged on help from an improbable source—a tiny band of Bedouin warriors. As guards, guides and raiders, the Bedouins protected Allied supply lines, led British units across the trackless desert, and earned respect for their courage under fire. All were members of the Desert Patrol, an elite, 650-man branch of Trans-Jordan's Army, the Arab Legion.

The Desert Patrol was the creation of John Bagot Glubb, a former British Army officer who entered the service of the Emir Abdullah, Trans-Jordan's ruler, in 1930. The Emir, impressed by Glubb's fluent Arabic and knowledge of Bedouin customs, commissioned him to raise a force to police the country's 28,000 square miles of desert.

Glubb recruited primarily among the Howeitat of southern Trans-Jordan—tribesmen who proved almost as intractable as they were fierce. The first volunteer, Awwadh ibn Hudeiba, so hated the idea of forming ranks that he flung down his uniform and stalked off, returning to his custom of raiding other tribes. Glubb curbed the Howeitat by threatening to police them with members of unfriendly tribes if they did not join. Eventually, these formidable desert fighters enlisted, forming the backbone of the Desert Patrol.

Glubb's next task was to teach his recruits to read and write. "In every desert outpost," he wrote, "wild, bearded faces could be seen crouching over copybooks, slowly tracing the alphabet, while horny hands gripped the pencil as they would have held a lance or rifle." Then after intensive training, the men were assigned to the Desert Patrol's long-range reconnaissance unit, the Camel Corps, or to its motorized strike force, the Desert Mechanized Regiment.

When it came to desert scouting or survival skills, there was nothing Glubb could teach his charges. "Each of his men," said a British officer who fought alongside the Desert Patrol, "was a walking guidebook to the desert." The Bedouins' familiarity with the terrain gave them a distinct advantage over their foe in 1941. "To the enemy," Glubb wrote, "the desert was a strange and hostile land, to be crossed as quickly as possible. To us it was home."

*A sergeant major of the Desert Patrol, armed with a .38-caliber Webley revolver and a silver-handled dagger, scans the horizon before remounting his camel.*

*A camel-mounted detachment of the Desert Patrol trots by its headquarters, a mud-walled fort at El Mafraq, 60 miles north of Amman. Similar forts, connected*

As a bandoleered sergeant looks on, a soldier carefully polishes his fighting knife.

by radio, were erected at strategic oases throughout Trans-Jordan.

A legionnaire squatting in a goat-hair tent roasts beans over the fire for a pot of coffee.

69

A Desert Patrol veteran takes the fingerprints of a youthful recruit.

A trainee sets a Bangalore torpedo to blast a gap through concertina wire.

At a training camp in Amman, Glubb's men practice firing an obsolete,

2-pounder field gun. In the field, the Desert Patrol traveled light, equipped with nothing more than Lee-Enfield rifles and old-fashioned machine guns.

*A detachment of legionnaires takes aim during rifle practice at El Mafraq. The camels were trained to lower their heads or to lie on their sides during actua*

Standing at attention, men of the Camel Corps await inspection alongside their kneeling mounts.

With riding sticks and rifles in their hands, legionnaires return to their base after a 1941 patrol.

*battles so that their riders could shoot over them.*

## FROM BEDOUIN BANDITS TO POPULAR HEROES

When the Desert Patrol cracked down on the ancient practice of intertribal camel rustling, many of the chastened offenders, deprived of a livelihood, enlisted in the Camel Corps. Riding pedigreed racing camels commandeered by Glubb, they were soon using their scouting and tracking expertise to run down thieves and rustlers, to protect desert caravans and to reconnoiter Trans-Jordan's 700 miles of barren borders. They penetrated the water-less areas of soft sand where wheeled vehicles could not travel. And they rode for up to 20 hours at a stretch, covering more than 100 miles in a single day.

Although patrol duty was spine-jarring and monotonous, it brought unexpected rewards. Outfitted in the Arab Legion's flowing buff robes and its red-and-white headdresses, the camel corpsmen cut impressive figures as they rode through the desert, crooning to their mounts to regulate their speed. "Tribesmen were soon complaining," Glubb reported, "that the prettiest girls would accept none but our soldiers as their lovers."

73

*Two soldiers man a Lewis machine gun on one of the Desert Patrol's six homemade armored cars. Designed by Glubb, a former Royal engineer, the vehicles had armor-plated bodies mounted on Ford truck chassis.*

# ROUTING THE ENEMY WITH FORD TRUCKS

The Desert Patrol's Mechanized Regiment, a crack force of 350 Bedouin infantrymen, plied the desert sands in six armored cars and 30 Ford trucks driven by daredevils who sped along at breakneck speeds. The Bedouins waged war just as they drove—with wild and happy abandon.

In July 1941, while supporting the British attack on Palmyra, Syria, a tiny detachment of the regiment was ambushed by a motorized company of Vichy French. Although outnumbered 5 to 1, Glubb's men held their ground while their armored cars pinned down the French with machine-gun fire. Then the feisty Bedouins charged headlong into the French ranks.

When the enemy fled in trucks, Glubb's warriors boarded their own vehicles and gave boisterous chase, brandishing their rifles and yelling bloodcurdling war cries. The terror-stricken Vichy drivers, unfamiliar with the terrain, drove into a sandy cul-de-sac. There the Frenchmen were quickly surrounded, dragged from their vehicles and disarmed. The final tally: two casualties among Glubb's men; 11 casualties and 80 prisoners among the French.

News of the victory spread quickly in the desert, and thousands of Bedouins volunteered for the Mechanized Regiment. "Our little campaign in Iraq and Palmyra," Glubb wrote later, "had invested the Arab Legion with a halo of glory."

At a July 1941 ceremony honoring the legion's victories in Iraq and Syria, men of the Desert Patrol's Mechanized Regiment pass in review with a color guard.

# 3

**An invasion orchestrated in Moscow and London**
**Installing an amenable new Shah in Teheran**
**The greatest Kremlin banquet since the days of the Czar**
**The many perils on the road to Tabriz**
**Scornful gibes from Josef Stalin**
**An offbeat outfit with "no fancy-pants dash whatever"**
**Building a mountain road "as smooth as Fifth Avenue"**
**Replacing the food the Russians commandeered**
**Soviet armies in American trucks**

In June of 1941, Winston Churchill hoped that Britain's ouster of the unfriendly government in Iraq, together with the British and Free French conquest of Syria, would make the Middle East safe for the Allies. But by July, Churchill smelled trouble in Iran and was laying plans to occupy the ancient kingdom, once known as Persia.

The German invasion of Russia on June 22 had invested Iran with great new importance in the strategic scheme of things. Britain and the Soviet Union could not afford to let Iran slip into the German camp. The country was crucial to the defense of India and its loss could jeopardize communications with the British Empire and the Commonwealth territories in the Far East. Moreover, Britain depended on oil from Iran, and that supply was indirectly threatened by the German armies now plunging deep into the Soviet Union.

But a British take-over in Iran would be more than a simple preemptive strike. It would open a new Allied supply route up through the so-called Persian Corridor to the battlefields of the Russian front. Such a logistical operation could—and would—have a significant impact upon the course of the War.

The problem that Churchill faced in Iran that summer of 1941 was closely akin to the recent troubles in Iraq and Syria: Local nationalists had become pro-German in reaction to the British and the Russians, who had contended for influence over the country for a century and more. Though Iran was avowedly neutral, reports reaching London told of more than 2,000 Germans at work there. Many were serving as technical advisers in the government of the ruler, Reza Shah Pahlavi. The British were convinced that the Germans were secretly building up a fifth column of Iranians sympathetic to Germany.

"Should Russia be defeated," Foreign Secretary Anthony Eden wrote to Churchill on July 22, "we shall have to be ready to occupy the Iranian oil fields; for in such an eventuality German pressure on the Iranians to turn us out would be irresistible."

The British broached the subject of Iran to the Russians and found them concerned enough about the German presence there to agree to military intervention if it became necessary. A joint plan of action was worked out in late July and early August. A British-Soviet note would be presented to the Shah, asking him to expel the Germans from Iran; if, as

# LIFE LINE TO THE RUSSIANS

expected, he refused to do so, troops of the two Allies would occupy the country.

The ultimatum was delivered to the Shah on August 17. In reply, the Shah offered to reduce the number of Germans in Iran, but insisted on retaining the technical and communications experts whom the British and Russians were particularly eager to evict. Churchill called the message "an unsatisfactory reply," and the invasion was scheduled for August 25. The Iranian Army was large for the Middle East—upward of 120,000 men—but it was ill-equipped and poorly trained. The Allies expected no serious problem.

On the appointed day, 40,000 Soviet troops in three mechanized columns drove south into Iran while two British divisions and part of another—19,000 men in all, mostly Indians—struck from Basra and other bases in Iraq. Indian infantry units advanced down the Shatt al Arab river from Basra in motorboats and paddle steamers and captured the Abadan oil refinery and adjacent Iranian ports at the head of the Persian Gulf. A mobile column under the command of Major General William Slim, who would later win fame in Burma, drove northeastward from Iraq into Luristan, seized Iranian oil fields and headed toward the Iranian capital, Teheran.

There was little fighting and few casualties. On August 27, the Iranian government began negotiating for an armistice. Three days later, British and Soviet forces met at the agreed-upon occupation line, running across northern Iran.

The campaign was over, but the Shah's political leanings were still in question. He continued to profess his neutrality. He did begin to oust the Germans. But he did not do enough to satisfy the Allies, who thoroughly distrusted him, and he did more than enough to convince his people that he was a British lackey. Clearly his position as monarch was untenable. So on September 16, he abdicated in favor of his son, the 22-year-old Muhammad Reza Pahlavi, and was forced into exile on the island of Mauritius in the Indian Ocean. Finally the Allies had their way: The Germans packed up and left Iran—after a last shopping spree in Teheran.

At the same time, the Iranian take-over was growing steadily more important to the Allies. Since a second front in Europe was still in the distant future (it was in fact three years away), something else had to be done quickly to relieve some of the pressure on the Soviet Union. Churchill had promised Stalin war matériel, including 200 fighter planes, "as soon as possible." He had also volunteered to share U.S. Lend-Lease aid and opened discussion with the Americans to expedite shipment of supplies Britain lacked or could not spare. When Stalin mentioned payment for the goods, Churchill assured him that "any assistance we can give you would better be on the same basis of comradeship as the American Lend-Lease bill, of which no formal account is kept in money."

This war aid had begun to move by sea soon after the German attack on the Soviet Union. But German U-boats and Luftwaffe planes based in occupied Norway were imperiling the Allied supply convoys bound for the northern Soviet ports of Murmansk and Archangel. And the Russians' need for supplies had become desperate. By late September, German armies had captured nearly one third of the Soviet Union's industry and much of its best agricultural land, in the process destroying whole Soviet armies and taking more than one million soldiers prisoner. British and American leaders feared that Stalin might soon be forced to negotiate a separate peace.

In hopes of bolstering the Russians, W. Averell Harriman and Lord Beaverbrook, the personal representatives of Roosevelt and Churchill, flew to Moscow in late September to discuss a long list of Lend-Lease supplies urgently requested by Stalin. The dictator was alternately friendly and abusive; on one occasion he disparaged the aid, implying that the anti-Communist Western powers gave it only to see the Russians and the Germans kill each other off. But Stalin still wanted prompt delivery of tanks, planes, antiaircraft guns, machine guns, rifles, aviation gasoline, aluminum and other raw materials, and large numbers of trucks.

Out of these discussions came an agreement on the quantities and delivery dates of Lend-Lease aid to the Soviet Union. Though American industry was still on a peacetime footing, the United States joined with Britain in pledging 1.5 million tons of war matériel by the end of June 1942. The so-called Moscow Protocol, the first of four Lend-Lease agreements with the Soviet Union, was signed on October 1, 1941, and it inspired one of Stalin's aides to exclaim, "Now we shall win the War!"

To celebrate the signing of the Moscow Protocol, Stalin

feted the British and American representatives in the white marble, glass and gold Catherine the Great Room at the Kremlin. The banquet, said to be the most elaborate function staged at the Kremlin since the czarist era, consolidated the new coalition of anti-German states, soon to be called the United Nations.

The United States and Great Britain had only a general idea of how to fulfill the commitment they had made to the Soviet Union. Funds had to be allocated to produce and transport the goods. Extensive facilities—ports, rails, roads—would have to be built, and laborers and technicians would have to be provided. The officials in charge of production and the services of supply knew that none of the many necessities was plentiful at the far end of the few feasible delivery routes.

It was already obvious that the two nations could not rely on the shorter route to Murmansk and Archangel. A valuable alternative was the route from the American West Coast to Vladivostok and other Soviet Far Eastern ports. But these ports were separated from the battlefront by the whole length of Asia; "any bullet sent by that route," said a U.S. official, "had to travel halfway around the world before it could be fired at a German." Moreover, the Far East route

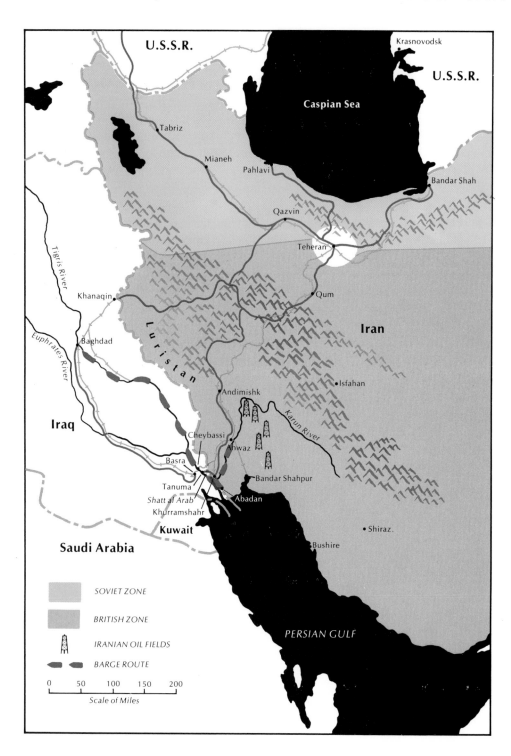

*After the British and Soviet take-over in August 1941, Iran was partitioned into three sectors: a Soviet zone of occupation (pink tint), an area centered on Teheran (circled) still under Iranian control, and a British zone of occupation (gray tint), later shared with the U.S. Persian Gulf Command. Lend-Lease war matériel for the Red Army was transported to transfer points in the Soviet zone over the Iranian State Railway and truck routes (red lines) from Iranian and Iraqi ports on the Persian Gulf and the Shatt al Arab waterway.*

passed through Japanese waters, and after the United States declared war on Japan in December 1941, only vessels of the Soviet Union, still uneasily at peace with Japan, were entrusted to transport American supplies, much of it raw materials and foodstuffs.

For war matériel, the safest, most reliable route would be the Persian Corridor, running from ports on the Persian Gulf, through Iran and portions of Iraq, to the Soviet border at the Caspian Sea. But it was much longer than the voyage to Murmansk; convoys from the United States would have to sail 15,000 miles round the Cape of Good Hope before they reached the gulf ports. And there the serious logistic problems also began.

Iran and Iraq, the two countries that shared the area between the gulf and the Caspian, covered an area of about 800,000 square miles. Iran alone was larger than Germany, France and England combined. The shortest routes from the gulf to the southern Soviet border ran nearly 1,000 miles through eastern Iraq and western Iran, across sun-scorched deserts and tiers of rugged mountains where temperatures at the higher altitudes sometimes dropped to −25° F.

The main supply artery was the single-track Iranian State Railway. After 12 years of construction by an international consortium, it had been completed in 1938 and was justly regarded as one of the engineering wonders of the world. Its track crossed 180 miles of desert from the Persian Gulf coast, climbed steeply for more than 100 miles through tunnels and across perilous bridges, then dropped 3,000 feet to Teheran, 500 miles from the start. Beyond Teheran, the railroad line split into two branches. One ran to Mianeh west of the Caspian Sea. The other branch ran northeastward,

through another 200 miles of lofty mountains, and descended to Bandar Shah on the Caspian Sea. In one mountainous section, 163 miles long, the track passed through 133 tunnels totaling 47 miles.

The normal peacetime traffic on the line was one passenger train every other day and one short freight train a week. The rolling stock was old-fashioned and poorly maintained. The trains were dispatched over a single telephone circuit, and they usually stopped when the phone went dead. The trains that failed to stop sometimes collided.

There were no first-class highways in Iran. The few paved roads, some built by the British during World War I, were narrow, hazardous affairs maintained sporadically by parties of villagers who filled holes with stones and dirt. Some stretches of roadway were no more than tracks followed for centuries by camel caravans.

The burden of preparing the Persian Corridor for the supply effort fell upon Lieut. General Sir Edward Quinan and his few thousand Indian occupation troops in Iran and Iraq, known as the Persia and Iraq Force, or Paiforce. To do the job and maintain security in both Iraq and its sector of Iran, Quinan's force was to be enlarged to 10 divisions. His orders, delivered in October after the signing of the Moscow Protocol, were "to develop such road, rail and river communications as are necessary to ensure the maximum possible delivery of supplies to Russia."

Merely to supply 10 full-strength British divisions (about 140,000 men, plus support units) was an enormous problem. The troops would require about 35,000 tons of ammunition to be prepared for three months of fighting. Paiforce would also need many times that tonnage in gasoline, oil,

*In the Iranian desert north of Abadan, Indian infantrymen patrol an oil pipeline a few days after the British-Soviet invasion on August 25, 1941. The giant Anglo-Iranian Oil Company slowed down but never ceased operation during the four-day take-over. Indeed, only 24 hours after the Iranians capitulated, it was again producing at capacity, pumping more than 200,000 barrels daily to oil tankers bound for British Empire ports.*

food, clothing, tools, spare parts for guns and vehicles, communications equipment, medical supplies, mobile workshops, and materials for building depots, bridges, defense works, hospitals, power stations and pump houses, and pipelines. Through the whole occupation, in fact, the British troops would use more of the incoming supplies than they forwarded to the Russians.

In October, the war matériel began trickling into the Persian Corridor from all over the globe. A share of British Lend-Lease aid from the United States was transshipped from English ports. The United Kingdom Commercial Company, a government purchasing agency, forwarded wool from Australia, aluminum and cobalt from Canada, jute and shellac from India, tea and rubber from Ceylon, coffee from East Africa, oilseeds from West Africa, hospital tents from Palestine, industrial diamonds from South Africa, machine tools from the United Kingdom.

By early 1942, the first direct consignments of U.S. Lend-Lease supplies began arriving from Boston and Philadelphia: wheat, flour, meat, eggs, milk, lard and butter for the half-starved Russians; leather, rubber boots, shoes, cloth and blankets for the Red Army; arms and ammunition and the explosives needed to manufacture more munitions; barbed wire and communications equipment; trucks, jeeps, scout cars and tanks; bombers and fighters, disassembled and packed in huge crates; rails and locomotives; petroleum, high-grade steel and aluminum, copper and other metals; dynamos, high-quality tools and dies; a complete hospital train—even toothpaste.

Inevitably, backlogs built up at the main British base of Basra, 75 miles up the Shatt, and the British could do little about it. Abadan was being used to the utmost for oil shipments, and all the primitive Persian Gulf ports together could not handle as much cargo as Basra—50,000 tons a month. Bandar Shahpur, the one gulf port linked to the Iranian State Railway, lay in the tidal flats east of the Shatt; its single jetty could berth only two large ships at a time. Khurramshahr, upriver at the junction of the Shatt with the Karun River, had one concrete jetty and two light jetties suitable only for barges. Bushire, a third of the way down the gulf coast, was impractical: Ships had to anchor seven miles offshore, and dhows ferried the cargoes to primitive quays.

To handle the swelling traffic, Khurramshahr was enlarged and entirely new facilities were built at Tanuma and Cheybassi, opposite Basra; all three were linked by new rail or road connections to the Iranian State Railway. The work was done by Indian Railway Construction Companies and British Army engineers, with valuable help from civil contractors and military engineers sent in by the United States. While the construction men built the new facilities, ships were unloaded helter-skelter by polyglot work gangs of Iranians, Iraqis, Indians and Chinese.

Basra was on the wrong side of the Shatt al Arab for easy connection to the Iranian railway, and so a second route was used. Supplies went first to Baghdad by a single track railway or by river. The Inland Water Transport section of the British Army had assembled a strange fleet of craft to ply the Tigris, including graceful Arab *mihailas,* a Turkish gunboat that had been a houseboat since retirement at the end of World War I, motorboats from America, prefabricated wooden pontoons, 500-ton barges, and even some rickety paddle steamers that had somehow survived a 4,000-mile ocean voyage across the Indian Ocean from Calcutta.

At Baghdad, the railborne goods had to be unloaded, ferried across the Tigris and reloaded on the line that ran to the town of Khanaqin on the Iranian border. From Khanaqin the supplies were taken by truck convoy into Iran and north to Tabriz, the capital of Azerbaijan Province.

The Khanaqin Lift, as this truck route became known, was a stern test of nerves, strength and stamina. The drivers, many of them Indians with little more than a few hours' experience in the vehicles, wrestled their lumbering trucks across 50 miles of sweltering plain, broken by gullies and strewn with stones and scrub, where a constant traffic of heavily laden donkeys passed along the road. At the Iranian border, where the route rose sharply into Luristan, the drivers stopped sweating and started shivering.

Since there were no staging posts along the route until 1943, the trucks traveled in self-sufficient convoys, each complete with doctor and medical vehicle. If a truck broke down, another would tow it to the next repair depot, perhaps 300 miles distant. The drivers had to negotiate mountain passes more than 7,000 feet high, and some of the hairpin bends were so tight that the long, 10-ton semitrailer trucks had to be backed up several times to get around. In winter, if a driver missed his gear shift on an ice-paved grade, his truck had only to slip back a few feet to plunge over a precipice into a snow-filled gorge. On the remote high plateaus, where the local road gangs left to work in the fields at harvest time, the surface was quickly broken by innumerable spine-jarring potholes.

After 700 miles of alternate danger and monotonous discomfort, the truck convoys finally arrived at Tabriz, where a railway led to the Soviet border 80 miles away. With only a brief break, the warriors of the road had to unload their trucks and overhaul them, then make the five-day return journey to Khanaqin. There they were allowed four days to recuperate and to prepare their vehicles once more for the hazards of the road.

During the nine months that one Indian truck company worked the Khanaqin Lift, many drivers made the trip to Tabriz 16 times. Three of the drivers were decorated by the Russians with the Order of the Red Star. The awards seemed penurious to one British driver. He snorted, "If I was Joe Stalin, I'd give the Red Star to the whole blooming lot."

In the meantime, 120 officers and 3,400 railroad men were toiling on the Iranian State Railway, struggling to deliver their trains intact to the Russians at Teheran. The broken-down rolling stock and the rugged terrain often defeated them. Some of the tunnels in the mountains spiraled upward inside the rock to gain the necessary height, so that the trains emerged high above the point where they had entered. All the tunnels were unventilated, and in the longest ones, the hot exhaust from the two or even three steam locomotives needed to haul a heavy train up the steep grades often raised the temperature to 180° F. To escape asphyxiation, the crews stoked up the boilers and set the regulators before they entered a tunnel, put wet rags over their faces and got down onto the step of the locomotives—as low as they could get. Sometimes, long, heavy trains failed to make steep grades and slipped back, forcing the crews to suffer this torture two or even three times.

It required incredible endurance to do this kind of work for 16 hours at a stretch, then to take five hours off and start again. It also called for a good deal of courage. The old-fashioned hook-and-link couplings on the Iranian freight cars frequently broke, and when the manual brakes proved

*British and American officers investigate a head-on collision of two Iranian freight trains running between Khurramshahr and Ahwaz. Such accidents, brought about by poor communications and faulty equipment, occurred with alarming frequency until 1943, when the Americans instituted a widespread safety program, including the installation of air brakes on most cars and rigid mechanical inspections at each terminal.*

# A POLISH ODYSSEY: THE DAWN OF FREEDOM IN IRAN

*Polish refugees at a transit camp outside Teheran welcome new arrivals. Few families left the Soviet Union intact, and many of the children were orphans.*

In 1942, the Persian Corridor became a two-way street: As the British delivered war matériel to the Russians in the north, the Soviet Union released to the British around 120,000 Polish soldiers and civilians who had been taken prisoner after the fall of Poland in 1939. In two giant exoduses, one in March and the other in August, the refugees were shipped across the Caspian Sea from Krasnovodsk in Soviet Turkmenia to Bandar Pahlavi, a small port on the Iranian shore, where a Polish staff and British supervisors had set up a huge reception center.

The long-suffering refugees were a pa-thetic sight as they shuffled off the ships. Many were half-starved, infected with lice, sick with typhus, malaria or dysentery. At the reception center, they were quickly given food, registered, run through delous-ing stations and quartered in sprawling tent cities. Sympathetic Iranians did what they could to help. They made a local hos-pital available and turned over a movie theater to shelter the weakest of the refu-gees. Iranian bakers worked long hours to supply the camp with bread.

From Bandar Pahlavi, the refugees were taken south in trucks to Qazvin, where the soldiers and the civilians were separated.

The troops headed west into Iraq to join the British occupation army, while the ci-vilians went east to transit camps on the outskirts of Teheran.

Soon both of the groups were broken up. Many of the soldiers went on to fight with distinction in the Allied invasion of Italy. Some civilians were sent abroad to find new homes in British Commonwealth countries. Though the great majority of the Poles never returned to their homeland, their odyssey had brought them something just as precious. "For us," a Polish officer wrote later, "the summer of 1942 was the dawn of freedom."

too weak to hold, parts of loaded trains might career backward until they crashed or were stopped by a steep upgrade. Brakemen who stayed aboard and saved the cars from disaster earned medals.

By dint of superhuman effort, the men on the Iranian railroad increased the line's average haul from 200 tons a day in 1941 to 740 tons a day in 1942. But even that was far short of Paiforce's quota of 2,000 tons a day. Paiforce had been assigned to deliver approximately 500,000 tons of the 1.5 million tons promised the Soviet Union in the nine months of the Moscow Protocol; but in all of 1942 it would hand over only 395,438 tons, 125,556 tons of it transported by truck.

In fact, Lend-Lease aid to the Soviet Union was everywhere falling short. During April, May and June 1942, German attacks on the Arctic convoy route claimed more than three out of every five tons leaving the United States for Murmansk. In July disaster struck Convoy PQ-17; out of 34 merchantmen 23 were sunk. The losses were so devastating that Churchill temporarily halted the northern convoys. Stalin considered this move an act of cowardice and said scornfully, ''Has the British Navy no sense of glory?''

Serious production difficulties in the United States also caused setbacks. From London, Harriman reported to Roosevelt that, while ''Britain was 100 per cent on schedule,'' the United States was 75 per cent behind. This problem was exacerbated by the increased needs of the United States armed forces after the Japanese attack on Pearl Harbor.

Stalin protested the American delay and inadequacy. He also renewed his demands for a second front. But the Americans still lacked the trained manpower to begin serious planning for a cross-Channel invasion of France, and the British faced a crisis in North Africa. In June 1942, Rommel took Tobruk and advanced to within 50 miles of Alexandria. He seemed to have the rich Nile delta within his grasp. As a countermeasure, the British and Americans agreed to undertake a counteroffensive with the modest number of troops available; they would land in Morocco and Algeria and strike Rommel's armies from behind.

The only way left to help the Russians directly was to step up the volume of supplies passing through the Persian Corridor. Not only would existing backlogs have to be cleared, but far more ambitious targets would have to be established.

The British and Americans, having failed to deliver all of the 1.5 million tons promised in the Moscow Protocol, now began talking about 4.4 million tons for the Second Protocol, ending in June 1943.

In July 1942, radios in Cairo, Baghdad, Basra and Teheran buzzed with coded messages as estimates and recommendations went back and forth. Churchill himself visited Teheran and so did Harriman. Out of all this activity came a plan, approved by the Combined Chiefs of Staff, directing that between July 1942 and June 1943 the Persian Corridor should carry 224,000 tons a month—more than half of the goods that would be delivered in all of 1942. The haulage quota for the Iranian State Railway was raised from 2,000 tons a day to 6,000.

Improvisation and sweat could no longer substitute for manpower—and plenty of it. Far from helping, the British troops in the corridor were a growing hindrance to the logistics effort. They were combat troops, not service troops; and as long-awaited reinforcements brought Paiforce almost up to its intended strength of 10 divisions by November 1942, their presence merely increased the supply drain. Clearly an extra army was needed, a special kind of army of railway engineers, stevedores and truckers, an army well equipped with all the hardware of a modern transport system.

Churchill and Roosevelt agreed that the United States should send in its own men and take over the running of the railway, the ports and the road haulage in Iran, leaving the British with all operations in Iraq, with the truck route to Tabriz, with river transport generally, and with the task of military security in both Iran and Iraq. Some British officers were alarmed and irked that foreigners would be in control of a communications line that was essential to the Empire. But British feelings of wounded pride were soon submerged in a tide of hard work.

The first sizable detachment of U.S. forces landed at Khurramshahr in December 1942. By April 1, 1943, Brigadier General Donald H. Connolly, a military engineer who had been serving in the headquarters of the Army Air Forces in Washington, had nearly 18,000 Americans in the field, plus large numbers of Iranians hired to unload freighters, drive trucks and work in assembly plants. By August his army had grown to nearly 30,000: port battalions, railway-operating battalions, road-maintenance groups, truck regiments, engineer battalions. It was known initially as the Persian Gulf Service Command, but the word "Service" seemed to carry an implication of general housework and it was dropped. "As the Persian Gulf Command," wrote one of its wags, "it could thenceforth perspire more cheerfully."

The PGC was a shambling, offbeat kind of unit; it had "no fancy-pants dash whatever," commented journalist Joel Sayre, who turned himself into its unofficial historian. Sayre said that on parade (an activity the Americans avoided whenever possible), the outfit resembled "a bunch of weary Texaco dealers," and he admitted that its ranks included many overage men, and troops who normally would have been disqualified by a draft board for poor eyesight and other physical disabilities. He recalled that once in Khurramshahr, a medical officer growled at him: "If anybody tells you fifty glass-eyed men landed this morning and got shoved in that longshore battalion, it's a dirty lie. There were only fifteen."

But disabilities and middle age did not prevent the men of the PGC from meeting their goals. They brought in 57 high-powered diesel locomotives and 1,650 freight cars, plus 150 ten-ton trucks, 656 seven-ton trucks and 2,600 basic 2½-ton trucks. In December 1942 Khurramshahr was a desolate cluster of mud buildings; by 1944 it was one of the world's busiest ports.

In mid-January 1943, the unloading time at Iranian ports had averaged 55 days per ship; one vessel spent 124 days in port. From then on, average unloading times continued to fall—to 51 days in April 1943, then to 18 days by Christmas that year and to eight days by September 1944.

The industrialization of the desert spread outward from Basra and Abadan in all directions. Trucks, arriving in gulf ports disassembled in crates, were hauled to assembly plants, put together by Iranian and Asian workers, loaded with supplies and driven to the Soviet zone, often before the ship that had brought them left the harbor. The British ran a truck assembly line at Bushire and another at their Basra base; they also had three factories producing drums and jerry cans for shipping oil and aviation fuel to the Soviet Union. The PGC ran two vehicle-assembly plants, one at Khurramshahr and the other near the mountains at Andimishk. Altogether these plants assembled and delivered 184,000 vehicles to the Russians between 1942 and 1945.

Meanwhile, at Abadan, an assembly line built by the Douglas Aircraft Company put together and turned over to Soviet pilots a total of nearly 4,000 fighters and bombers. In addition, 995 aircraft were flown in by an arm of the U.S. Army Air Forces, the Air Transport Command, which piloted them from Brazil across the South Atlantic to the coast of West Africa, and from there across central Africa to Basra and Abadan.

The American drivers in the PGC's truck regiments were appalled by the condition of the roads in the Persian Corridor. Truck tires that lasted up to 80,000 miles in America were worn out after only 4,000 miles in Iran, and the jarring that the drivers took was sometimes so severe that they steered their trucks while standing on the running boards to give their aching backs a rest. Although the truck drivers represented only one tenth of the American manpower, they accounted for one third of the PGC's hospital cases, their most frequent complaint being lower-back injury.

The main American truck route, from Khurramshahr to Qazvin in the Soviet occupation zone 90 miles west of Teheran, was constantly under construction or repair. The British had made a valiant effort at road improvement with virtually no modern machinery to help them; they had done the work with men and donkeys—67,000 men and 14,000

*Arriving at Qazvin in the Soviet zone on March 4, 1943, GI drivers in the first U.S. truck convoy eat a stand-up meal while waiting for their Lend-Lease goods to be inspected by the Russians. The 46 trucks had made the 466-mile journey from Andimishk in four days.*

donkeys at the peak. But the Americans were equipped with road rollers, asphalt cookers and bulldozers, and they accomplished some remarkable feats of engineering. Across the 150 miles from Khurramshahr to Andimishk, the last town before the mountains, the engineers built what one admirer called a "real, sure-enough road," wide enough for three trucks abreast "and as smooth as Fifth Avenue." After three months of backbreaking toil, they worked to within sight of Andimishk. But it was all in vain. The floods of March 1943 washed away so much of their handiwork that they had to start again from scratch.

By July 1943, the route to Qazvin was carrying 19,000 tons a month, and by January 1944 the figure had risen to 36,000. If the grand total of 457,475 tons delivered to the Russians by road could have been placed in a single convoy of standard American 2½-ton trucks, the line would have stretched bumper to bumper from Baltimore to Chicago.

The PGC's biggest contribution came in railroading. The Americans brought to bear on the Iranian State Railway everything the British had lacked: ample manpower, freight cars with air brakes, and above all, powerful diesel locomotives, which could traverse terrain obstacles that had frequently stopped the steam locomotives. As the diesels replaced the steam locomotives, the torture of the long, suffocating tunnels came to an end. The air-braked boxcars reduced the high accident rate that had plagued the British. New signaling and communications systems improved the rudimentary traffic control. The tonnages mounted. During the period of American operation, the daily average was 3,804 tons. The grand total of all supplies conveyed to the Soviet Union by rail was 3,347,768 tons, about 60 per cent of the nearly six million tons transported north through the Persian Corridor.

By the middle of 1943, the problems that had slowed down the logistics effort in the corridor were steadily being eliminated. The tide-turning victory of Soviet armies at Stalingrad in February had ended the vague threat of a German invasion of Iran from the north and permitted the British to begin sending supply-consuming Paiforce units to North Africa. The Persian Gulf Command was solidifying its routes and busily improving its posts with comfortable barracks, showers and recreation halls. But month after uneventful month of unloading and transporting matériel, maintaining vehicles and working shifts at assembly plants created a new problem: boredom.

With few exceptions, the Americans who served in the PGC considered their tour of duty in Iran a form of cruel and unusual punishment. It was not just that the weather was abominable and the work grueling; there was practically nothing to do in off-duty hours. The men invented all sorts of absurd games to while away the time. In a sport known as the Perspiration Handicap, they competed to see who could fill a C-ration can with sweat first.

The Army did its best to provide the GIs with recreation facilities. All along the routes to the Soviet zone, PXs and service clubs sprang up, frequently made from the packing cases that had brought in disassembled trucks and aircraft. Troupes of entertainers, including Soviet dancers and musicians, toured the isolated posts along the railway, and the Army Special Services Division showed Western movies in improvised theaters. In areas where Paiforce and the PGC shared operations, British troops saw American film shows and American troops drank British beer.

The American Red Cross sent young women into the corridor to console the servicemen with coffee, doughnuts and conversation. The women went through an ordeal of their own. First came the shock of open drains and cockroaches, and jackals that prowled remote camps at night. Then there was the job of fending off lovelorn GIs, routing Peeping Toms and Iranian suitors and getting used to the pervasive odor of greasy Iranian mutton cooking. And always there were unexpected difficulties: the struggle to stay on the job while suffering from diarrhea, the attempt to create the Christmas spirit in the desert when the temperature was 100° F., the losing effort to keep up appearances in a climate that ruined the complexion.

"Don't envy you kids a bit," a newspaperman in Cairo told a Red Cross woman on her way to Iran. "You'll leave here looking nineteen and come back looking ninety." She soon agreed—after catching malaria and sand-fly fever and going temporarily bald (the doctor explained it was quite normal to lose one's hair after a high fever).

The only real bright spot for the Americans was Teheran, a busy cosmopolitan city located between the British and Russian zones. The soldiery of the three nations rubbed elbows with the rich and the poor of Iran, with Polish refugees *(page 82)*, Free French, Arabs, Turks, Kurds and Armenians. There was something for everyone in Teheran. Although the American soldiers did not make any headway with the veiled Iranian women, they did find plenty of drinking places with belly dancers. The officers crowded into Teheran's best hotel, the Imperial Palace, which had been converted into an officers' billet, and they spent hours in the bar of the government-operated Ferdowsi Hotel, swapping stories with British officers over glasses of vodka and vermouth. The Russians, who were under strict orders not to fraternize, simply disappeared from the city streets during their off-duty hours; they holed up in their barracks, singing to pass the time.

American consultants replaced the ousted Germans in the young Shah's government. Joseph Sheridan, who had earned millions as a wholesale grocer in Cairo, served as food adviser and fought a losing battle to break the black market in wheat. Agricultural adviser Luther W. Winsor attempted to persuade uninterested Iranian landowners to invest in crop irrigation. Financial, medical and military advisers tried to institute reforms in their fields. For the most part, the Iranians listened intently to their representations but opposed change. They turned down a compulsory program of inoculation against typhus, typhoid and smallpox, even though seven out of 10 Iranian children died before reaching the age of nine.

One American adviser who met with uncommon success was Colonel H. Norman Schwarzkopf, a West Pointer who had been superintendent of the New Jersey State Police during the Lindbergh kidnapping case in the early 1930s.

Schwarzkopf, a brusque, stocky man with close-cropped graying hair, was hired by Iran to reform the ragtag rural police force, which an assistant, U.S. Army Captain William Preston, described as "a dumping ground of Iranian Army men who had gotten into trouble."

Schwarzkopf persuaded the young Shah to accept a series of basic reforms. After weeding out the incompetent officers, he reequipped the men with decent weapons, dressed them in snappy new uniforms and raised their pay from nine to 35 dollars a month. With training and discipline, the police became an effective 20,000-man security force.

There were many problems that the Americans and the British were unable to solve. The occupation of Iran had caused runaway inflation, doubling and redoubling the price of many necessities. The Iranians resented the foreign troops, and the Shah requested that the soldiers have as little contact as possible with the civilians. The Allies' monopoly of the transportation system disrupted everyday business. The Iranians complained that the Soviet occupation authorities had set up two puppet governments in their zone. Worse, the Soviet zone was "the bread basket of Iran," and the Russians had caused critical food shortages—and widespread riots—by shipping home huge quantities of local produce. The Americans and British were forced to compensate for the difference by shipping in extra quantities of wheat and rice.

The Americans and the British continued delivering supplies to the Soviet Union long after the Red Army took the offensive and began driving the Germans westward. September 1944 was the peak month, with more than 190,000 tons changing hands in the corridor. Target Zero, an Ameri-

*The young Shah of Allied-occupied Iran, Muhammad Reza Pahlavi, plays table tennis with an American sergeant in the game room of one of his palaces in Teheran. In addition to cultivating the good will of the American soldiers, the Shah increasingly sought U.S. military, economic and technical assistance to counterbalance British and Soviet influence.*

can plan for phasing out shipments by June 1945, went into effect in December 1944, and in July 1945, two months after the end of the war in Europe, the last consignment of cargo cleared the Persian Corridor. The men of Paiforce and the PGC were also gradually reduced to zero: The last Americans sailed away on December 30, 1945, and the last British group left on March 2. The Russians, under considerable prodding, finally agreed to respect the territorial integrity of Iran, and pulled out of their zone in May 1946.

In the final analysis, the importance of Lend-Lease aid to the Soviet Union was as hard to calculate as it had been to deliver. To the Western Allies, the quantities were enormous: 5,767,301 tons went through the Persian Corridor, slightly more than the tonnage transported to Murmansk and Archangel; the Soviet-operated Far East route had run up the impressive total of 9,232,605 million tons, though the supplies were officially classified as nonmilitary goods.

But the Soviet leaders claimed that the grand total of 19.6 million Lend-Lease tons amounted to no more than 4 per cent of the nation's wartime industrial output. In fact, the Russians had worked an industrial miracle, building vast new complexes of factories and steel mills beyond the Urals. Since Soviet production statistics were unavailable to Western experts, they found it hard to dispute the 4 per cent figure. Some American and British experts estimated that 10 per cent was closer to the truth.

Even though the total Lend-Lease tonnage was small compared with Soviet production, the large amounts of specific strategic goods had an important effect on the fighting on the Russian front. American power-generating equipment accounted for one fifth of the total Soviet increase in such machinery during the War. Lend-Lease field telephones and wire rebuilt the disrupted communications systems of the Red Army. American additives boosted the octane of Soviet gasoline.

Without doubt, the 184,000 American trucks and other vehicles assembled in the Persian Corridor were the most useful of all the Lend-Lease supplies, as Stalin had foreseen. They helped the Red Army to make enormous improvements in its mobility, so that by 1944 Soviet mechanized units in Western Europe were advancing at an average rate of 20 miles a day. "If you happen to see a photograph of Russian troops entering a German city," Joel Sayre wrote, "you might notice the trucks they were riding in. If they were American, as they were almost sure to be, it is a good bet that they were run up by the PGC."

No less significant was the effect of Lend-Lease on Allied morale. Though the Soviet government made few public references to aid from the West, the Russian people from Leningrad to Samarkand had eaten American Spam, and bread made of American wheat, and had seen British and American fighter planes defending their cities; many civilians, as well as the Soviet troops in American trucks, knew that the United States and Britain were trying to help.

The supply effort boosted the morale of the givers as well as the receivers. The Western Allies knew that the Soviet Union was paying a terrible price in lives and suffering, and they took satisfaction in donating the goods and the labor to deliver it. The official Paiforce historian proudly summed up the spirit of the British-American endeavor: "The Russians needed the stuff, and they were going to get it."

# HELP FROM THE IRANIANS

*Impoverished Iranian villagers gather to beg food and cigarettes from the drivers of an American truck convoy loaded with goods for the Soviet Union.*

# FROM CONFRONTATION TO ACCOMMODATION

The East and the West, an old culture and a modern one, confronted each other when, in August 1941, British and Soviet armored columns invaded the ancient and neutral kingdom of Iran to assure the passage of Lend-Lease supplies to the Soviet Union. The encounter came as a shock to the 16 million Iranians, who bitterly resented the invaders, and also to the Allies, who were appalled by the country's primitive transportation system. But a massive accommodation soon began.

The fatalistic Iranians resigned themselves to occupation, as their forefathers had often done since Alexander the Great conquered the Persian Empire, and they tried to profit from it. More than 100,000 Iranians of many ethnic stocks—Persians, Armenians, Turks, Kurds, Arabs—went to work for the Allies as stevedores, road builders, truck drivers and assembly-plant workers. American troops, who joined the occupation in December 1942, found that many Iranians were quick to learn new skills—and just as quick to exploit them. A number of drivers trained by the Americans left to work for the Russians, who paid higher wages.

For their part, the Allies adjusted to the customs of the land. Antagonistic ethnic groups, such as the Persians and the Arabs, were kept apart on assembly lines. Work shifts during the Islamic holy month of Ramadan were rearranged so that Muslims, who fasted until sunset, worked at night and were replaced by Armenian Christians during the day.

In spite of the accommodations, relations between the Iranians and the Allies were always uneasy. When an Iranian worker died in a plant accident, the rumor spread that he had been murdered by American soldiers, and 250 employees quit in protest. Petty theft by Iranians, and Allied countermeasures, added to the strain. Nonetheless, with the Iranians' help the Persian Corridor grew into a mighty supply line, funneling ever-increasing amounts of matériel to the Soviet Union—more than two million tons in 1944 alone.

*A black American soldier supervises the loading of a truck by a group of Iranian workers. Initially, the Iranian laborers resented working under black troops, but their indignation faded after a few weeks of joint effort.*

*At the port in Khurramshahr, Iranian Arabs carry sacks of American flour from a barge to a storage shed on the dock. Some harbor workers were capable of lifting bulky loads that weighed as much as 500 pounds.*

LOCOMOTIVES

TRUCK TIR

GASOLINE DRUMS

TAN

AMMUNITION

STEEL BASES FOR DOCK PILIN

*Iranian workers unload a profusion of U.S. Lend-Lease goods—everything from locomotives to long-grain rice. The enormous crane at upper left, brought ove*

LEAD INGOTS

DIESEL TURBO-CHARGERS

WIRE

TRUCKS

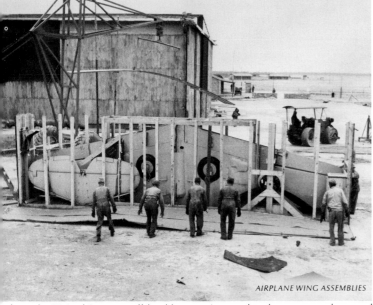

AIRPLANE WING ASSEMBLIES

RICE

*from the United States to off-load locomotives and tanks, consumed so much power that during its operation the entire town of Ahwaz had to be blacked out.*

*Searching for stolen goods, a patrol boat carrying British and American security troops halts an Iranian dhow in the Shatt al Arab near Khurramshahr,*

## BLACKMAIL, PETTY THEFT AND HIGHWAY ROBBERY

American goods, pouring into Iran by the millions of tons, were a natural target for theft by two groups: the armed tribes who controlled the mountainous regions and the poor harbor workers who had to live from hand to mouth. Between them, they caused a never-ending security problem for the Allies.

The Americans negotiated "friendship pacts" with, and paid blackmail to, various tribal khans who guaranteed the safe passage of goods through their territory. This price—often no more than a case of rifles—was well spent. In areas where no agreements existed, American truck convoys and rail shipments were regularly looted, despite the presence of Red Army and Indian guards.

In the shops and camps, all manner of items disappeared—valve caps, distribu-

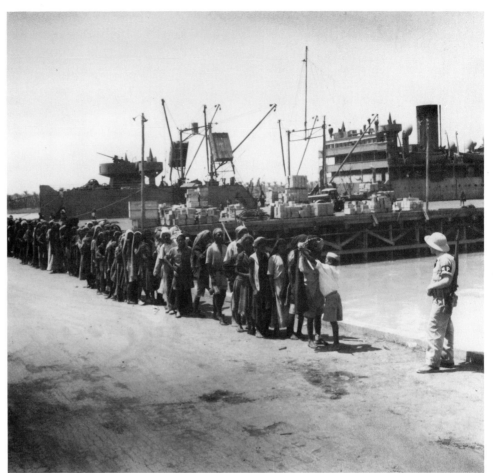
Iranian workers leaving their shift are searched by a local youth and his American MP supervisor.

the principal harbor for Lend-Lease shipments.

tor parts, tires, light bulbs, tools. Much more serious was the communications-crippling theft of copper telephone wire, which nomads regularly cut down in long lengths to make jewelry. The U.S. Army estimated that it had to replace no less than 250 miles of telephone line in the three years of operations in Iran.

Hunting for bandits outside Ahwaz, a U.S. officer questions a local sheik with the aid of an interpreter.

An Iranian mason manufactures mud bricks for the construction of a U.S. Army camp at Andimishk.

In an Abadan plant, a barefoot Kurd polishes the windows of a newly assembled A-20 light bomber.

## STRONG BACKS AND ANCIENT CRAFTS

Though most of the workers did physical labor in the railyards and on the roads and docks, a few Iranians became skilled crane operators and many learned to assemble complex machines such as trucks and aircraft from crated parts. Yet, for the Americans, the most impressive thing about the Iranians was the way local artisans often accomplished the work of modern technology by using their traditional crafts.

*Compensating for an early shortage of locomotives, Iranian railyard workers strain to push a freight car loaded with grain from a siding onto the main line.*

U.S. Army headquarters in Teheran received its water from *ganats*, Iran's ancient subterranean aqueducts, which were kept sanitary and free-flowing not by Army engineers but by artisans whose craft dated back to 700 B.C. Squatting in narrow air shafts 100 feet beneath the ground, they reinforced worn-out walls with clay and kept the channel silt-free with their short-handled spades and leather buckets.

The power shortage made widespread air conditioning all but impossible, yet Iranian masons rendered it largely unnecessary. Using mud bricks they constructed well-insulated barracks, mess halls and hospitals that remained comfortable year round. One mason built a cold-storage warehouse whose four-foot-thick walls enabled refrigeration units to maintain temperatures below freezing even when outside temperatures soared above 100° F.

Joining a convoy of trucks for the long drive north to Teheran, an Iranian driver has his orders verified by a Red Army guard working at the Soviet inspection station in Andimishk.

# AN ALLIED SUCCESS, AN IRANIAN VICTORY

At the outset of the supply effort, the Iranians had angrily complained that the Allies were monopolizing their national railroad, crowding out their own necessities and displacing pilgrims traveling to the holy city of Qum. But after three years of back-breaking labor by 15,000 Iranians and the importation of American freight cars and locomotives, the railroad was carrying 30 times its daily prewar tonnage—and many more pilgrims to boot.

What is more, the Americans had also built and upgraded large sections of the highways leading from the Persian Gulf to the Soviet border. The Americans supplied the trucks, and within one year their training schools graduated 7,500 Iranian drivers, many of whom man-handled the 10-ton trucks over roads the Iranians helped to build. In the first six months of 1944, trucks delivered 145,818 tons of supplies to the Soviet Union, and half of the drivers were Iranians.

Ultimately, the old triumphed over the new. By the end of 1944, the Allies had begun withdrawing, and gradually most of the workers resumed their ancient ways.

Decorated with the flags of Iran, Great Britain, the U.S.S.R. and the U.S., the

freight train hauling the 1½ millionth ton of American aid to the Russians is saluted by a Red Army honor guard as it pulls out of Teheran on July 28, 1944.

"Madagascar is stealthy," wrote Rupert Croft-Cooke, who served there as a British Army sergeant. "The naked feet of the Malagasy in the soft dust, the motionless leaves of the tropical trees, the black, unblinking eyes of the frightened and watchful people, the low voices and the quiet birds—there is a hush over it which is almost one of death."

Against that little-known Indian Ocean island, British Empire forces in the spring of 1942 launched the Allies' first large-scale operation combining sea, land and air forces. Compared with the War's great combined operations, such as the Allied invasions of Sicily, Italy and Normandy, the Madagascar campaign was little more than a bizarre jungle sideshow. It featured unopposed landings, marathon marches (one of which took units of the King's African Rifles 500 miles in 56 days), battles against biting insects and skirmishes against Vichy French leaders who were more interested in saving face than in holding Madagascar. Yet in the makeshift Allied planning of the War's early years, Madagascar held a prominent strategic place.

The island, more than 1,000 miles long from south to north, is separated from Mozambique on the southeast African coast by the 250-mile-wide Mozambique Channel. So long as Axis warships and aircraft made the Mediterranean too dangerous for routine Allied shipping, the channel would have to serve as the main British sea-lane around the Cape of Good Hope to Egypt, India and the recently opened Persian Corridor to the Soviet Union. But the channel was dominated by Madagascar, whose government took orders from Vichy, which in turn took orders from Germany.

Vichy in the summer of 1941 had meekly submitted to the occupation of French Indochina by Japanese troops. In early February, 1942, two months after Japan's entry into the War as Germany's Axis partner, Winston Churchill expressed the fear that Madagascar might suffer the same fate. "The Japanese," he said, "might well turn up at Madagascar one of these fine days and Vichy will offer no more resistance to them there than in French Indochina." About the same time, a Vichy official announced that his government would not hesitate to ask Japan to defend Madagascar.

Britain's concern over Madagascar increased as Japanese conquests shattered the Allied eastern flank in the Indian Ocean. By February 15, 1942, the entire Malay Peninsula, including Singapore, was in Japanese hands. The Dutch East

# ASSAULT ON MADAGASCAR

Indies soon fell. In March, Rangoon was captured and Japanese troops began swarming northward through Burma. On March 23 the Japanese thrust westward toward Ceylon, home of the British Eastern Fleet, by occupying the Andaman and Nicobar Islands (page 102), dependencies of British India in the Bay of Bengal.

These developments, the British felt, might enable the Germans to coordinate a land offensive in the Middle East with a Japanese naval campaign off the coast of Africa. In March, in fact, the German High Command was working on a grandiose plan to conquer Egypt and Persia and link up with the Japanese on the shores of the Indian Ocean.

The Churchill government was determined to deny Madagascar's bases to Japanese submarines and to prevent the loss or impairment of Britain's shipping life line. To achieve these ends, Churchill and the British Chiefs of Staff decided in March to mount a preemptive invasion of Madagascar.

The force scraped together for the operation had as its nucleus the 29th Independent Brigade, made up of the 1st Royal Scots Fusiliers and the 2nd Royal Welsh Fusiliers, the 2nd East Lancashire Regiment and the 2nd South Lancashire Regiment. The troops were all hard-bitten regulars, trained for amphibious landings. Their commander was Brigadier F. W. Festing, a mettlesome officer who liked to ride into battle at the head of his troops. Four other units were put under Festing's command: a special force of six medium Valentine tanks and six light Tetrarch tanks, a field-artillery battery, an antiaircraft troop and the No. 5 Commando Squadron.

The land units were rounded out by one third of the 5th Infantry Division, which had been earmarked for India, where General Sir Archibald Wavell was awaiting a Japanese invasion that never materialized. This force, the 17th Brigade Group, consisted of three infantry battalions, a field-artillery regiment and a company of field engineers who would soon be called upon to perform feats never covered in their training.

The combined invasion units, which were designated Force 121, had a total strength of 13,000 troops. In overall command of the land forces was Major General Robert Sturges of the Royal Marines who, as a survivor of the Gallipoli debacle in World War I, came about as close as anyone in Britain's armed forces to being an expert in beachhead warfare. The operation was code-named *Ironclad*.

Late in March 1942 the troopships of Force 121 steamed from British ports and gathered in the Irish Sea. The destination of the expedition was still unknown to the men who would make the landings. And the techniques of the operation were a mystery to a large part of the force; unlike the troops of the 29th Independent Brigade and the Commandos, the men of the 17th Brigade Group had never received amphibious training of any sort. But the officers and men could scarcely help noticing that the davits of the troopships were hung not with lifeboats but with assault landing craft. Shortly after leaving port, Lieut. Colonel J. W. Hinchcliffe, commanding the 2nd Battalion of the Northamptonshire Regiment, went below and told his adjutant: "At the bottom of the Secret and Confidential box I think you will find a large blue book labeled 'Combined Operations.' Will you let me have it, please?"

Hinchcliffe and other officers hastily studied up on the techniques of amphibious landings. En route, they even began training their men to get in and out of mock landing craft that had been drawn on the deck or constructed from benches and boards.

Off Freetown, the capital and port city of Sierra Leone on Africa's west coast, the troop convoy joined with Royal Navy warships under the command of Rear Admiral Edward N. Syfret, a graying officer who was a close friend of Churchill's. Considering the Royal Navy's strained resources (among other disasters, the battleship *Prince of Wales* and the battle cruiser *Repulse* had recently been sunk by Japanese aircraft operating out of French Indochina), the British Chiefs of Staff had put together a respectable fleet for the Madagascar operation. It consisted of the battleship *Ramillies*, the aircraft carriers *Illustrious* and *Indomitable*, the cruisers *Devonshire* and *Hermione*, nine destroyers, six corvettes and six minesweepers.

In late April, Force 121 rounded the Cape of Good Hope, and on April 28, after a five-day stop for supplies at Durban, it sailed north into the Mozambique Channel as if taking the regular route to the Middle East.

To starboard lay the land mass of mysterious Madagascar.

Discovered by 16th Century Portuguese explorers, the island had since seen all manner of outsiders come and go—pirates, Arab and European slave traders, Christian missionaries, and budding British empire-builders, who quickly gave Madagascar up as a bad job. But the French, whose interest in the island dated from the 17th Century, proved to be more persistent. In 1895, a French force landed on Madagascar and managed to manhandle its guns to the capital, Tananarive, located in the center of the island. The gunners opened fire on the palace of Queen Ranavalona III, the last of Madagascar's indigenous monarchs. As the story was later told, the second shot passed through a palace window and landed squarely on the royal couch—while that article of furniture was fortuitously unoccupied. The Queen prudently surrendered; Madagascar was under French control from then on.

From tidy, white stucco enclaves surrounded by jungle, French colonial administrators carried on a brisk export trade in coffee and cocoa, sugar and vanilla, and maize and tobacco. Madagascar's graphite mines were the richest in the world, and from Madagascar's cattle population, estimated at an astounding 10 million, came lucrative exports of tinned beef.

Aside from bouts with malarial, dengue, blackwater and sand-fly fevers, the French on Madagascar lived an agreeable life. The bureaucrats and their wives had local labor to tend their houses, work their gardens and serve the ritual *apéritifs* on verandas overlooking palm-fringed beaches and blue seas. On their visits to tribal villages in the outlands, the administrators rode in *filanjana*—litters carried in relays by two four-man teams of porters. One team would trot a short distance along a rough trail, then the four relief men would take over, scarcely missing a step.

After the fall of France, General Charles de Gaulle had urged Madagascar and other colonial governments to renounce Vichy in favor of the Allied cause. To forestall any such untoward occurrence, Vichy had dispatched to Tananarive a new governor general in the person of Armand Annet, a veteran bureaucrat who would never have dreamed of disobeying his home office—in this case the Vichy Ministry of Colonies. Ever since Annet's arrival in April of 1941, Madagascar's public buildings had been bedecked with 10-foot-high posters of Vichy's 84-year-old head of state, Marshal Henri Philippe Pétain.

As it happened, such propaganda measures were hardly necessary, since members of the French hierarchy in Madagascar had already decided to remain loyal to Vichy. For one thing, they had no wish to jeopardize their pensions. As an American observer later explained, "Their personnel folders, and the money they had paid into the retirement fund, were not with General de Gaulle in London. They were in Paris, in Occupied France, and Vichy had access to the documents."

Neither would there be any uprising on behalf of the Allies by Madagascar's population, which had little interest in the foreigners' quarrels. The people were known collectively as the Malagasy or the Malgache. Their origins were shrouded by the past; during a remote era they had migrated from nearby Africa and from some distant eastern hori-

## JAPAN'S PIONEERS IN THE INDIAN OCEAN

In March 1942, while the British were finalizing plans to invade Madagascar, the Japanese overran Sumatra and the British-owned Andaman Islands, extending their empire all the way into the Bay of Bengal. Riding the crest of the Japanese advance came pioneering young soldiers and sailors to change these jungle outposts into an impregnable defense line. It was exciting duty on an exotic frontier.

But the Allied invasions never materialized. As the tide of war shifted against Japan, the Bay of Bengal became a backwater. Instead of fighting the enemy, the men simply wasted away from disease, malnutrition and sheer hopelessness. "We were more dead than the dead on Saipan," said a Naval officer who was finally taken off Andaman by the British in 1945. "Before the true defeat occurred, we had already died of a psychological banzai attack."

*Building an airstrip in the Andamans in 1942, a Japanese Naval engineer driving a tractor clears a jungle field while others in his unit haul logs.*

zon, possibly Indonesia. Now they were divided into at least 18 groups, including the Merina ("Those from the Country Where One Can See Far"), the Antandroy ("The People of the Thorny Brambles"), the Mahafaly ("Those Who Put Taboos on Things") and the Tsimihety ("The People Who Do Not Cut Their Hair").

The Malagasy lived in wooden houses roofed with banana leaves; they wore cotton clothes and broad-brimmed hats of woven sisal. Many males had been conscripted into French service and now wore the red fezzes of the French African military forces.

The island battlefield was jungle or bush country. Trade winds from the Indian Ocean dumped the heavy rains that fed Madagascar's palm trees, banana plants and hardwood forests—and turned the narrow, rutted roads into a red porridge. However, the western coastland along the Mozambique Channel was dry bush country, cut off from the east by highlands covered with mahogany forests.

The British objective was the magnificent port of Diégo-Suarez, on the eastern side of Madagascar's northern tip. One of the world's great anchorages, Diégo-Suarez was large enough to accommodate the entire Royal Navy (or, for that matter, the Japanese Navy). For a seaborne invader, the only entrance into the harbor was through a mile-wide strait protected by eight French batteries of 75mm and 90mm guns, which, though obsolete, were to be avoided.

There was a back door to the harbor on Madagascar's west coast: Forces put ashore at two bays there could march only 21 miles across the island's tapering tip and assault Diégo-Suarez from the rear.

The British planned to go in by the back door. And so, shortly before 3 o'clock on the moonlit morning of May 5, Royal Navy minesweepers began clearing the way toward the landing beaches on Courrier Bay and, just to its south, Ambararata Bay. The invasion of Madagascar had begun.

In all of Madagascar, the Vichy French had perhaps 8,000 troops, three quarters of them indifferent Malagasy conscripts; most of the rest were black soldiers from Senegal, and they were tough troopers. Concentrated in and around Diégo-Suarez were 1,500 to 3,000 men, including gun crews who were supposed to man coastal batteries defending the harbor and eastern bays. At this hour almost all the

Vichy forces were asleep, confident that they would never be called on to repel an invasion attempt. The Vichy command was certain that the guns defending the Diégo-Suarez harbor were sufficiently intimidating, while the western bays abounded in such hazards as small islands, shoals, reefs and heavily mined channels. Of the Ambararata defenses a French staff report declared, "Firing at night is not contemplated, the entrance to the bay being considered impossible at night."

The British invaders, however, made short work of the hazards that lay on their approaches. Following safe paths that the minesweepers had cleared and marked with buoys, the convoy ships crept in, anchored, and at 4:30 a.m. began sending troops ashore. By 6:30 approximately 2,000 men had been landed.

On the other side of the isthmus, outside Diégo-Suarez Bay, the British had mounted various efforts to deceive the French into thinking that the invasion would come in from

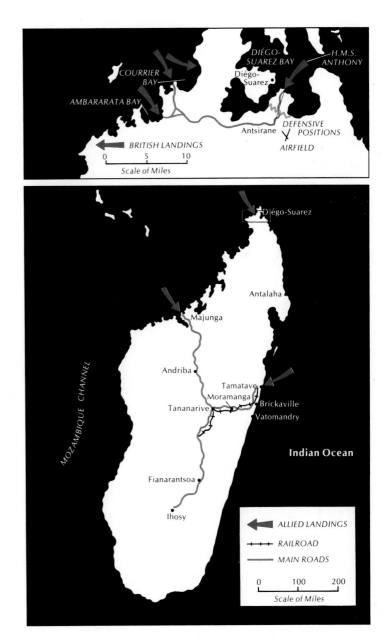

*The two-phase British campaign on Madagascar started in May of 1942 with amphibious landings (inset) at Courrier Bay and Ambararata Bay, designed to capture the harbor of Diégo-Suarez and the Vichy naval base at Antsirane. Four months later, when the British decided to seize the rest of the island, landings were made at Majunga and Tamatave, with both forces assigned to link up in Tananarive, Madagascar's capital.*

the east. The cruiser *Hermione* put on a fine pyrotechnic display, simulating a naval bombardment with rockets and star shells. Leaflets explaining British motives and demanding an immediate surrender were dropped by carrier planes on Vichy military installations around Diégo-Suarez. At the same time, 18 Swordfish from the aircraft carrier *Illustrious* bombed and torpedoed the French ships within the anchorage, sinking a submarine and setting ablaze the sloop *D'Entrecasteaux.* Six Albacores and eight Sea-Hurricanes from the carrier *Indomitable* then strafed the airfield about six miles to the south of Diégo-Suarez; more than 20 French fighter planes stationed there never got into battle. Finally, dummies resembling paratroopers were dropped in a valley close to Diégo-Suarez, causing the defenders to send reserve troops there.

The western landings met with practically no resistance. Going ashore at Courrier Bay, the Commandos and a company of East Lancashires immediately seized the single, unmanned coastal battery, then entered a nearby barracks, where they found a lone sentry brewing his morning coffee, and captured six French officers and 90 Malagasy troops in their beds. The men of the Courrier Bay force, pushing overland through mangrove swamps and thick bush country, fought flies and mosquitoes—but very little else. By 4:30 p.m. they had entered the town of Diégo-Suarez, which a French guidebook admitted was, ''unfortunately, not yet a fine city.'' An American visitor had bluntly called it ''a dirty armpit of a town.''

The British objective lay across a mile-wide bay: the French naval base at Antsirane, which included a 26,000-ton dry dock, a radio station and a fully equipped submarine base. The Commandos had expected to find fishing boats to transport them across the bay, but none were found. And so they were forced to remain in Diégo-Suarez, out of the rest of the action.

Like the Courrier Bay landings, those farther south near the village of Ambararata had been unhampered by Vichy defenders. British Sergeant Croft-Cooke recalled that the main feature of the assault was the ''noisy good humor of the beach landing parties who swore and gave instructions and bullied one another with such blasphemous bonhommie that they might have been a chorus of 'Jack My Hearties' in a musical comedy.''

With the Welsh Fusiliers in the lead and the Scots close behind, the 29th Independent Brigade swung off on the road leading to Antsirane and its naval base, 21 miles distant. ''There was no sound of firing, no glimpse of the enemy, nothing to break the warm peace of the day,'' wrote Croft-Cooke. ''Ten miles or more of the distance were covered before we ever saw anything but red earth and florid vegetation.''

Then occurred one of those odd incidents that came to characterize the Madagascar campaign—and this one would prove costly in lives. Two French Naval officers, on a private fishing and swimming trip to the west coast, were taken prisoner. Still hopeful of seizing Antsirane without bloodshed, British commanders decided to send one of the captives with a letter to the town's governor demanding surrender. The French officer went off in his own car and, violating his parole, spread the word that the British were coming from the west, not the east.

Late that morning the infantry encountered the first Vichy defenders on the road to Antsirane. Brigadier Festing, riding

Malagasy troops conscripted into Vichy's Madagascar army do their morning calisthenics in front of the palace at Tananarive. The easygoing Malagasy sometimes showed up late for drills and duty assignments, infuriating their French officers and later prompting their British captors to describe any indefinite period of time as ''a Malagasy hour.''

ahead of his troops by several hundred yards, heard shots from a nearby ridgeline, and his driver was wounded in the hand—the first British casualty of the invasion. After a few minutes, two Valentine tanks and one Tetrarch clattered to a halt on the roadway. The brigadier strode briskly among them, whacking their turrets with a long stick and instructing the crewmen as they popped out their heads. The tanks roared ahead, silenced the snipers and passed on. But then the French reopened fire, and it took a bayonet charge to put them to rout.

The march continued. The men were tiring beneath the broiling sun when the vanguard descended a hill and came to a bridge spanning a small river. There stood a corrugated iron building bearing the incongruous painted legend: ROBINSON'S HOTEL. It was taken over as brigade headquarters, and the proprietor, an ancient Chinese, bustled about clucking cheerfully in atrocious French and dispensing a concoction of hot tea, sugar and rum.

Just ahead, three miles short of Antsirane, lay the town's final defense line. Anchored on both flanks by mangrove swamps, it consisted of two redoubts connected by trenches, and it was manned by French officers and Senegalese and Malagasy troops, all forewarned.

Festing sent his tanks against these defenses, but his lead Valentine was hit and put out of action by French field guns. Three more Valentines were stopped in their tracks and two

light Tetrarchs were set ablaze. Then Festing ordered a frontal attack by the infantry; it, too, petered out.

The next attack was scheduled to begin during the predawn hours, and General Sturges confidently looked forward to "a good scrap which would end when we ate breakfast in Antsirane." As the men made ready for battle, the hills around them blazed with fires that had been set to prevent enemy snipers from crawling through the high grass toward the British encampment. Sergeant Croft-Cooke later recalled with awe "this fiery night among palm and banana trees, the earth like hot powder underfoot and the sky a glory of starlight, with stretchers being carried and stories brought from our positions a few hundred yards away."

According to plan, the South Lancashires worked their way around to the right, struggled across rocky ground and penetrated all the way to the shoreline south of Antsirane. There, cut off from the main force and hampered by badly broken terrain and mangrove swamps, the troops split into small units and fought as commandos. One group swung behind the Vichy defense line and plagued it with fire from the rear; another spread confusion by stampeding captured packhorses and mules; still others seized the radio station and a barracks. More than 200 prisoners were taken.

But General Sturges knew nothing of the South Lancashire regiment's exploits; the Lancs' backpack radio sets had failed, and Sturges, when he heard nothing from the men, feared they had met with disaster. Meanwhile, it was clear by 7 a.m. that the frontal attack by Festing's infantry had fizzled. "It was," Sturges said, "an unhappy moment."

The stalemate held throughout the morning of May 6. At 2 p.m., Sturges returned to the landing area and went aboard the battleship Ramillies, which was standing guard over the troopships. It seemed to be a time for desperate deeds, and Sturges had just such a venture in mind. At the general's urging, Admiral Syfret agreed to an attempt to distract the enemy by sending the destroyer Anthony into Diégo-Suarez Bay for an assault by 50 Marines on the Antsirane docks. But Syfret considered the effort a forlorn hope and reconciled himself to the loss of his destroyer.

Within 35 minutes, 50 Marines under Captain Martin Price were aboard the Anthony, which left immediately at high speed to steam the 100 miles or so round to the other side of the island. Just before 8 p.m. the ship neared the high

*Armand Annet, the French Vichy Governor General of Madagascar, put up a bold front when he learned on May 5, 1942, that British invaders had landed at Diégo-Suarez, 450 miles north of his headquarters in Tananarive. Annet ordered posters printed proclaiming: "We are all ready for the supreme sacrifice. The French flag at Diégo will be defended to the last." But Annet himself did all his defending a safe distance from the British, whom he never saw until he surrendered.*

cliffs that marked the harbor entrance. "Action Stations" sounded. Down below on the forecastle mess deck, the landing party was ready. The moon would not rise for another hour, and the break in the cliffs was hidden against the dark silhouette of high ground behind. The ship's captain, Lieut. Commander J. M. Hodges, had never before seen this coast. But he found the gap and ordered full speed ahead.

The *Anthony* shot through the strait into the harbor at 30 knots. Then the French guns opened fire. To the Marines crouching below it seemed as if the enemy cannon were firing within a few feet of them. The destroyer raced eight miles across the harbor, running a gantlet of French artillery all the way. She overshot the jetty at the dockyard, but Hodges checked his speed and brought her in stern to.

The Marines hurried ashore. Shells were bursting around them, and desultory small-arms fire came from the jetty and the wooded hills behind. But the landing party made its way through the dockyard, and the *Anthony*, her job done, steamed at high speed back through the strait, answering French fire with her antiaircraft and 4.7-inch guns.

The 50 Marines were alone in the enemy-held town, its docks aflame from bombing attacks earlier that day. By chance Price and his men made their way to the French artillery commander's house and, after climbing 100 feet up a steep bank, established themselves in its compound. Price then sent half his force to secure the naval depot.

At the depot the 25 men, led by a young lieutenant named James Powell, were greeted by feeble rifle fire. In reply the Marines lobbed a few hand grenades. Within moments the depot commander came out carrying a white flag. After Powell had accepted the surrender, a French bugler

sounded an unfamiliar call. The Marines thought that he had sounded the "Alarm" and immediately swarmed all over him. Someone explained that the bugler had simply blown the French "Cease-fire." The Marines apologized.

Upon entering the depot, Powell and his sergeant discovered a number of Frenchmen sitting around. Summoning up his schoolboy French, Powell commanded: *"Levez les mains!"* The Frenchmen put up their hands. Powell wondered, "What the hell do I do now?" He noticed a door on the far side of the room and shouted, *"Ouvrez la porte!"* The French seemed not to have understood.

Powell tried the door himself, but it was locked. "Quite suddenly," Powell recalled, "I remembered a James Cagney picture I had seen when I was a young sublieutenant; Cagney shot out the lock in this gangster scene. So I thought I would do it!" Powell took two shots at the lock, damaging it without opening the door. His sergeant, a veteran soldier, solved the problem with a burst of submachine-gun fire.

Inside were more than 50 British prisoners, including a British agent who had been scheduled to be shot in the morning. Powell armed the men with French weapons, doubling the size of his raiding party.

Coincident with the Marines' attack on Antsirane, Brigadier Festing's force had renewed its offensive and broken through. The French defenders, warned by telephone of the danger in their rear, broke and ran. British troops were soon marching into the town through the Malagasy quarter, where the light from burning roofs threw flickering shadows on the whitewashed walls. The Vichy batteries at the harbor entrance were discouraged by a brief naval bombardment and surrendered at midmorning on May 7. After the French

## THE LUCKY MISTAKES THAT SAVED A FLEET

In March 1942, as Japanese armies consolidated their new Southeast Asian conquests and invaded Burma, Tokyo ordered a climactic attack on Ceylon by Vice Admiral Chuichi Nagumo's First Air Fleet. Nagumo, fresh from spectacular raids on Pearl Harbor and Darwin, Australia, envisioned few difficulties in destroying the 29 aging warships of Britain's ragged Eastern Fleet at their Ceylon bases, Colombo and Trincomalee. The victory would give Japan control of the Indian Ocean and cut Allied access to India and Australia.

The Japanese failed—and by a curious

set of events. As at Pearl Harbor, Admiral Nagumo planned an early-morning raid on Ceylon's airfields, docks and anchorages. However, this time the element of surprise was lost; on March 28, the British had decoded a message predicting the attack, but at some unnamed date.

Vice Admiral Sir James Somerville, the Eastern Fleet commander, now made an egregious error. With more courage than good sense, he ordered his 29 ships to intercept the far superior Japanese carrier force. The fleet set sail at once—and fate decreed a compensating error. As the British warships searched for the Japanese, they began to run low on fuel. All but four had to divert to a secret haven in the Maldive Islands, 600 miles south of Ceylon.

When 127 Japanese bombers attacked Colombo at 7:40 a.m. on April 5, they found the skies abuzz with British fighters, but the harbor was bare. In an hour-long battle, the British lost 27 planes and shot down 19 of the enemy's. In the next four days, Nagumo's task force searched far and wide for the British fleet. But Somerville, now belatedly aware of the dangers, kept most of his ships hidden in the Maldives, and those that ventured out avoided combat whenever possible.

The Japanese did manage to find and sink seven of the vessels, including the cruisers *Dorsetshire* and *Cornwall (right)*. But the rest of the fleet escaped, and the Japanese eventually retired, without ever gaining control of the Indian Ocean.

mines had been swept, Admiral Syfret steamed triumphantly into harbor on board the *Ramillies,* followed by several other warships.

With the British forces in firm control of Diégo-Suarez, Winston Churchill on May 10 made a radio broadcast announcing the successful landing on Madagascar. To keep the operation secret, he continued, extraordinary preinvasion security measures had been taken. Security had been so stringent that not even de Gaulle had been told of the invasion until after the troops landed.

Always quick to take offense at any real or imagined slight to the Free French, the general later wrote that the news had "brought my uneasiness and irritation to their peak," especially since he had repeatedly urged the British to land a Free French invasion force on Madagascar. The general now argued that the defeated Vichyites must be replaced by Free French administrators. The British avoided any commitment, leading de Gaulle to suspect the worst. The Allies, he wrote, were excluding Free France so as "to dispose of her lands and substance, fragment by fragment, perhaps even to take advantage of this dispersal to allot to themselves, here and there, parcels of her property."

Churchill insisted, "We have no ulterior motive about Madagascar." But de Gaulle's demands for a Free French administration fell on deaf ears. In fact, the Allies had already firmly decided against working with representatives of the proud and contentious de Gaulle: It would be much easier to keep the pliable Vichy incumbents in office—under British supervision, of course.

Toward that end, Vichy functionaries of lower rank, from schoolmasters to policemen and customs officers, were assembled in the Diégo-Suarez town hall and informed that if they stayed on the job their salaries would be continued. The reaction was unanimous: "If we volunteer to serve under the English we may lose our pensions. What we want is to be *ordered* to carry on."

The matter was easily arranged.

From their perching place in Diégo-Suarez, the British forces hoped to negotiate the surrender of the rest of Madagascar, and a great deal of long-distance dickering was carried on between them and Governor General Annet, still safely ensconced in Tananarive. But Annet was determined not to capitulate, and the British, stuck for the time being where they were, soon settled into a daily routine. Since the Vichy administrators in Diégo-Suarez seemed to be performing their duties satisfactorily, there was little else for the British to do but sip the sweet local rum (usually mixed with orange juice) or saunter into the countryside to admire the purple bougainvillaea.

But the tranquillity of Diégo-Suarez was soon broken. Late in May, four big Japanese I-class submarines entered the Mozambique Channel from the south in search of Allied warships. Disappointed with their findings, the submarines then converged on Diégo-Suarez. There, on the evening of May 30, a midget submarine skillfully penetrated the harbor and, before the anchored warships or the shore batteries there could react, damaged the battleship *Ramillies* and sank a tanker.

Amid the general confusion, the submarine nearly made good her escape. But she ran aground on a reef and her two crewmen swam ashore north of the harbor. The British sent

*The Dorsetshire and the Cornwall evade bombers off Ceylon.*     *Clinging to wreckage, hundreds of Dorsetshire survivors await rescue.*

out search parties. Three days later, a patrol cornered and killed the two Japanese.

The British commanders naturally concluded that the Japanese submarines were operating out of the Vichy ports in the south. Actually, the midget submarine had been launched from one of the big I-boats, and the I-boats were being serviced by two auxiliary cruisers. Nevertheless, the British launched a series of air strikes at the Vichy ports, using South African bombers now based at the airfield near Diégo-Suarez. Of course the air raids did nothing to curb the submarines' depredations. In June, the I-boats sank 14 ships totaling 57,000 tons. In July, the toll rose to 20 ships and 94,000 tons.

The British now decided that they could put the Vichy ports out of business only by capturing them. Their decision was reinforced by South Africa's doughty and influential Prime Minister, Jan Christiaan Smuts, who urged London to "make a clean job" of the work begun at Diégo-Suarez by seizing Madagascar in its entirety.

So in mid-August a follow-up campaign was planned to take place before the monsoon rains arrived in October. Many new troops would be involved: The British 5th Division had departed for India in May and June and was replaced by an East African brigade and several small South African units. The campaign was a three-part operation code-named *Stream Line Jane*.

The "Stream" part of the campaign was to be an amphibious assault at night by the 29th Independent Brigade against the port of Majunga, which lay about 320 miles down Madagascar's west coast. In the "Line" part of the plan, a force composed of elements of the 22nd East African Brigade, plus a South African armored-car squadron and a team of field engineers, would land with the 29th Brigade, leave Majunga the instant the port was captured and race down the road that led 250 miles southeast to Tananarive. The objective was to seize two critical bridges whose demolition by the Vichy French forces would seriously delay the planned advance toward Tananarive. Having secured the bridges, the detachment would await the arrival of the main force of the East African Brigade—three battalions of the King's African Rifles. The entire force would then push on to Madagascar's capital.

For the "Jane" attack, the 29th Independent Brigade, having secured Majunga, would reembark, sail around the northern end of Madagascar, then storm the east-coast port of Tamatave, 140 miles northeast of Tananarive and connected to the capital not only by road but by one of Madagascar's few rail lines. Moving inland, the brigade would eventually hook up with the East and South Africans, thereby establishing a line of communication across the entire width of Madagascar.

To lull any enemy suspicions, the 29th Brigade and a South African armored-car squadron were transported in late August to Mombasa, the chief port of Kenya on the east coast of Africa; there the brigade ostentatiously engaged in a number of field exercises, while the rumor was assiduously circulated that its next move would be to India. On September 9, the Mombasa troop convoy and its escorts—including the flagship cruiser *Birmingham,* the aircraft carrier *Illustrious* and the Dutch cruiser *Heemskerck*—made rendezvous in a dead-calm Mozambique Channel with the ships bringing the East Africans down from Diégo-Suarez.

*Major General Robert G. Sturges (second from right), the overall commander of the land force during the British seaborne assault on Diégo-Suarez in May 1942, examines a chart of Madagascar with his Naval commander, Rear Admiral Edward N. Syfret (seated, left), Brigadier F. W. Festing, commander of the 29th Independent Brigade (standing), and a Royal Navy captain. In his report on the landing, Syfret noted that "co-operation between the services was most cordial."*

That tranquil seascape would not last for long. The assault on Majunga—which would become known as the "Battle before Breakfast"—was only a few hours away.

At about 3 o'clock on the morning of September 10, 1942, Majunga's military commander, a man named Martins, was rudely aroused from his slumber by an agitated messenger with news that the British were landing about nine miles north of the palm-fringed town. Martins sent the troops of his small garrison rushing toward the danger point. He remained prudently behind.

The British could hardly have asked for greater cooperation. The landings to the north had been made by detachments of the East Lancs and Welsh Fusiliers as a feint aimed at drawing the defenders out of Majunga. The decoy units easily avoided Martins' troops. Their closest approach to a confrontation came when a handful of Malagasy soldiers suddenly popped out of a house beside the path—and just as suddenly vanished into a banana grove.

At 5:20 a.m., as dawn tinted the sky, British carrier aircraft staged a noisy but harmless demonstration over Majunga while lead elements of the 29th Independent Brigade were put ashore at the town's docks, which they cleared against only token opposition.

Martins was slightly wounded in the left arm. He was taken prisoner by a group led by a British colonel who demanded that Martins order the town's surrender.

"Did my men fight well?" Martins asked wistfully. "Magnificently!" replied the colonel, somehow managing to keep a straight face.

Thereupon, Martins, his honor satisfied, agreed to capitulate. But a crisis of military etiquette then came to the fore: No bugle could be found to blow the "Cease-fire." Martins kept shouting for a *clairon* until a British officer found an alternative. Discovering Martins' wife locked in her bedroom, he persuaded her to prevent a further effusion of blood by lending him a sheet and a broom. Under the improvised white flag, the inventive officer, the British colonel and Martins toured the town—and the surrender of Majunga was accomplished.

By 7:30 a.m., the Battle before Breakfast had ended. By noon, British officers and French functionaries were amiably drinking and dining in Majunga's cafés. At 10:40, South African armored cars and Nyasalanders of the King's African Rifles, transported by truck, were rolling ahead toward the crucial bridges on the road to Tananarive.

The attack toward the capital might have been a wearisome venture had it not been for the helpful Malagasy. A British war correspondent who made the trip wrote that the Malagasy's disinterest in the fight "did not prevent them from turning out in their thousands to build roadblocks when told to by the French, or from turning out in their thousands to pull them down again when told to by our political officer. Sometimes they did not need telling, and when our men arrived we often found them happily at work pulling down the obstacles they had just put up."

The roadblocks were not the only obstacles to the British advance. At many small streams the wooden bridges had been dismantled. But the frugal French had hidden the planks in nearby brush, where they were easily found and quickly put back into place.

Only rarely did the Vichy forces attempt to make a stand.

British troops dash out of a landing craft and storm a deserted beach at Tamatave on Madagascar's east coast on September 18, 1942. Watching the men search for the enemy in empty machine-gun posts and rifle pits, a British correspondent wrote: "It was like a Hollywood assault, which was being held up by the failure of the opposition half of the cast to put in an appearance on time."

To meet those infrequent martial displays, the South and East Africans used a simple but unfailing attack pattern. No sooner was a defended obstacle encountered than the armored cars, mortars and artillery would open up with covering fire. A platoon would draw the Vichy fire by advancing frontally until pinned down. Meanwhile, two other platoons would work their way through the bush to attack the enemy line, which was almost never held in depth, from the flanks or the rear.

The system worked beautifully for two or three days—until the Africans arrived in the neighborhood of Andriba, a mountain village 150 miles from Majunga and 110 miles from Tananarive. There stood an undismantled stone roadblock, and behind it, hidden on a ridge in foxholes camouflaged by tarpaulins and burned grass, lay a company of tough Senegalese, armed with machine guns and rifles, who held their position in depth.

Two East Africans immediately fell wounded, and the rest of their platoon was pinned down. Following their familiar tactic, two accompanying platoons deployed in flanking movements. One of them, however, tried to turn the enemy-held ridge too soon, and its British commander was killed.

In this critical instant, an East African sergeant named Odillo assumed command of the platoon and led it in a murderous charge. Swinging their *pangas*—curved-bladed, machete-like weapons up to three feet long—the Africans killed a French officer and a noncom who had been in charge of a key machine-gun position. Then they overran the Senegalese.

"The Senegalese were very brave," recalled a British reporter. "There was nothing but to go for it hammer and tongs, which they did. Occasionally, after firing to the last second, one of the Senegalese would jump out and try to scuttle off through our lines. We dropped a number of them like rabbits."

The King's African Rifles had lost one officer killed and another wounded, four infantrymen killed and another eight wounded. The Senegalese had suffered a larger but unspecified number of casualties. "That evening, in Andriba hospital," reported the British journalist, "the extraordinary sight was seen of wounded Nyasalanders and Senegalese lying side by side in adjacent beds. A few hours before they had been fighting each other furiously; now they were the best of friends."

The Vichy forces made a few more attempts to halt the Africans' advance, but none was so strong and savage as the defense at Andriba had been. The Africans pressed on, suffering only light casualties. They reached Tananarive on the afternoon of September 23 and found it undefended. That evening an announcement was made on Radio Tananarive: "This is a British officer speaking. At 5 p.m. today our troops occupied Tananarive. Everything is quiet. That is all."

Madagascar's capital was at last in Allied hands. But Madagascar's devotedly Vichy Governor General was not: Armand Annet had fled to the town of Fianarantsoa, 190 miles to the south. On September 25, the East African infantry and the South African armored cars set out to find him.

A week after the East Africans had begun their march from Majunga to Tananarive, the third phase of Operation *Stream Line Jane* was put into motion. By early morning on September 18 the task force and the ships carrying the 29th Inde-

*An honor guard of the King's African Rifles is reviewed by British Lieut. General Sir William Platt after the capitulation of Madagascar. During the last eight weeks of the campaign, the Africans fought their way through 500 miles of bush country and more than 3,000 roadblocks. "The whole lot never went to sleep at one time," a British officer marveled. "If one company was moving roadblocks by day, a second took over at night, and a third was ready to go forward in the morning."*

pendent Brigade were off the east-coast port of Tamatave.

The shoreline at Tamatave, lying in the path of the trade winds, was battered by heavy surf, and Allied planners wished to avoid an assault in landing craft. Instead, they hoped that an ultimatum, followed if necessary by a naval bombardment, would do the trick. At 5:40 a.m., British commanders sailed into the harbor on the *Birmingham* and began negotiations by radio with the *chef de région* in Tamatave. It was no use. That functionary, like his Vichy colleagues throughout Madagascar, was determined to avoid the dishonor of surrendering without a show of resistance.

The British made one last effort at persuasion. At 7:30 a.m., a launch from the *Birmingham* sped in toward Tamatave, flying a white flag of truce. As it neared the shore, shells from the French shore batteries raised spouts of water a safe distance from the little craft. The launch swung about and returned to the warship at full throttle.

Almost immediately the warships did some token cannonading of their own; the British wished to capture Tamatave, not to demolish it.

The Vichyites did not overdo their face-saving show of resistance. After precisely three minutes of naval bombardment, they ran up a white flag on a pole on Tamatave's waterfront. Well before noon, Tamatave was in British hands, and units of the South Lancashires and Royal Welsh Fusiliers were on the way to Brickaville, about 65 miles to the south, from where they hoped to ride by rail to Tananarive.

At Brickaville, the troops found no rail transportation; the French authorities had foresightedly removed their locomotives to Moramanga, about 70 miles up the line. So the South Lancs improvised one of the War's oddest marches. They discovered a number of small flatcars. The troops jumped into the cars and away they went—pushed up the railroad tracks by relays of Malagasy helpers.

While en route to Tananarive they received reports that it had already been captured. They pressed on to Moramanga and there, on September 25, they linked up with a detachment of the King's African Rifles. The British line of communications across Madagascar was complete.

It remained for the fierce black fighters of the King's African Rifles and the white South Africans to bring the Madagascar campaign to its conclusion. For 40 frustrating days they struggled southward in pursuit of the elusive Governor General Annet and the last remnants of the Vichy forces on Madagascar. Annet drove his Malagasy troops to desperate labors. They barred the way with a profusion of roadblocks; along one half-mile stretch some 800 trees had been felled, and within another mile and a half, 29 stone walls had been erected, the largest of which was 18 feet thick. Mile-long stretches of roadway were littered with stones—some of them as large as melons—that had to be removed before the trucks were able to travel on. Time after time, small Vichy units set up ambushes. In one such trap, a hidden machine gun opened fire on a British radio truck and wounded a dozen Africans.

The Africans pressed on, hiking for days through swirling mists. On October 18 they received reports that their unseen enemy was preparing an enormous ambush five miles ahead. There lay a U-shaped arc of hills, its prongs pointing to the north. If the Africans were to continue along their present route, they would barge into the "U" and be caught in converging fire.

Instead, the Tanganyikan battalion of the King's African Rifles was divided in two, and the halves were sent on 30-mile marches around the "U," meeting again in the enemy's rear. Then, on October 19, the Kenya battalion advanced just far enough into the trap to draw enemy fire. At this point the Tanganyikans opened up from the rear with everything they had, catching the enemy troops in the middle of their own ambush. More than 800 Vichyites swiftly surrendered, with no loss on the British side.

The shooting war on Madagascar was almost over. After nearly five weeks of marching from Tananarive, the Africans at last entered Fianarantsoa, where Annet was supposed to be holding out. He was gone again, this time to Ihosy, about 100 miles southwest. The Africans moved after him. They were still marching when, on November 5, they received an envoy from Annet asking for the terms of surrender. Hostilities ceased at 2 p.m., and Annet signed the articles of capitulation shortly after midnight.

All Madagascar was firmly in Allied hands. Its deepwater ports—crucial to control of the passageway to India and the Persian Corridor—were now beyond the grasp of the Axis. The island once more lay silent and brooding beneath the tropical sun.

# THE BATTLE OF BOREDOM

To pass the time, two U.S. Marines stationed on Midway Island play beach ball with a Japanese plastic weather balloon sent up by distant meteorologists.

# INVENTIVE PURSUITS FOR LONG, IDLE DAYS

"Monotony, monotony, all is monotony," a GI moaned in a letter to *Yank* from his Pacific outpost. His was a sentiment shared by thousands of fellow servicemen garrisoned in the War's out-of-the-way places, where frequently the only fight was against ennui.

At remote bases in the Middle East, Greenland, Iceland, the Aleutians and the South Pacific, the Americans endured a relentless procession of days as bland as their steady diet of B and C and K rations. Harsh climates—temperatures ranging from −50° F. to 150° F. in the shade—often made outdoor recreation impossible. Poor transportation barred the way to USO troupes, liquor supplies and new movies. Payday was usually on time, but it seemed pointless in places that offered nowhere to spend the money.

Combat casualties were scarce at such posts, but boredom took a heavy toll. An Army medical report noted that in the Arctic "chronic depression was practically universal." Some men cracked under the strain; they were evacuated and later given so-called Section Eight discharges for "emotional maladjustment." But the great majority of the men managed to beat the crushing monotony with a variety of inventive activities.

Some soldiers turned to academic pursuits to ward off the blues. GIs in Alaska founded the "Bering Institute," giving tutelage in economics, math, bookkeeping and music appreciation. One amateur botanist compiled a field book of every plant on the Aleutian island of Amchitka.

In their isolation, the soldiers reserved a special affection for birds and animals, often domesticating local species for pets. In Greenland, a GI succeeded in training native falcons to hunt from his wrist after reading up on falconry in the small post library. For a seven-man rescue team snowed in at a Greenland outpost, the only diversion for a time was a simple wager on how many puppies their pregnant sledge dog Elizabeth would whelp. "Admittedly the lottery idea would not appeal to the seasoned USO veterans," remarked Staff Sergeant Arthur Hall. "But in that ice-locked hell it helped keep the bunch of us from getting a Section Eight."

*Marines on quiet Trinidad Island spend the midnight hour rounding up a quarter-ton sea tortoise, a tasty alternative to their lackluster chow.*

*Two madcap U.S. soldiers stationed on Kiska in the Aleutians take turns scrubbing each other down outside their snow-covered tents on a December day.*

A U.S. Coastguardsman stationed in the
Arctic goes over the fundamentals of softball
with a willing pair of Eskimo rookies.

Turbaned trainers coach mounted American
servicemen at the starting line of a donkey race,
one of the events at a Red Cross carnival
in Khurramshahr, a city in southwestern Iran.

Towed by a landing craft, a Coastguardsman
crouching on a homemade surfboard
skims through the Pacific waters off Guam.

A rambunctious trio of monkeys explores an amused GI in Dutch Guiana.

A GI fondles his pet wolf cub at a forward base in the Aleutians.

On a jeep, a baby kangaroo licks the fingers of a U.S. airman in Australia.

At a base in the South Pacific, a cockatoo nibbles at a Marine's cigarette.

On Midway, a Marine affectionately nuzzles his finger-trained fairy tern.

An Army private stationed in North Africa offers a tidbit to his pet stork.

A long-tailed coatimundi—an omnivorous cousin of the raccoon—stands on tiptoe for a snack from his amused airman friend on Ascension Island.

From an amphibious tractor in the shoals off their South Pacific island base, Marines ring a school of fish with rifle fire. Stunned by the concussion, the fish were easily scooped up.

In a mud-pit arena at a Pacific island rest camp, Marines stage a messy free-for-all. When the brawling got out of hand, judges bopped the offending parties with tent pegs.

Marines on an isle in the Pacific line up their coconut crabs for a race across the sand. The crustaceans called for delicate handling; their huge pincers could mangle fingers.

# 5

In the spring of 1942, while Japanese forces were winning victory after victory in Southeast Asia and the South Pacific, Imperial General Headquarters strategists in Tokyo cast enterprising glances toward the bleak Aleutian Islands in the North Pacific. The shortest route from Japan to the United States closely followed the 1,200-mile-long chain of more than 70 islands from Attu, 650 miles northeast of Japan's big naval base in the Kurile Islands, to Umnak, just off the coast of the Alaska Peninsula. Obviously the Aleutians could be used as steppingstones for an invasion of North America— or for an invasion of Japan, if the Americans ever recovered from their disastrous naval losses at Pearl Harbor.

The possibility of a Japanese attack on the Aleutians worried the U.S. Joint Chiefs of Staff. Only 45,000 American servicemen were on duty in all of Alaska, and barely 13,000 of these were stationed on the Alaska Peninsula and on the two defended Aleutian Islands, Unalaska and Umnak, just to the west. The American commanders recalled uneasily that the prophet of air power, Billy Mitchell, had predicted that any invasion of the United States would come along the Aleutian chain.

The loss of the Aleutians could have serious consequences even if the Japanese advanced no farther. Soviet cargo ships were now docking at Seattle, picking up Lend-Lease supplies and delivering the goods to Vladivostok at the Pacific terminus of the Trans-Siberian Railroad. Currently Japan and the Soviet Union were not at war, but if that situation changed, Japanese planes and warships based on Attu Island or neighboring Kiska would surely wreak havoc on the Soviet supply line. The cities of the U.S. West Coast and the north-south shipping lanes would be vulnerable to attack as well.

And so the Americans fretted about the Aleutians, even though an invasion would pose great difficulties for the Japanese. While the U.S. presence in the islands was pitifully weak, the Aleutians were fiercely defended, from end to end and in all seasons, by the worst weather in the world.

All manner of foul phenomena were bred by the collision of the warm Japan Current and the frigid waters of the Bering Sea. In this massive weather engine, terrific winds were suddenly unleashed, and no one could predict their direction from one minute to the next. Depending on the season, these fickle tempests would blow snow or rain almost hori-

# THEATER OF FRUSTRATION

zontally (hence the GI joke, "It never rains in the Aleutians; it rains in Siberia and blows over"). Destroyers, wallowing in the huge wind-lashed seas, sometimes rolled so far that their stacks shipped water. On the islands, the indigenous Aleuts combated the winds by burying their huts as deep as they could in the soil under the muskeg, whose thick spongy mat of vegetation passed for solid ground.

And then there was the fog. For long periods through most of the year, the islands were swaddled in blankets of wet, woolly fog. Flying was hazardous in the extreme; at times the fog would lift to 50 feet or so above the water, and then pilots would drop beneath the ceiling, flying so close to the water that their propellers' slip stream scooped out white wakes. To compound the difficulties of navigation, the Aleutian mountains were salted with magnetic lodestones that threw compasses into a vertigo.

The Aleutians were, in short, utterly lacking in appeal. But the Japanese, who had fished the Aleutian waters for generations, knew the worst about the weather and were not discouraged by it. They would soon invade the islands, though primarily to prevent the Americans from using them to invade Japan. And of course the loss of U.S. territory and the threat to the mainland would force the Americans to stage a reinvasion.

Predictably, the Aleutian fighting was by turns ludicrous and infuriating. The airmen, playing blindman's buff in the fog, bombed whales instead of enemy ships, often reported sinking the same submarine-shaped rock and lost far more planes to the weather than to enemy gunfire. The sailors fought only one sea battle—an old-fashioned ship-to-ship slugging match in which aircraft took no part. The soldiers fought only one important land battle, in which most of the casualties were caused by trench foot and exposure. Mercifully, the Americans and the Japanese had weightier business elsewhere and thus could commit only small forces to the Aleutian sideshow.

In the end, the men who campaigned in the cold northern wasteland agreed with the jaundiced view of Lieut. Commander Samuel Eliot Morison, who was commissioned by President Roosevelt to write a Naval history of the War. "The Aleutians theater," wrote Morison, "might well be called the Theater of Military Frustration. Both sides would have done well to leave the Aleutians to the Aleuts."

As dawn approached on June 3, 1942, Rear Admiral Kakuji Kakuta stood waiting impatiently on his flagship, the aircraft carrier *Ryujo*, in Aleutian waters about 180 miles south of Unalaska Island. Arrayed around him was the rest of the 2nd Carrier Striking Force of the Japanese Northern Area Force: the carrier *Junyo*, three destroyers, two heavy cruisers and an oiler. The carrier force was followed at a distance by light cruisers, troop transports and support craft necessary for assault landings.

Kakuta's mission was to bomb Dutch Harbor, the U.S. naval base on Unalaska Island, just 100 miles off the tip of the Alaskan mainland. Then, if all went well, he would screen the landing of ground troops on three of the westernmost islands: Attu, Kiska and Adak.

The takeoff of Kakuta's planes was delayed by a heavy mist that prolonged the darkness. After warming up their engines for half an hour, the pilots roared off into the murk. The planes from the *Junyo* were soon forced back by the fog, but the 13 attack bombers and their three fighter escorts from the *Ryujo* pressed on. Since the poor visibility made formation flying impossible, the planes headed singly for Dutch Harbor, navigating by dead reckoning.

The Americans expected an attack of some sort. A few weeks before, a top-secret code-breaking group at Pearl Harbor had read Japanese radio traffic and pieced together an enormous battle plan involving Admiral Isoroku Yamamoto and his Combined Fleet. The Japanese were on their way to Midway to annihilate the remnants of Admiral Chester W. Nimitz' U.S. Pacific Fleet. Yamamoto's attack was to be masked by a powerful sideswipe at the Aleutians.

Nimitz had entrusted the Naval defense of the Aleutians to Rear Admiral Robert A. Theobald and had scraped together a modest force for him to fight with. All told, Theobald commanded 37 warships; his main strength consisted of two heavy cruisers, three light cruisers, 13 destroyers and six antique S-type submarines.

On the islands, the patrol wings of PBY Catalina flying boats had been alerted, and the meager forces on Umnak and Unalaska had been beefed up to a strength of 10,000 men. At Umnak, a new airstrip had been feverishly bulldozed into the four-foot-deep layer of volcanic ash laid down by the eruption of Katmai Volcano in 1912. The unstable surface, overlaid with steel mesh, was so elastic that it could bounce a landing plane 30 feet in the air. Fliers said that it was like landing on an inner-spring mattress.

Though the Japanese strike force was expected, nobody knew just where it would attack or how to find it in the execrable weather. On the morning of June 3, Theobald and his warships were 500 miles southeast of Kakuta's task force, which put them completely out of the ensuing action.

The first of the Japanese planes arrived undetected at Dutch Harbor at 5:45 a.m. But the base was on guard. The everlasting fog had lifted somewhat, and as the fighters swept low between the rugged promontories guarding the entrance to the harbor, antiaircraft gun crews opened fire from their batteries dug into the rocks. The seven ships in the harbor added to the flak curtain as they struggled to raise steam and get under way. The transport *President Fillmore* fired her own deck guns and a battery of 37mm guns that she was delivering to the Aleutian defenders. The ship spat so much flak that observers reported her afire.

Five minutes after the fighters made their first pass over the harbor, four bombers came into view from the southwest. They dropped 16 bombs, 14 of them on the barracks at Fort Mears, the Army base next to Dutch Harbor. Two white-frame barracks and three Quonset huts were blown to splinters, killing 25 men and wounding 25 more. The next three bombers overshot the base, their bombs falling harmlessly into the tundra beyond. Three more bombers damaged the radio station and destroyed a Quonset hut.

The last wave of three bombers aimed for the base's old wooden oil tanks. They missed the tanks but hit a pillbox and a truck, killing two men.

Once the bombers had finished their work, the fighters returned to strafe the base. They caught Navy Lieutenant Jack F. Litsey trying to take off in his Catalina. "A radioman was shot through the hand," recalled an ensign in the crew. "His hand was resting on another man's back and the bullet passed through his hand and killed the man underneath. Another man jumped from the plane to swim ashore. He was drowned." Litsey ran his plane onto the beach, put out a small fire and counted 38 bullet holes in one wing.

Against these losses, the antiaircraft gunners of Dutch Harbor had managed to shoot down only one Zero. (It was not found till five weeks later, only slightly damaged, on a small island 20 miles from the base.) The raid was over before Dutch Harbor could get any air support from the U.S. Army's Fourteenth Tactical Air Force, which had 33 Curtiss P-40 fighters and 17 assorted bombers based on neighboring Umnak Island and at Cold Bay on the Alaska Peninsula.

Immediately after the raid, the base's PBY pilots of Patrol Wing 4 received an urgent new order: "Carry out your scouting plan to the limits of your fuel." For a week they had been flying 14-hour searches in their great, fat bluegray flying boats; now they were to come in only to gas up. And some of the Catalinas, which were so dangerously slow and awkward that their crews called them Blue Coffins, were further encumbered with two 2,000-pound torpedoes mounted under their wings. Improbable though it seemed, the ponderous birds were supposed to attack the Japanese warships if they found any.

In late afternoon of that first day, a Catalina piloted by Lieutenant (jg.) Lucius D. Campbell broke through a wall of mist and found part of the Japanese task force. Two carriers and several cruisers and escorting destroyers were steaming along at the edge of a squall about 80 miles to the south of Umnak.

In hopes of establishing the warships' course and destination, Campbell tracked them for two hours, ducking in and out of the fog bank to evade the carriers' Zeroes and the flak from the warships. He stayed until his rudder was shot loose, the plane ripped by bullets and afire, one man wounded and the fuel tank punctured. Too late, he broke away. With the last of his gas leaking out, he made a miraculous, no-rudder, no-power landing at sea. A Coast Guard cutter picked up the crew three hours later. Two other Catalinas were ordered out to take over Campbell's vigil. They were never heard from and did not return.

Still other Catalinas searched throughout the night, and shortly after dawn on June 4, a PBY piloted by Lieutenant Charles Perkins found the warships again, well to the south of Umnak Island. Perkins radioed for help and circled in the murk above the Japanese ships until he had barely enough gas to make it back to Dutch Harbor. But before he left, Perkins attempted a torpedo run. It backfired. A flak hit disabled one engine, and he had to limp home on the other.

Shortly after Perkins left the scene, two B-26 Marauders, speedy medium bombers, arrived from Cold Bay in answer to his call. Flying just above the wavetops, the two planes, piloted by Captains George W. Thornbrough and Henry S. Taylor, nearly crashed into the two Japanese carriers before they saw them in the mist.

Thornbrough was carrying a torpedo, a naval weapon about which he, as an Army flier, knew almost nothing. Somehow he had picked up the notion that a torpedo could be armed by diving it through air at 350 miles an hour. Accordingly, he climbed, then dived and released his "fish." His aim was perfect; the long, heavy weapon hit squarely on the flight deck—and rolled over the side.

Ignoring orders to orbit and wait for more B-26s, Thornbrough returned to Cold Bay sobbing with rage and frustration. He reloaded with 500-pound bombs, weapons he knew, and took off. He was never seen again.

Meanwhile, pilot Taylor had made a torpedo run on a Japanese carrier. But the fog distorted his vision; he came in too close to launch his torpedoes and was barely able to pull up in time to clear the ship's superstructure. Then the bomber bucked, and Taylor and his copilot, Second Lieutenant John Nealon, felt a rush of wind. The nose of the plane had been hit, and the bombardier's glass turret had been smashed. The bombardier crouched there, hands over his face, blood streaming through his fingers.

Taylor and Nealon hauled the wounded man out of the turret. Then at 6,500 feet, they slid into an attack run. It was a good thing they had moved the bombardier; two more hits blew off the rest of the nose.

During the bombing run, the tail gunner began yelling that his gun was jammed—just as a Zero attacked from the rear. "Fix that gun and quit yelling!" Nealon shouted back. The startled tail gunner cleared the jam and shot down the Zero. But by now the enemy ships had vanished in the fog. Somehow Taylor managed to hold his plane together on the 100-mile flight back to Cold Bay.

That afternoon the Japanese launched their second attack on Dutch Harbor. Beginning at 6 p.m., 10 fighters, followed closely by 11 dive bombers, strafed the Naval air station. The bombs destroyed four new fuel-oil tanks and scored hits on a warehouse, an empty aircraft hangar and an old ship that had been beached for use as a barracks. At 6:21, another wave of three bombers attacked, but their bombs fell harmlessly into the harbor. The final wave of five bombers attacked at 6:25 and managed to hit a gun emplacement, killing four men. This brought the total casualties at Dutch Harbor to 43 killed and about 50 wounded.

The Japanese planes retired to their carriers. Pilots from the *Junyo* had chosen to rendezvous at the western end of Unalaska Island, unaware of the newly built U.S. landing field on Umnak. Much to their surprise, eight Japanese planes were met by eight American P-40s. In the ensuing melee, the Americans shot down two bombers and two fighters and damaged a third bomber so heavily that it crashed before reaching the *Junyo*. The Americans lost two P-40s, one of which crash-landed safely.

The next day, June 5, the Japanese task force withdrew to the west. Admiral Kakuta and the invasion forces had received somewhat garbled orders following Yamamoto's debacle in the Battle of Midway, and, for a time, they did not know whether to proceed with the planned invasions of the

*Flame and smoke billow skyward from U.S. Army barracks hit by Japanese bombs during the air raid on Dutch Harbor on June 3. The dense smoke spread quickly and obscured most of the area from the Japanese, who dropped the rest of their bombs haphazardly.*

# A WILDERNESS HIGHWAY BUILT TO DEFEND THE NORTHWEST

In the spring of 1942, about 10,000 troops of the U.S. Army Corps of Engineers descended upon a handful of sleepy towns in Alaska and western Canada. They had been sent to this unlikely front by American defense planners, who, fearing Japanese advances into the North Pacific, had decided to build a road that would connect and supply far-flung U.S. bases in Alaska and a string of airfields under construction in the Canadian West.

To the amusement of oldtimers who knew the formidable difficulties of the region, the Army announced that the Alcan Highway would be open to military traffic in just eight months, before winter set in.

Seven regiments of engineers went to work, along with several thousand Ameri-can and Canadian contractors. Starting out with their heavy earth-moving equipment at scattered points along the route, they sprinted toward each other, working seven days a week. They hacked their way through dense forests, laid long sections of log roadway over swampy terrain and built scores of bridges.

In spite of maddening swarms of enor-

Surveying the wild northland, an engineer measures the difference in elevation between two points.

Swiftly cleared and graded, a dirt stretch of the

mous mosquitoes and temperatures that soon afterward dipped to −50° F., the engineers met their ambitious deadline. On the 20th of November, in a roadside ceremony near Kluane Lake in the Yukon, the snipping of a red, white and blue ribbon opened the Alcan Highway. The first truck to travel the 1,500-mile length of the road rolled into Fairbanks the next day.

*Alcan Highway carries trucks ahead. When completed, the road zigzagged 1,500 miles (inset) from Dawson Creek, British Columbia, to Big Delta, Alaska.*

127

three islands. Finally, Yamamoto canceled the Adak landing and ordered them to take Attu and Kiska.

In the second week of June, the Japanese troops, 2,500 in all, went ashore and took over. On Attu, the only Americans found by the men of the 301st Independent Infantry Battalion were Mr. and Mrs. Charles Jones, an elderly couple, who ran a weather station and taught school in the Aleutian village. The Joneses tried to commit suicide. He succeeded; his wife and the Aleuts were sent to Japan as prisoners.

On Kiska, the 3rd Special Landing Force captured nine of the 10 Navy enlisted men who were manning a weather station. Aerographer's Mate First Class William House managed to escape, and for 50 days thereafter he subsisted on worms and grass along the shore of the island. Then he surrendered and was later sent to Japan.

The capture of Attu and Kiska completed the Japanese invasion of the Aleutians. Imperial General Headquarters never laid plans to advance any farther toward the North American mainland.

In mainland Alaska and the continental United States, the stunning news that Japanese troops had occupied American territory caused consternation among the public. Panicky people called for action to prevent the Japanese from invading the West Coast. U.S. military planners were less concerned; after studying the situation, most of them had come to the conclusion that the mainland was beyond the reach of the Japanese. Major General Simon Bolivar Buckner Jr.,

the Army's top officer in Alaska, said: ''They might make it, but it would be their grandchildren who finally got there; and by then they would all be American citizens anyway.''

Nevertheless, Admiral Ernest J. King, the Commander in Chief of the U.S. Fleet, was determined to evict the Japanese from American soil. He urged Admiral Nimitz to ''explore and press all possible active measures'' to push them out. Nimitz complied, but gave proper priority to more urgent matters. The U.S. campaign to liberate the conquered islands would take 14 weary months.

The American counterattack began in a small way on June 11 with a three-day bombing blitz. The Japanese were consolidating their beachhead on Kiska, and the island's spacious harbor was full of targets. The burden of the attack fell first on the Catalinas, now basing on the tender *Gillis*, an ancient converted destroyer moored off Atka Island, 350 miles east of Kiska. Gassed up and laden with 500-pound bombs, the PBYs lumbered westward below the fog. But the pilots, considering it suicidal to poke into the harbor in plain view of all the gunners on ship and shore, climbed up through the murk before reaching the island. In the sunlight above the fog, they took a bearing on the 4,000-foot-high Kiska Volcano and headed south, counting the seconds.

When they estimated that the harbor was directly below, they called upon their matronly craft to masquerade as dive bombers and plunged down through the mists at more than

*Technicians examine a late-model Zero fighter that crashed during the Japanese attack on Dutch Harbor on June 3, 1942. Although the plane wound up on its back, the soft, watery muskeg prevented its destruction; it was shipped to the United States, where it was repaired and flown in order to determine its performance secrets. Later, it was used as the star attraction in a War Bonds drive.*

*A Japanese color guard slogs through slushy snow in the unopposed June 7, 1942, Attu landing. The photo was displayed proudly in Japanese newspapers, which compared Attu's inhospitable summer to winter at home.*

200 miles per hour, nearly twice a Catalina's modest cruising speed. As the PBYs broke into the clear below the fog, the bombardiers took a quick look for a target and dumped their bombs. Then it took all the muscle of both pilot and copilot heaving at the controls to pull 17 tons of aircraft out of the dive and send the Catalinas straining to climb to safety in the fog.

The PBY crews claimed to have damaged three warships and two Japanese seaplanes. But since they had little time for accurate observation, the damage they did was not nearly as clear as the price they paid for the effort. One PBY went into its dive and was never seen again. Another came home with so many bullet holes that it sank upon landing. A third returned with two men dead and another wounded.

On June 14 the PBYs ran into a new enemy weapon over Kiska: Zero fighters equipped with floats so that they could operate out of Kiska Harbor. (The Japanese had no earth-moving equipment and would spend months hacking out an airfield by manual labor.) Though the Zeroes' floats reduced their performance, the fighters were much too fast and agile for the Catalinas. To save the PBYs for normal patrol and rescue duty, they were immediately excused from further dive bombing.

In place of the PBYs, the Army's Eleventh Air Force brought up a dozen bombers—B-17 Flying Fortresses and B-24 Liberators—to the trampoline-like runway at Umnak. All summer the heavyweights flew when the weather permitted, which was not often. When they were able to reach Kiska, they usually had to bomb blind from above the fog. Apparently most of their bombs were swallowed up by the muck of the tundra. An intelligence report summed up: "It is unlikely that raids by these aircraft possessed much more than nuisance value. Certainly none of the enemy's operations was impeded to a significant extent."

If anything, Admiral Theobald's warships had a harder time than the airplanes. For the sailors, every patrol was an endless, nerve-racking affair; they were constantly fighting thick fog, treacherous winds, mountainous seas, unpredictable currents and uncharted reefs. It was a special kind of torture for a sailor to go on deck watch in heavy weather; even in June, temperatures often went well below freezing.

"It took half an hour for a man to dress before going on the bridge," said a submarine skipper. "This usually consisted of heavy woolen underwear, followed by a heavy woolen hunting shirt, plus two pairs of woolen submarine trousers, plus three pairs of heavy wool socks, a pair of aviator's fleece-lined boots and large flexible rubber boots over those. Then, on top of all this, sponge-rubber-lined trousers, more sweaters and a sponge-lined parka." Once a lookout encased himself in this cocoon and went topside, he had to be lashed tightly to the bridge to keep from being bashed against the superstructure or washed overboard.

Two submarines were lost soon after the Japanese landed. The *S-27*, groping through the fog in late June, ran hard

aground on a reef off Amchitka Island. Her crew abandoned ship and took refuge in an old Aleut church until some PBYs came to the rescue a week later. The *Grunion,* a more modern fleet boat, disappeared in July after reporting that she had sunk two Japanese submarine chasers.

But the submarines did enjoy some success. On July 4 near Attu, the *Triton* sent the Japanese destroyer *Nenohi* to the bottom with two torpedoes. The next day, the *Growler* crept to the entrance of Kiska Harbor, sank one destroyer and severely damaged two others.

But Theobald and his surface fleet met with frustration at every turn. In late July, a force of cruisers and destroyers made two attempts to bombard Kiska; both forays were repulsed by fog, and in the second one, three minesweepers and a destroyer were damaged in collisions. Theobald gave up in disgust and turned over the next mission to Rear Admiral William W. Smith.

Smith made a third attempt on August 7. At 4:30 p.m., after running in and out of heavy mists all day, the task force plowed into a fog bank so dense that the bow of a ship was invisible from the bridge. On the cruiser *Indianapolis,* Lieut. Commander John Tatom climbed the ladder up the foremast to get a better look. From there he saw an astonishing sight: the masts of the other ships sticking up through the shallow fog bank like straws out of a vanilla soda.

Then Lieutenant Robert A. O'Neill, the pilot of the *Indianapolis'* light observation plane that had been launched in the soup, radioed that the firing course was clear. Admiral Smith, who had been sorely tempted to give up the attack, reached a decision. "Take them in for 30 minutes, turn on the firing course, and commence shooting," he ordered.

At 7:55, the ships commenced firing into Kiska Harbor over an eminence called South Head. The long-range bombardment went on for a satisfying length of time and used up 400 tons of ammunition. Finally at 8:21, Smith called a halt. Reconnaissance planes later reported that the bombardment had done minor damage.

The dubious results of air and sea strikes to date prompted interservice discussions of tactics—and an absurd feud between two top commanders. In order to cause the Japanese serious discomfiture, the Army and Army Air Forces generals wanted to build an airstrip within fighter-plane range of Kiska, which would permit fighter-escorted bombing raids.

They picked Tanaga, 160 miles east of Kiska, for the new base. The Navy disagreed, preferring Adak, which was 50 miles farther from Kiska but which had a good harbor. The disagreement did not seem critical—at first.

But then General Buckner started the trouble. One evening, while relaxing over drinks with Admiral Theobald and other officers, Buckner fished out a bit of playful doggerel he had written. It obviously teased Theobald for his reluctance to order operations in foggy weather:

*In far Alaska's icy spray, I stand beside my binnacle*
*And scan the waters through the fog for fear some*
*    rocky pinnacle*
*Projecting from unfathomed depths may break my*
*    hull asunder*
*And place my name upon the list of those who*
*    made a blunder.*

Theobald, a man once described as "having one of the best brains and worst dispositions in the Navy," was incensed. After seething over the verse for two days, he sent Buckner a letter, spiced with polite insults, that renounced any further contact save for unavoidable military duty. Theobald considered the matter momentous enough to send a copy of the letter and the verse to Admiral King, who forwarded both to General George C. Marshall, the U.S. Army Chief of Staff. Marshall investigated the officers' quarrel, but postponed any action.

The Joint Chiefs of Staff quickly decided the original argument over the new base in favor of the Navy; the airfield would be built on Adak. It turned out to be a fortunate choice. When the engineers went ashore, they found a flooded tidal flat with a hard bottom. In less than two weeks they drained the basin and laid down steel matting for a landing strip. By September 14 the base was operational, and a flight of 31 P-38 Lightnings and 16 B-24s took off on the first fighter-escorted bombing strike to Kiska. Soon a number of B-26 Marauders and B-25 Mitchell medium bombers also took up residence on Adak.

In spite of the wild gales that portended winter, many sorties were flown to Kiska and even to Attu, 170 miles farther to the west. The planes sank half a dozen ships at anchor in Kiska Harbor, damaged others, strafed bivouac areas and shot a number of float-equipped Zeroes out of the sky.

*Marston and a comrade mush across the snow toward a base.*

*Eskimo scouts form up to drill with their World War I rifles.*

## "MUKTUK" MARSTON AND ALASKA'S TUNDRA ARMY

After the Japanese attacked the Aleutians in June 1942, the Governor of Alaska empowered Major Marvin "Muktuk" Marston to "build a native army" to defend the territory against further aggression. Marston, an Arctic veteran who had earned his nickname by consuming enormous quantities of *muktuk*, or whale blubber, raised a militia of nearly 3,500 men and a few unauthorized women sharpshooters.

Marston placed his home guard in 78 coastal villages and regularly inspected them in long journeys by boat, plane and dog sledge. But Marston's militia needed little supervision. Its members faithfully patrolled 5,000 miles of Aleutian coastline and 200,000 square miles of tundra, rescuing a number of downed U.S. airmen.

The militia even saw action of a sort. From their home islands, the Japanese sent aloft bomb-carrying balloons with timers linked to the altitude-control units; the balloons, carried east by the prevailing winds, were expected to reach the United States 80 to 120 hours later, then descend and release incendiary bombs. Muktuk's marksmen shot down at least 18 balloons.

*In a photograph he inscribed to a friend, Major Marvin "Muktuk" Marston relaxes with his Husky pup. Marston first visited Alaska as a 15-year-old merchant seaman and immediately became, he said, "a sourdough at heart."*

Still, air raids alone could not win back Kiska and Attu; the islands would have to be taken at some future date by ground troops in battle with the Japanese. To prepare for the day when an invasion force could be mustered, the Army and the Navy agreed to establish a staging area on an uninhabited island closer to their two goals.

For the next move, Admiral Theobald wanted to occupy Amchitka, a narrow, low-lying island only 90 miles from Kiska. Again the Army disagreed and again the Joint Chiefs decided in Theobald's favor. But this time Theobald's antagonistic attitude overstrained his superiors' tolerance. Admiral Nimitz, acting in the interest of interservice harmony, relieved Theobald and replaced him with Rear Admiral

Thomas C. Kinkaid, a strong, business-like leader who found it unnecessary to quarrel with the Army commanders.

On January 12, 1943, four troop transports ferried a 2,000-man combat team into desolate Constantine Harbor on Amchitka. The soldiers were wading peacefully ashore through freezing brine when the usual Aleutian troubles began. The destroyer *Worden* was caught in a contrary current and driven against a rocky outcrop; 14 sailors drowned before the crew was rescued, leaving the destroyer to be battered to wreckage by the surf. Then a raging gale drove into the harbor's funnel-like mouth. One troop transport dragged her anchors and ran hard aground. Most of the landing craft were smashed on the beach, and thereafter cargo was unloaded by heaving it off the sides of ships and letting the surf

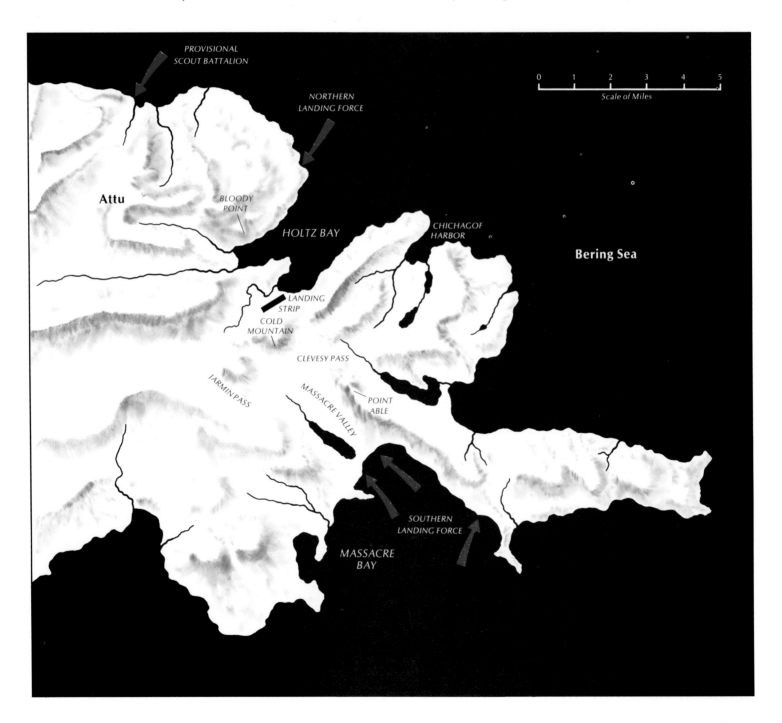

carry it in. Men worked waist-deep in the bone-chilling chop to haul the crates ashore.

After the storm, the troops started building a camp on squishy tundra that quickly broke up under the weight of GI boots and the churning tires of jeeps. By the second day the men were laboring, eating and sleeping in shin-deep mud. At night they were rocked to sleep by the dull grumbling of mild earth tremors.

After a few days, opposition appeared. The float Zeroes discovered Amchitka's new occupants and took to coming over in the afternoons with light, wing-mounted bombs. Their favorite target was the stranded transport, but most of their bombs landed in the tundra.

In the meantime, as on Adak, the engineers found a hard-bottomed tidal flat and within three weeks they had built another airstrip. Eight P-40s arrived on February 16, and the pilots gave a warm welcome to the Zeroes when they paid their regular visit that afternoon. Two Zeroes were shot down in flames, to the cheers of watching GIs.

The Americans' occupation of Amchitka, coming after their move to Adak, caused grave concern among the Japanese top commanders. They reasoned, incorrectly, that the enemy would not be pressing westward so assiduously unless he intended to use the Aleutians as a land bridge to the Kuriles and northern Japan. They hastened to reinforce the garrisons on both Attu and Kiska and exhorted the troops to redouble efforts to carve out airstrips. On February 5, orders went out from Imperial General Headquarters "to hold the western Aleutians at all costs and to carry out preparations for war" in the Kuriles.

The stepped-up preparations by both sides set the stage for the sole naval battle fought in the Aleutian theater. The delivery of troops and supplies to Kiska and Attu was deemed so important by the Japanese that Vice Admiral Boshiro Hosogaya, commander of the Northern Area Force (and Kakuta's superior), began using his warships to escort the transports and cargo ships bound for the Aleutians. And U.S. warships were patrolling vigorously to intercept the Japanese ships. So it was that on March 26, a U.S. task group—consisting of the heavy cruiser *Salt Lake City*, the light cruiser *Richmond* and four destroyers—happened to be on a collision course with a Japanese flotilla in the waters off Siberia's Komandorski Islands, about 180 miles west of Attu.

An hour before dawn, just as the American crews were finishing breakfast, the radarmen on two U.S. warships simultaneously reported contact with five enemy ships about 10 miles to the north. To the radarmen and the lookouts, they appeared to be transports, and the task-group commander, Rear Admiral Charles H. McMorris, gleefully ordered his ships to close. McMorris later confessed that he expected "a Roman holiday."

But shortly after 8 a.m., McMorris got a rude shock. Just as his ships approached firing range, lookouts spied two enemy heavy cruisers coming in on the starboard bow. Then two light cruisers hove into view. In fact, McMorris had run into the heavy cruisers *Nachi* and *Maya*, the light cruisers *Tama* and *Abukuma*, four destroyers and two fast, heavily armed merchant cruisers.

Though McMorris was outnumbered 2 to 1 by the Japanese, he chose to accept battle. He thought he could cut out the transports and get away before the enemy could cause him any great harm. And he was willing to gamble that the Japanese would make a mistake.

The Japanese opened fire at 8:40, and for three and a quarter hours the three heavy cruisers traded salvos at ranges of up to 12 miles. The smaller U.S. ships deployed to shield the *Salt Lake City*.

The first Japanese shells straddled the *Richmond*, McMorris' flagship, but the enemy gunners abruptly shifted their attention to the bigger *Salt Lake City*. Two minutes later the *Salt Lake City* drew first blood, hitting the *Nachi* with her third and fourth salvos and starting a small fire. It was extinguished quickly. At 8:50 the *Nachi* took two more hits, which damaged her communications and killed several men on the bridge. Minutes later she was hit harder and took heavier casualties; a shell penetrated her torpedo compartment and exploded.

Through much of the battle, the *Richmond* and the *Salt Lake City* had luck with a maneuver called "chasing the salvos"; assuming that an enemy who sees his shells miss will correct his range or firing angle for the next salvo, a captain would turn his ship toward the splashes. If all went well, the next salvo would scream by harmlessly.

Between chasing salvos and just plain zigzagging, Captain Bertram Rodgers, skipper of the *Salt Lake City*, led a

The U.S. plan to recapture Attu Island called for five separate landings (arrows) involving 11,000 men. The main Southern Force was to land at Massacre Bay and seize the Jarmin and Clevesy mountain passes, which opened into the island's interior valleys. The smaller Northern Force, with support from a scout battalion, was to clear the shores of Holtz Bay and then join up with the Southern Force for a final attack on the enemy's strongest positions near Chichagof Harbor.

charmed life. His executive officer, Commander Worthington Bitler, recalled: "The skipper would ask, 'Well, Worthy, which way shall we turn next?'

"I'd answer, 'Your guesses have been perfect so far, Captain. Guess again!' He'd swing right or left, and the spot we would have been in would be plowed up with 10 or 15 eight-inch shells.

"The skipper would then look at me with a grin just like a schoolboy. 'Fooled 'em again, Worthy!' It was uncanny."

But the *Salt Lake City* ran out of luck at 9:10 a.m. A shell penetrated her armor below the waterline, ruptured her oil tanks and exploded three feet from the after engine room. Crewmen stopped the flow of oil into the engine room and plugged the shell hole. The cruiser kept on fighting at full speed. An hour later she was hit again. Several of her compartments flooded.

But then at 11:03, she took another blow and the concussion compounded the damage. Sea water flooded into the engine room, and oil spurted into the after gyro compartment. Damage-control parties struggled to stanch her wounds, the men frantically working armpit-deep in spilled oil and icy sea water, plugging leaks with anything that came to hand, including their shirts. The water that spewed into the fuel tanks extinguished the boilers one by one.

At 11:55 the *Salt Lake City* went dead in the water. A U.S. destroyer quickly laid down a smoke screen to conceal the crippled warship, and the other destroyers raced toward the Japanese, hoping to deliver a torpedo attack. The *Richmond* came charging in to take off the cruiser's crew.

Just then, with victory at hand, Hosogaya unaccountably ordered a withdrawal. At 12:03 he fired a farewell salvo and turned his ships westward. The *Salt Lake City's* crewmen were left to tend their ship in grateful bewilderment. The final battle entry in the cruiser's log said: "This day the hand of Divine Providence lay over the ship."

Hosogaya had his reasons for retiring. As he explained to his superiors, he was low on ammunition and fuel; he did not realize that the *Salt Lake City* lay dead under her smoke screen; and he expected U.S. bombers to arrive from Amchitka or Adak. For his failure the high command fired him.

The Americans had come out ahead in spite of the damage to the *Salt Lake City* and the loss of seven men dead, five on the destroyer *Bailey* and two on the *Salt Lake City*. The Japanese reinforcements headed for Attu had been turned back, and that was vital. For now the time of the final hand-to-hand struggle was drawing near.

The U.S. Joint Chiefs of Staff had decided to invade Attu in the spring of 1943. They had chosen Attu as the target in preference to Kiska for sound military reasons: More important campaigns—now including operations in North Africa and the build-up for the invasions of Sicily, Italy and Normandy—meant that the U.S. simply could not muster the ships, manpower and matériel that would be needed to overwhelm Kiska, which reconnaissance had shown to be more heavily defended than Attu. The Americans would skip Kiska and then, from Attu farther west and Amchitka to the east, interdict it by sea and air. The Attu operation would be the first of the War in which U.S. forces bypassed a strong enemy base to attack a weaker one closer to Japan—a technique they would later use over and over again in island-hopping campaigns across the Pacific.

Americans were new to the techniques of amphibious warfare in the spring of 1943. They had only their landings

*American infantrymen, pinned down in Attu's Massacre Valley, return the fire of Japanese snipers dug in on the fog-shrouded mountains. The Americans resumed their advance after the battleship Nevada bombarded the enemy positions. Then, said an officer, "dead Japanese, hunks of artillery, pieces of guns, and arms and legs rolled down out of the fog."*

in North Africa and Guadalcanal to guide them, and neither operation was of much use in preparing for a landing on a subarctic island. They made many mistakes.

The 7th Infantry Division, the outfit that would bear the brunt of the fighting, had been trained in the California desert for action as a motorized unit in North Africa. In January 1943, the men were transferred across the state to Fort Ord, near Monterey, to practice amphibious operations. Of course the sun-drenched California beaches gave them no conception of the problems they would face on the Aleutian tundra. And they went through their landing drills with only a small fraction of the supplies and heavy equipment they would have to carry in for the actual battle.

The Americans settled for inadequate reconnaissance, no doubt because of the difficulty of penetrating the Aleutian fogs. At first they thought that the Japanese garrison on Attu had only 500 men and that cleaning it out would take three days. The estimate was later raised, but not until the island had been secured—after three weeks of tough fighting— did they learn that Attu had more than 2,300 defenders.

The invasion was planned on sketchy knowledge of Attu's terrain. The most detailed map available was a Coast and Geodetic Survey chart that showed the topography only to 1,000 yards in from the shoreline. The interior—an area cut by deep valleys and ridges rising to 3,000 feet—was a blank, and whole companies could get lost there and wander around aimlessly for days. The coastal waters were also largely a blank; printed on the chart was a warning to ships not to approach closer than two and a half miles because of uncharted shallows and rocks. This meant that the landing craft would have a long trip to shore in the fog.

The Americans' worst mistake was their dress and gear. Most of the troops would go ashore wearing ordinary winter uniforms that provided little protection from the Aleutian rain and wind. And the troops' high-topped leather boots were not the waterproof footgear needed for Attu's soggy tundra. Moreover, as a security measure, the winter gear was not issued until the men were aboard ship, and they had no chance to break in their boots. On Attu their cold, wet feet would be rubbed raw, often leading to gangrene.

The assault plan that finally evolved was a complicated one for an operation involving less than a full division. It called for two main landings, on the northern and southern coasts of the 20-mile-wide island (map, page 132). These forces would fight toward each other, then turn east together and drive seven miles to the main Japanese positions at the eastern tip of the island. In addition, a small unit called the Provisional Scout Battalion would come ashore seven miles west of the Northern Force to divert enemy attention from the main landings.

The Northern Force, the smaller of the two main groups, was made up of the 1st Battalion of the 17th Infantry Regiment, a battery of field artillery and supporting troops. It was commanded by Lieut. Colonel Albert V. Hartl. The Southern Force, under Colonel Edward P. Earle, consisted of the 2nd and 3rd Battalions of the 17th, the 2nd Battalion of the 32nd

*Medics carry a disabled GI—one of hundreds of frostbite or trench-foot victims—to a jeep for evacuation to an Attu aid station. It was impossible for many soldiers, ducking enemy fire in water-filled foxholes, to take proper care of their feet: rubbing them to keep up circulation and changing often into dry socks.*

Regiment and three field-artillery batteries. The 1st and 3rd Battalions of the 32nd and two batteries of field artillery would remain on board ship as a floating reserve. In all, the assault force and floating reserve numbered about 11,000 men. The 4th Infantry Regiment would be held in tactical reserve on Adak.

To preserve the element of surprise, no preinvasion bombardment was planned. But the ground troops would have plenty of heavy support if they needed it: Three battleships, the *Nevada*, the *Idaho* and the *Pennsylvania*, would be on call, as well as the bombers from Adak, Amchitka and the escort carrier *Nassau*.

The invasion force sailed from San Francisco on April 24, reaching Cold Bay on the 30th. D-day was set for May 7, and the ships arrived off Attu in time. But thick fog and howling winds postponed the assault. To kill time and avoid detection, the convoy steamed far north into the Bering Sea.

The delay turned out to be a stroke of good luck. The Japanese on Attu had been warned by the Kiska garrison of threatening U.S. ship movements, and for a week they guarded their beaches and manned their artillery day and night. But as the days passed and no enemy ships emerged from the fog, the men on Attu decided that it was a false alarm. On May 9 they stood down from their guns. On May 11 the U.S. invasion force arrived offshore.

The first Americans to land were 200 troops of the Provisional Scout Battalion, who had been brought in close to the north coast by the submarines *Narwhal* and *Nautilus*. They came ashore at 3 a.m. and soon afterward were joined by the remaining 400 men of their unit, landed from the destroyer *Kane*. They began climbing through the mountains in search of a way east toward the main enemy positions, at Holtz Bay and Chichagof Harbor.

At 4:15 p.m., the Northern Force started going ashore on the north coast just to the west of Holtz Bay; the men hit a tiny sandspit so narrow and rocky that only two landing craft could beach at one time.

The landing was unopposed and evidently unnoticed—until after 6 p.m. Then a platoon working eastward from the beach saw four Japanese soldiers strolling toward them. The Americans killed two of the men, but the others managed to escape to warn their comrades of the American presence.

By 9:30 p.m., 1,100 men were struggling up the steep, slippery bluff 75 yards behind the beach. Signalmen wrestled their heavy spools of wire up the hill, sometimes falling in the squishy mud. On the beach, GIs sloshed through the surf, pulling handcarts loaded down with gear. Gun crews strained to haul their artillery pieces into position. Infantrymen stacked their rifles here and there on the beach and went to work digging foxholes.

In the meantime, on the south side of the island the invasion was not going well. There the fog had socked in solidly and stayed without a break. H-hour, originally set for 7:40 a.m., was postponed from hour to hour. All through the delay the landing craft, laden with troops and gear, milled around the transports.

Finally at 3:30 p.m. someone decided that something had to be done. A destroyer, navigating by radar, began leading the small boats in, guiding them by blowing her whistle and keeping a searchlight trained astern. A reporter aboard a landing craft wrote: "We trailed in her wake, spread out on either side a disorderly procession. Each wave leader had six boats and each had his own ideas about speed and position. Boats surged ahead, fell back, crossed over, heaved in one another's churning wakes.

"Always ahead went our squeaking Pied Piper with its crazy whistle and one glaring eye."

Fortunately for the men of the Southern Force, there were no Japanese on the beach when they finally found it—in fog so thick that a man 10 feet ahead was invisible. By full dark—around 10 p.m. in the long subarctic summer day—all the men were ashore, learning about other repugnant Aleutian features. Within 75 yards of the beach, the tractors pulling the 105mm howitzers were hopelessly mired, spinning their treads in the tundra. The guns had to be emplaced where they stood, and their crews hurried about scrounging around for steel matting and whatever solid detritus they could find to keep the howitzers from sinking too deep to be trained on any target.

Next morning the Americans found plenty of Japanese to fight. The men of the Northern Force struggled up through snow and rocks to a crest that—given the events of the day—would come to be known as Bloody Point. Overnight, Japanese units had dug in on that ridge, and the Americans had to drive past them and southward down a

*A line of black dots against the snow, the Provisional Scout Battalion inches along a rugged mountainside toward the main Japanese defenses at the eastern end of Attu. It took the mountain-trained troops more than a day to negotiate the seven miles from their north-shore landing zone to a point overlooking the Japanese position. Then, exhausted, the Americans covered the remaining few hundred yards to their attack position by sliding down the slope on the seats of their pants.*

steep slope to the planned meeting with the Southern Force.

After a breakfast of cold K rations, the GIs began creeping forward, upslope into the fog. A few riflemen traded desultory shots with unseen enemy snipers. Lieut. Colonel Hartl ordered one of his three companies to circle to the right and take the crest by climbing a deep gully that ran diagonally up the ridge. The company moved partway up the hill and entered the gully. The fog was lifting now, and the Japanese on the crest spotted them. The Americans were pinned down in the gully by heavy enemy fire from machine guns, light mortars, rifles and—from 9 a.m. onward—artillery. For the next 12 hours the GIs would stay there, unable to advance or to retreat, lying in the mud in their enfiladed ditch or shivering in foxholes full of frigid seepage.

Hartl's two other companies spent the remainder of the day struggling to relieve the troops trapped in the gully. They would crawl on their bellies straight up the mountain for a short distance, only to be driven back by Japanese artillery. At times they withdrew to a safe distance so that their own artillery from the beach or the battleships offshore could pound the crest of the ridge. Periodically, waves of Lightning fighters and Liberator bombers from Amchitka and Grumman F4F Wildcats from the *Nassau* made bombing and strafing runs.

The GIs started an all-out drive for the top at about 5 p.m., after a furious naval barrage. An hour and a half later, they had managed to crawl and scramble up the ridge, driving a number of enemy troops down the far side. Now heavy enemy artillery fire forced them to back off a little, but they moved laterally to a sheltered position on the crest. And there they held.

At 7:30 the Japanese counterattacked—a fierce charge with hand grenades and fixed bayonets. As hand-to-hand fighting raged, the Japanese turned their antiaircraft guns onto the crest with the shells fused to explode a few feet over the heads of the men struggling there. Shrapnel rained down on the Americans and Japanese alike, and the concussion of the exploding shells knocked men over like discarded rag dolls. The battle lasted 22 minutes and the Americans held on. Bloody Point was theirs.

During the night, the survivors from the gully made their way down to the battalion aid station. Some walked. Those who could not were carried by aid men. Most of the immo-

bilized men were victims of their boots. Their feet were frozen, blue and shriveled. Only exposure to the air could save them from gangrene and, perhaps, amputation.

On D-day-plus-1, the GIs of the Southern Force got their chance to suffer. Their mission was to push north about three miles up a broad, gently rising valley; it, and the adjacent bay, bore the name Massacre in commemoration of the slaughter of hundreds of Aleuts by Russian fur trappers more than a century before. At the head of the valley lay two passes that led to the rendezvous with the Northern Force.

The advance went smoothly at first, but when the lead companies were a mile or so into Massacre Valley, all hell broke loose. The steep ridges on each side were alive with Japanese troops, well-armed with mortars and machine guns. And their camouflage was perfect: Though the valley floor was clear, fog hung low and thick on the sides of the mountains. The Japanese simply fired blind through the fog into the valley and hit the Americans.

The valley floor became a purgatory of exploding shells and whining bullets. GIs fell dead or wounded. Men who tried to run fell with heavy splashes in the sopping-wet tundra, their ankles sprained or their legs wrenched as they stepped into hidden potholes overgrown with muskeg and covered with snow or slush. The muskeg was so thick that the men could hack out only small coffin-shaped pits, which filled with water almost at once. Men lay for hours on end in the water or took cover in one of the icy streambeds that crisscrossed the terrain.

Soon the GIs were so weak and wet and shivering with cold that concerted action was impossible. When the platoon leaders and squad leaders signaled an advance, some of their men rose and staggered ahead, but some could not get up and they would have to be carried out later with the wounded. When Colonel Earle went forward to find out why his men were not advancing, he was killed by a sniper.

The advance of the Southern Force bogged down completely. D-day-plus-2 brought no change. By the third day, the limping procession of trench-foot cases began to reach the aid stations. By the fourth day, most of the victims had to be carried.

Whenever the fog lifted a little, the Japanese positions were battered by the *Nevada* off the south beach, by the

*Pennsylvania* and the *Idaho* in the north, by lesser warships ringing the eastern end of the island, and occasionally by Wildcat fighters. None of this seemed to do much except to leave dirty gashes in the snow, and the cost ran high. Three Wildcats got caught in a sudden windstorm and crashed.

The days with little progress wore on the nerves of Major General Albert E. Brown, commander of all the ground forces. He asked for reinforcements. As early as D-plus-2—May 13—a large part of the shipboard reserve was committed. That eased the situation, but then Brown wanted large amounts of engineering and road-building equipment. Admiral Kinkaid, in overall charge of the operation, correctly interpreted the requests as proof that the Southern Force was stuck and that the entire battle was going nowhere. The admiral had a worry of his own—that his ships were tarrying too long off Attu within bomber range of Paramushir Island, the Japanese base on the Kurile Islands. So Kinkaid relieved Brown and replaced him with Major General Eugene Landrum from Adak.

Landrum came ashore May 16 and immediately ordered the men on the valley floor to begin fighting up the slopes, into the snow, fog and rocks where the Japanese were. In fact, the change in command had little to do with the dramatic American successes of the following day.

While the Southern Force had been stalled for almost a week in the valley, the men of the Northern Force had consolidated their gains and moved forward slowly but steadily. By May 16 they were within striking distance of the northern end of the passes that the Southern Force had to take to escape from the valley. The Japanese commander, Colonel Yasuyo Yamazaki, abandoned Jarmin Pass, the more westerly of the two, during the predawn darkness of May 17. He knew that he could not prevent the linkup of the U.S. pincers, so he chose to concentrate his troops for a strong defense of Clevesy Pass in the east, thus denying the Americans the principal route to Chichagof Harbor at the eastern end of the island. The next day the Americans shook hands in Jarmin Pass—and the fight for Clevesy Pass began.

Elements of three regiments fought for Clevesy Pass from May 18 to May 21. One flank of the pass lay in the shadow of a steep, snow-covered eminence called Cold Mountain. Two companies of the 17th Regiment crawled up the jagged slope, often hand over hand, on the morning of May 20. A GI was hit near the top and fell 500 feet in long, loose bounces until a rock outcropping stopped what was left of him. His buddies kept going and took the top of Cold Mountain in a racket of gunfire and grenade explosions that echoed in the valley below.

The other side of the pass was dominated by a sharp escarpment named Point Able. For four days patrols from the 32nd Regiment tried to clear it. They were driven back by the Japanese at the top, one of whom yelled insults in passable English.

Finally on May 21, two platoons of the 32nd fought their way up to the top in the early-morning gloom. On the tiny, deeply entrenched crest they killed 25 enemy soldiers. The last Japanese alive killed two Americans with his submachine gun, then leaped off the peak screaming.

The fall of Clevesy Pass sealed the fate of the Japanese on Attu. The Americans had isolated the Japanese on the

*At battle's end on Attu, a Japanese soldier who fought to the death despite severe chest wounds lies sprawled in a wrecked dugout at Holtz Bay. The hundreds of Japanese who chose to die rather than surrender to the enemy inspired propagandists in Tokyo to compare the defense of Attu to another heroic last-ditch stand—by the Texans at the Alamo.*

cramped eastern end of the island and now possessed the high ground. All that remained for the GIs was to push downslope to Chichagof, mopping up as they went. But it would prove to be a grisly job.

The Japanese did not retreat. They had dug a deep, extensive system of trenches, mortar pits and foxholes before the Americans landed, and now they defended their positions to the death. Many of the Japanese were killed in their rock-lined dugouts amid tidy piles of unused grenades, unopened boxes of rations and unspent ammunition.

The Japanese would not surrender even if they could fight no longer. When a company of GIs took a jagged ridge, they found enemy soldiers sitting in their holes, shaken and confused by the action. GIs who knew a few words of Japanese yelled to them, telling them to come out with their hands up. There was no response. The Americans had been asked by intelligence officers to take prisoners for interrogation, but men who had tried to oblige got killed for their pains. So the GIs moved from hole to hole lobbing grenades down on the stunned enemy soldiers.

The Japanese continued to fight hard, and it sometimes took heroic measures to crack their positions. One such fight took place on a ridge between Holtz Bay and Chichagof Harbor. Lieut. Colonel John Finn and the men of four companies were meeting with stiff resistance from a high, snowy plateau on the far side of a steep saddle perhaps 100 yards away. While some troops saturated the plateau with fire from eight heavy machine guns and eight mortars, other GIs moved to the attack. They ran down into the saddle, then clawed their way up the other side. Finn could

see no Japanese, only the crablike GIs crawling upslope.

When the scrambling figures were almost at the lip of the plateau, the covering fire lifted. At once the hidden Japanese reacted, rolling grenades down the snowy incline. Two Americans fell backward and lay still, legs pointing uphill. The rest slid and rolled down the hill.

The covering fire started up again and kept up until the ragged line of crawling figures of the GIs reached the top. Again Japanese grenades began to explode among them.

Again the line skidded backward down the hill—except for one man. He hunched for a moment at the edge of the plateau. Then he pulled himself upright, stepped over the edge and stood silhouetted against the snow. Oblivious of enemy fire, he went through a series of movements that almost had the quality of a ballet.

For a moment, the man seemed to dance on tiptoes, holding his rifle across his belly. He stopped, pointed the rifle at the ground and fired. He stepped back, then forward, putting each foot down with precision. He pointed the rifle down and fired again. He moved forward again, snatched a grenade from his belt, pulled the pin, dropped it and danced away. He drew back and worked his rifle, apparently trying to reload. He reached to his belt and fumbled with his bayonet. For a moment he seemed undecided. Then he ran forward and, grabbing the rifle by the muzzle, brought the butt down with a full, deliberate swing. Four times he raised the clubbed rifle and smashed it down. Then he stepped to the edge of the plateau and crooked an arm at the men below.

Lieut. Colonel Finn ran down into the saddle and hauled himself up the slope onto the plateau. There he grabbed

*GIs visit the graves of their buddies at a cemetery on Attu. More than 2,500 American and Japanese soldiers died in the course of the brutal 20-day battle for the island.*

Captain Robert Johnson, in command of the two companies now on top.

"Who was that God-blessed fool?" he demanded.

"That's him," Johnson said, pointing to a figure sitting on a rock. "Mirich's his name. George Mirich. He's got three bullets in his left arm. He wouldn't have clubbed those guys but his ammo was gone and his bayonet was smashed."

"You're a sergeant," Finn said to Mirich. "Go get that arm dressed."

By nightfall on May 28 the bulk of the American forces were poised for the final assault on Chichagof Harbor. General Landrum had decided to finish off the battle of Attu with an all-out attack the next morning.

Sometime during the night of May 28, Colonel Yamazaki reached a decision of his own. Out of 2,300 men on hand when the invasion came, he had about 1,000 still able to bear arms. He decided to counterattack. His plan was desperate. His men would break out of the Chichagof Harbor area, killing as they went, with the ultimate aim of getting through Clevesy Pass to the U.S. artillery position on a nearby hill. He would capture the massed howitzers, turn them on the Americans in Massacre Valley and hold them at bay until help came from Paramushir Island.

The men wounded too seriously to walk were given a choice: pistols with which to kill themselves or, for the few who could not do the deed, a lethal injection of morphine. The walking wounded were told to arm themselves and come along. By now weapons and ammunition were in short supply; some men had only bayonets lashed to sticks.

At 3 a.m. Yamazaki led his ragtag force up the valley. They fell upon Company B of the 32nd Regiment in the valley and part of Company L of the 17th on a rise. At first, the attack was silent; Americans were bayoneted in their sleeping bags. But then wild firing began and grenades exploded all around. The confused survivors of Company B fled in disorder, some running barefooted through the icy muck.

The Japanese overran a tented aid station, slaughtering the medics and the wounded in their cots. But then a sort of mass hysteria seized Yamazaki's men. They began screaming and charging pointlessly hither and yon, breaking off in small groups. Some GIs who lived through the night of horror thought they were drunk. A few of the Japanese simply sat down among the Americans they had just killed and gorged themselves on American rations.

The main body of Japanese held together after a fashion and got into Clevesy Pass. There they fell upon the division engineers. Alerted by the gunfire down below, the engineers had organized a defense line. Cooks and bulldozer drivers grabbed any handy weapon and fought hard. They stopped the Japanese in the pass.

Now the strange behavior of Yamazaki's men turned even more irrational—to the Americans at least. The Japanese gave up trying to slaughter Americans and turned to killing themselves. Mostly they did it with grenades, holding them against forehead, breast or belly. Hundreds finished themselves, screaming as they did so. In the dawn the valley was full of headless, handless, scooped-out corpses.

The mass suicide left the Americans numb with shock. "I am glad they're dead, really glad of it," said the division chaplain as he walked among the corpses. "That worries me. How can I go back to my church when I've got it in me to be glad men are dead? But now I'm glad they're dead."

The battle for Attu was soon finished. Out of Yamazaki's 2,300 men, 29 were taken prisoner. The rest were dead. The battle had cost the Americans 549 killed and 1,148 wounded—in addition to the 2,100 men who were listed as casualties because of trench foot, exposure and shock.

Yamazaki's counterattack—the first banzai charge of the War—ended the Aleutian fighting, although a failure of reconnaissance would keep the Americans in the dark until they assaulted Kiska 10 weeks later. That invasion was an enormous operation involving more than 34,000 ground troops, including 5,500 Canadians, and an armada of three battleships, one heavy cruiser, one light cruiser, 19 destroyers, 15 transports, four cargo vessels, three fast minesweepers, two tugs, one harbor tug, a surveying ship, 24 heavy bombers, 44 medium bombers, 28 dive bombers, 12 patrol bombers and 60 fighters.

The landings went off without a hitch on August 15. But after four days of probing for opposition in vain, the invaders finally realized that the Japanese, undetected, had evacuated Kiska about three weeks earlier. The only living things left on the island were a few dogs, the abandoned pets of lonely Japanese soldiers who had slipped away under cover of the everlasting Aleutian fog.

# THE GI VS. THE ELEMENTS

Flying past an Aleutian peak, a transport hauling supplies through the islands is silhouetted against one of the area's many natural hazards: impenetrable fog.

# MISERABLE DUTY ON THE INTOLERABLE ISLANDS

*Standing on wooden planks outside his pyramidal tent, a GI tests the depth of the ever-present, shifting, sometimes bottomless Aleutian mud.*

The U.S. servicemen on duty in the Aleutian Islands were pitted against adversaries even tougher than the Japanese: the intractable terrain and the scourging climate. Through much of the year, the islands were plagued by fog, sometimes so thick that a man could see nothing a dozen feet away. Freakish gales called williwaws screamed in from the sea with wind speeds of 100 miles an hour, and some brought torrential rains and blinding blizzards. The ground rarely froze in the Aleutians, thanks to the warm Japan Current, but the wind and dampness sometimes drove temperatures down to zero.

The islands' tundra terrain was a fit companion to the atrocious weather. The springy mat of muskeg vegetation fought the blades of the GIs' bulldozers, and once the thick layer was stripped away, the men had to toil in deep, dark mud to build camps, roads and airstrips. There were no trees—none at all—to break the wind, a fact that the men combined with another conspicuous shortage in a sardonic saying: "There is a woman behind every tree in the Aleutians." "Living conditions are terrible," an officer summed up in his diary. "Our tents are pitched on excavations that overlook the perpetual marsh, and heated by tiny metal coal stoves because there is no natural fuel on the island. The floor is covered with three inches of water, and it is rising."

It took engineers and construction battalions weeks of frustrating labor to carve out each new base. And for the men who were assigned to maintain these facilities, there was no alternative but to endure the endless bad weather and the unremitting hardships.

But occasionally a break in the weather gave a lift to the spirit. "Whenever the sun shines for more than an hour," said an Army medic, "I get so happy it's almost pathological." In the summertime, some of the GIs wandered into the inland valleys and admired the brilliant wild flowers. A Navy officer who captained a supply tug recalled: "Once I sat on top of a mountain on Attu. It was so clear I could look right up the island chain 170 miles to Kiska. I was so awed that I cried. It was the most beautiful thing I ever saw."

A bulldozer attacks the Aleutian muskeg, a thick, tensile blanket of vegetation. Once punctured, it became a quagmire that bogged down men and machines.

U.S. Navy Seabees lay down a runway of interlocking steel links. With numbed fingers, the men had to join 80,000 segments, each weighing 65 pounds.

Two soldiers start digging out their Quonset hut after a snowstorm. Gale-force winter winds frequently built up snowdrifts to a height of 15 feet and more.

*A heated tent shelters mechanics while they work on the engine of a P-40 fighter. But there is no protection for the man checking instruments in the cockpit.*

## BATTLING THE COLD TO KEEP THEM FLYING

At the airfield on Umnak Island, oil-sump fires were kept burning in 50-gallon drums on the flight line so that airplane mechanics could warm their hands while arming and checking the aircraft. This practice was followed routinely in the midsummer months, and it warned newcomers of what they could expect when winter came.

The subarctic winters were made brutally cold by wind-blown snow and sleet. It took only minutes of exposure to freeze a man's eyelids together, and a drop of icy high-octane gasoline on the skin raised a huge blister. Yet crewmen had to stand in the open for hours on end to fuel up a sin-gle B-17 for a bombing mission over the Japanese-held western islands, Kiska and Attu. Frequently, the planes' engines refused to start until their cylinders had been thawed out with a blowtorch.

Then the fliers' ordeal began. By the time the PBY flying boats lifted off from the harbors, their windscreens were coated with frozen sea spray, dangerously reducing visibility. In the bombers flying above the weather, cabin temperatures dropped to −85° F., and the ice that formed on the wings of the planes steadily reduced their speeds, increased their gas consumption and made them hazardous to fly. And when the bombers finally managed to return, the ground crewmen sometimes had to spend two hours scraping them clean of a ton of ice.

*Struggling against an Aleutian williwaw, a soldier is held motionless at a 45-degree angle by the force of the wind. During a windstorm, many men skipped meals rather than risk the short walk to the mess hall.*

*A Navy PBY lies on its back, overturned by a williwaw at Dutch Harbor in November of 1942. Ground crews could repair a plane like this one within 24 hours; total wrecks supplied parts for the planes still flying.*

# WILD WINDS OF THE WILLIWAW

More terrible than the snow and the cold were the powerful, erratic, Aleutian windstorms. "People just can't picture a wind that goes up and down, east and west, all the time," wrote reporter Howard Handleman. "The williwaw goes down the back of your neck, up the front of your trousers and into both pants pockets at once."

Williwaws sucked planes out of their hangars, flipped them over or carried them away. A particularly violent williwaw on Adak was clocked at 110 miles an hour—before still-stronger winds ripped off the anemometer cups that were used to measure wind velocity. For weeks afterward the men retold the joke about three apocryphal sea gulls that made a forced landing after their feathers were all blown off.

But it was no joke to be caught in a williwaw. Many soldiers were injured by winds that knocked them down or pelted them with flying rubble. One victim said: "I was walking along in a high wind when this here outhouse came sailing out of nowhere and pinned me to a hut." He was unconscious for three days.

Mount Tulik, a long-dormant volcano on Umnak Island, erupts on June 4, 1945, adding a rain of ash to the GIs' discomfort. The troops were on alert to

abandon the island in case of a major lava flow. They were grievously disappointed when the eruption subsided and the evacuation was called off.

# AIRMEN'S NIGHTMARE: PEA-SOUP FOGS

The Aleutian fogs were the bane of the fliers' existence. A fog might come to stay for days on end, socking in the airfield; then again, fogs would sometimes roll through in a matter of minutes. One pilot, who had come in for landing on a clear field but overshot the strip, later said, "By the time I got back, the field was shut tight and I was hanging there with mountains all around me." He finally followed a radio beam down to a safe landing.

The fog accounted for many of the 63 planes lost in the autumn of 1942, a period in which only nine Aleutian-based planes were shot down in combat. Some of the pilots, unable to see the end of the runway, crashed on takeoff or landing; others, disoriented by the fog, got lost and were never found. On a single fogbound mission from Umnak to Kiska, five planes went down: Four crashed trying to land and one simply did not return.

The airmen complained bitterly about being required to fly excessively hazardous missions, but some brass hats in the States replied that the men were exaggerating the weather conditions. Then in December 1942, a visiting inspector general went along on a bombing mission. On the way back his pilot found that two airfields were socked in solid by a pea-soup fog. Unable to land, he ran out of fuel. The B-24 crashed at sea, breaking the general's collarbone. A flying boat quickly rescued all hands. But after that the Aleutian airmen were never again accused of exaggerating weather reports.

*FIRST MINUTE*

*TENTH MINUTE*

A dramatic sequence of pictures taken by Life photographer Dmitri Kessel shows the Aleutian fog closing

FOURTH MINUTE

SEVENTH MINUTE

FOURTEENTH MINUTE

SEVENTEENTH MINUTE

in on Adak Island. Between the first picture and the last one, only 17 minutes elapsed. Formed over the water, the fog was driven inland by the rising wind.

# AIRLINE TO EVERYWHERE

Weary fliers await a ride to the transient barracks at Casablanca's Cazes Field, one of the busiest of the 250 Air Transport Command bases worldwide.

# AMERICA'S EVER-READY AIR-FREIGHT EXPRESS

In the summer of 1942, as the German Afrika Korps drove deep into Egypt, the British Eighth Army ran completely out of antitank shell fuses. Within 15 hours of calling for help, the British received 15 tons of fuses, thanks to an emergency airlift by the U.S. Air Transport Command.

In January of 1943, General Douglas MacArthur dispatched an urgent appeal for assistance: His troops fighting in the Solomon Islands had depleted their supply of hand grenades. Within three days, the Air Transport Command had flown in five and one half tons of grenades from an arsenal in Utah.

That same year, a vital military hospital in Nome, Alaska, was destroyed by fire. Within 36 hours, an entire set of duplicate medical equipment—everything from surgical gloves to beds—had been flown to Nome by cargo planes of the Air Transport Command.

Such logistical feats became routine for the ATC, the world's largest airline. Established to slash time and distance when the War would not wait, the ATC hopscotched about the globe between far-flung air bases, ferrying thousands of new bombers and fighter planes to combat zones and moving more than 100,000 tons of supplies a month. Its cargo was as diverse as its routes. The command's 3,700 aircraft, said an official Air Force history, hauled "everything from bulldozers to blood plasma, from college professors to Hollywood entertainers, from high-explosive ammunition to the most delicate signal equipment, from eminent scientists to obscure technicians, from heads of state to the ordinary GI." On return trips, the planes often served as aerial ambulances, bringing back wounded soldiers for medical treatment in the States.

ATC supplies flown from India over the Himalayas to China—the famed "Hump" route—kept the Chinese in the War. General Claire Chennault of the Flying Tigers said, with only slight exaggeration, "Every vehicle, every gallon of fuel, every round of ammunition, every weapon that found its way into Free China during nearly three years was flown in from India by air."

An ATC crewman catnaps in a hammock under his B-25. The exhausting schedules taught the aircrews to sleep when and where they could.

A formation of C-47s assembles at dawn over the huge ATC base at Natal, Brazil, before setting out on the 2,797-mile flight to Africa. Once over the ocean, such formations routinely scattered because, as an ATC officer said, at night or in bad weather "one thing which his instruments will not tell a pilot is that he is too close to another plane."

Senegalese levies and their French officers join ATC fliers in a solemn procession for the funeral of a pilot who crashed near Eknes Field outside Dakar. Situated at Africa's most westerly point, the base was a way-stop for eastbound ATC planes crossing the Atlantic Ocean from Natal, Brazil.

A C-47 cargo plane passes over the Great Pyramids at Giza, nine miles southwest of Cairo, on its way to a landing at the ATC's Payne Field. The sprawling air base, built from scratch on the desert, was the hub of North African routes that continued on to Teheran, Iran, and Karachi, India.

160

Villagers from Jorhat—a hamlet near the Indian-Burmese border—
cool off in a bathing pool alongside a C-46 under repair at an ATC field.
Ground crews at Jorhat and other bases in India were bedeviled by
summer temperatures that often soared above 130° F. and an average
rainfall of 200 inches during the five-month-long monsoon season.

Carved from a coral atoll 1,337 miles south of Hawaii, this ATC base on palmy Christmas Island was one stop on a "milk run" bringing mail, magazines and movies to military outposts throughout the South Pacific.

A C-46 comes in for a landing at Luliang, China, an ATC base opened in August of 1944 to accommodate increased air traffic over the Hump. The water-buffalo-drawn cart lumbering alongside the hardpan runway exemplified the primitive conditions that the ATC had to face in China: Local laborers pumped aviation fuel from drums by hand and accurate weather reports were rare. Groused one passenger, "The present system is that if you can see the end of the runway, it's safe to take off."

# 6

In 1941, few people outside of the southwest Pacific knew much about the long arc of islands north of Australia and south of the Philippines. They were not the soft South Sea Islands of song and romantic story. Beyond their white beaches lay impenetrable jungle, thick cane fields, man-high razor grass and, often, rugged mountains. Many of the islands were populated by fierce tribesmen only half-weaned from cannibalism. All of the islands teemed with snakes and leeches, mosquitoes and tropical amoebae that could cause illness as painful and as deadly as an enemy bullet. The names of the islands would become synonyms for jungle fighting of the ugliest sort: Borneo, New Guinea, New Britain, the Solomons, Timor.

All of the islands were to some degree strategically important. The Dutch East Indies—particularly Borneo and Java—contained oil fields, rubber plantations and mineral deposits vital to Japan's imperial ambitions. Timor and the Solomons lacked such wealth, but they were stepping-stones to Australia. Even if the Japanese were halted short of the island continent, possession of Timor and the Solomons would put them astride vital shipping lanes stretching east and west across the Pacific and Indian Oceans. So, for one strategic reason or another, the islands were fought for, conquered and reconquered in campaigns as raw and as hard as the islands themselves.

When the Japanese struck southward in 1941, four divisions of Australian troops were far away, contesting for the Middle East or manning the defenses of Malaya and Singapore. Most of the Australian Army's remaining strength—about 34,000 troops—was incorporated into the American-British-Dutch-Australian (ABDA) Command in the waning days of 1941. They would have to fight a cruel defensive war on every primitive island coveted by the Japanese.

Thousands of men would perish in obscure battles at places unknown even to mapmakers. Bypassed garrisons lost contact with their headquarters and were presumed lost, only to pop up alive and fighting many months later. Downed airmen and shipwrecked sailors alike struggled for weeks or months to survive enemy pursuers and hellish jungles, often aided by the coastwatchers—Australians, New Zealanders and a handful of other peoples who remained behind to report on enemy activity after the islands had been overrun. Prisoners of war labored, starved and died in

# GUERRILLAS OF THE JUNGLE

brackish backwaters without word of their whereabouts ever reaching home. In rain forest and mountain ravine, commando-trained bands played deadly games of hide-and-seek with the enemy.

Timor, which rose from the sea only 500 miles to the northwest of the great north Australian harbor at Darwin, was a natural target for early Japanese conquest. The 300-mile-long island, its eastern half Portuguese and its western half Dutch, guarded a vital shipping lane through the Torres Strait, north of Australia, and across the Timor Sea to Java and the Indian Ocean. The capture of Timor by the Japanese would force the Allies to ferry supplies destined for Java and Singapore an additional 2,500 miles around the south coast of Australia. To defend against this possibility, the 40th Battalion of the Australian 2nd Imperial Force was sent to Kupang, the capital of Dutch Timor, on December 12, 1941. Along with 500 Dutch soldiers and colonial auxiliaries already stationed at Kupang and elsewhere on the island, the 1,700-man group—code-named Sparrow Force—was supposed to thwart Japanese designs on Timor.

At the same time, the British government had been exerting diplomatic pressure on the government of neutral Portugal to transfer a large force of its own troops to Timor. The closest Portuguese soldiers were stationed in eastern Africa at Mozambique, some 6,000 miles from the island of Timor. And when the Portuguese attempted to send 500 troops to Timor in mid-December, the Japanese, who were by then in control of most of the seas of Southeast Asia, refused the Portuguese request for safe conduct, thus forcing the troopship to turn back to Mozambique.

On December 17, Sparrow Force undertook one of the first Allied offensive actions of the war in the Pacific. If the Portuguese were unable to protect their half of Timor, the Australians and Dutch would. One hundred and fifty-five men of the 2nd Independent Company of the 2nd Imperial Force—familiarly known as the 2nd/2nd—were dispatched to Dili, the capital of Portuguese Timor. Five days later, the remainder of the 2nd/2nd, an additional 151 men, joined their mates at Dili.

The 2nd/2nd was no ordinary outfit. Secretly formed and rigorously trained in commando tactics in Australia's rugged outback, it was one of three such all-volunteer companies originally scheduled for special operations in the Middle East. Each of the men had mastered several skills, could handle all the standard infantry weapons and could operate a radio or draw a contour map with equal competence. Every third man was armed with a Thompson submachine gun and all were expert with explosives, the piano-wire garrote, the deadly Fairburn hand-to-hand combat knife and the techniques of laying mantraps and setting ambushes. Furthermore, life on the sprawling cattle and sheep stations of the Australian frontier had taught most of the men how to butcher and preserve game, find and purify water, and survive in a hostile environment.

To the men of the 2nd/2nd, the posting to Dili was unpleasant in the extreme. Dili, on the northern coast of the island, was a malarial amphitheater whose few roads quickly dwindled into footpaths as they ascended into what one observer described as a "lunatic, contorted, tangled mass of mountains." A number of the mountains were more than 9,000 feet high. The place was brutally hot in the dry season; the rainy season lasted from November through June, and the overflowing rivers made the island difficult either to defend or to attack.

The 2nd/2nd landed at Dili and easily secured the landing beaches. Behind it followed a complement of 260 Dutch troops from Kupang, making a force of 566 men in all. The Portuguese Governor and his small contingent of local militiamen offered no armed opposition—though the governor did lodge an angry verbal protest over this violation of Portuguese neutrality.

Despite their protests, the Portuguese could scarcely deny that the harbor at Dili and its airfield, about a mile and a half from town, were openly coveted by the Japanese. Freighters out of Kobe regularly took soundings of the harbor; as far back as 1934, visiting "agricultural specialists" had sent soil samples from the airstrip back to naval intelligence headquarters at Yokosuka. The Portuguese customs even now held a quantity of impounded meteorological equipment shipped "by mistake" to the Japanese consul. If the Japanese took Dili, they would make the larger Dutch base at Kupang untenable and cut Australia's supply lines to India and South Africa.

So the 2nd/2nd established itself around the airfield, emplacing Bren guns and mortars, digging strong points and, more realistically, planting explosives to demolish the runways. The Dutch occupied the palatial buildings of the Asia Investment Company in town; the firm, a German front, owned empty offices, warehouses and laboratories built to process gold, oil, coffee, rubber and tobacco, all awaiting the day when Portugal might bend to German persuasion or Japanese force.

While the Dutch continued to maintain their traditional aloofness from the local population, the happy-go-lucky Australians adopted the diminutive islanders and were soon conversant in the local language. While the company commander, Major Alan Spence, kept busy on the diplomatic front smoothing the ruffled feathers of the Portuguese Governor, Spence's second-in-command, Captain B. J. Callinan, quietly led patrols far into the interior to map every ridge and footpath and mark the most likely spots for ambushes and supply caches.

Despite the difficult terrain, these excursions into cooler climes were popular with the Aussies, who relished the respite from the sweltering, airless bowl around Dili harbor. But, because several senior Portuguese officials had disappeared and were rumored to be mustering men for a fight against the invaders, the Australians also had to "stand to" every night at their trenches and gun positions around the airfield, and they soon fell victim to a much more deadly enemy—the Anopheles mosquito.

By early January, all but 50 of the Australians were unfit for duty. Some had been stricken with an especially debilitating form of malaria; they had failed to take their daily dose of quinine, which was issued in the form of an evil-tasting powder. Others were suffering from dysentery; they had failed to purify contaminated drinking water. For an outfit that supposedly was elite, the 2nd/2nd was making some very embarrassing and amateurish errors at the outset.

Major Spence decided to move the company headquarters from the miasmal coastal lowlands to Three Spurs, a more healthful spot on a ridgeline overlooking Dili. There the sick men benefited from an uncontaminated water supply, cool breezes in the evening, fewer mosquitoes and a stock of palatable quinine tablets donated by the Dutch. The men were soon back on their feet, shaky but much wiser for their ordeal.

Toward the end of January, Japanese planes started paying more frequent visits to Dili and the surrounding area; on one occasion they strafed the town and the airfield. Major Spence needed no further warning that an enemy invasion was imminent. He and his men began preparations for what would be their only salvation—flight-and-fight operations in the interior.

Most of the 2nd/2nd was ordered inland to the village of Railaco, four miles beyond Three Spurs. This group move included 50 reinforcements, newly arrived from Australia, and all the spare troops from the airfield defense unit, which was left to carry on with only 20 men. From Railaco, the main body explored ever deeper into the mountainous interior, winning the confidence of the local people and the Portuguese district officials on whom they would depend for help. The Dutch at Dili also began moving supplies inland. Their commanding officer, Colonel Nicholas van Straaten, planned to retreat to Kupang, 160 miles to the west, in case of an invasion.

The Japanese invasion of Timor, accompanied by an air raid on Darwin, began on February 19, four days after the fall of Singapore. Assaults on key coastal points were made by 6,000 troops of Major General Takeo Ito's Eastern Force, who numbered among them a regiment of the 38th Division, which had taken Hong Kong. That night, 5,000 troops

On the Japanese-conquered island of Timor, Australian signalmen of the 2nd/2nd Independent Company tinker with a short-wave radio, which they had put together to communicate with Australia, nearly 500 miles away. In April 1942, the 2nd/2nd's headquarters in Darwin had picked up their first signal, sent on another homemade radio. But their superiors suspected a Japanese ruse, and the isolated Aussies were required to transmit a series of code words before Darwin agreed to air-drop them supplies.

went ashore in the vicinity of Kupang, while a force of 1,000 men descended on Dili and the airfield, having landed somewhere between them.

Shortly before midnight on the 19th, an Australian sentry at the airfield reported to the unit commander, Lieutenant C. F. G. McKenzie, that he heard strange, unidentifiable noises coming from the direction of Dili. McKenzie, alarmed, telephoned Captain Callinan, who was visiting Colonel van Straaten in Dili, and told him about the strange noises. McKenzie suggested that it was the sound of a Japanese invasion force and—since reinforcements from the 2nd/2nd were at Three Spurs, too far away to arrive in time—asked that Straaten send some Dutch troops to bolster the airfield defenses. Callinan ordered McKenzie to send out a patrol to investigate, then gave the telephone to Straaten, who poohpoohed the idea of an invasion.

Soon after the colonel hung up, his Dili headquarters was battered by a quick succession of eight shells—shells that were aimed well enough to miss the Japanese consulate building next door. Straaten then concluded that the shelling came from a Japanese submarine in the harbor, and he ordered his artillery to fire back.

At the airfield, McKenzie saw the bursting shells and made out two ships—a warship and a troop transport. He phoned the ill tidings to Straaten, who stubbornly clung to his submarine theory.

Meanwhile, McKenzie's group had set up a machine gun at the edge of the airstrip overlooking the road to Dili. The men heard voices coming toward them and held their fire, thinking that the Dutch might be sending reinforcements after all. Finally, the Australians recognized the troops as Japanese and opened fire. Moments later, Japanese hand grenades landed nearby, killing one man and seriously wounding another.

During the skirmish, an Aussie private managed to crawl into the underbrush and make his way back to McKenzie, whose command post was at the airfield. Meanwhile, the lieutenant again phoned Dili. Callinan answered; he heard, he later said, "the unmistakable sound of the Bren gun in action, followed by two loud explosions and the telephone went dead." The line had been cut by a Japanese shell.

In desperation, McKenzie decided to send a messenger, Private C. E. Doyle, to report that the Japanese were attacking and to tell Callinan that his men would hold them off as long as possible. An Aussie recalled the messenger's ludicrous departure: "Doyle mounted an old Dutch push bicycle, called farewell to his friends, then crouching low over the handle bars, pushed off. The sight of a dashing Australian riding a push bicycle hell for leather through their lines must have amazed the Japanese to such an extent that they did not open up."

Doyle managed to get through to Callinan; he reported the situation at the airfield and then raced back to join his comrades. The Australians were outnumbered, but they had their guns zeroed in on the approaches to the airstrip, and they picked off the Japanese infiltrators who tried to close in on their position.

At dawn, though, McKenzie knew that it was time to retreat, that the Japanese would soon see that only a handful of Aussies were holding them off. Along with the rest of the airfield unit, he slipped away toward Dili, leaving behind three gunners and two demolitions men under Corporal Kevin Curran. While Curran and the sappers set their fuses, the gunners gave them covering fire. Then the demolition charges exploded all over the runways, and Curran led his men through smoke and cascading dirt toward a prepared hide-out high on a nearby ridge.

The six men made good their escape, and so did most of McKenzie's squad. The 2nd/2nd had lost 18 men in the retreat. One man had been killed and two others captured defending the airfield, and 15 men, heading for Dili on leave, had been captured by the Japanese before they could reach the town. Of the 15 prisoners, three were summarily executed by their captors. (A fourth was bayoneted in the neck, and left for dead. He managed to crawl off into the brush, where he was succored by friendly local people; he later rejoined the 2nd/2nd.)

At the same time, with 5,000 ground troops already ashore in and around Kupang, 630 Japanese paratroopers were dropped there to soften the Allied defenses. The paratroopers, said witnesses, did not fight as a coherent force. Instead, many of them climbed palm trees and fought as snipers. As such they were easy pickings for Sparrow Force, which killed all but 78 of them. Nevertheless, the Allies were quickly outflanked, overrun and forced to surrender. Only a

# THE SPY MISSION OF DR. DE BRUIJN

*Dr. de Bruijn (center) sits surrounded by members of his New Guinea spy group: khaki-clad Dutch colonial policemen and nearly naked Papuans.*

In December of 1942, a seaplane from Melbourne, Australia, landed on a lake at Enarotali, an outpost deep in the malarial jungles of Japanese-held Dutch New Guinea. Aboard were Dr. Jean Victor de Bruijn, at the age of 29 a veteran Dutch colonial administrator who had served in the New Guinea interior since 1939, and a Dutch radioman, Rudy Gout. While on medical leave in Australia, de Bruijn had volunteered to spy on the Japanese for General Douglas MacArthur's Allied Intelligence Bureau.

De Bruijn soon learned that the Japanese were building an air base near his coastal supply depot. He radioed Melbourne this valuable information and began recruiting and training Papuan men to report enemy movements. Soon his little force numbered 38 men, including eight policemen from other Dutch colonies who had helped de Bruijn before the Japanese invasion. De Bruijn also organized some Papuans into a farming co-

Radioman Gout rests between transmissions.

Papuan women cultivate vegetables in a communal garden that was used to feed the spy ring.

Working from dugout canoes, women within Dr. de Bruijn's community harvest crayfish from a lake near their camp in the New Guinea highlands.

operative to grow food for the spy ring.

In June 1943, de Bruijn and his band narrowly escaped a Japanese attack that leveled their outpost. Thereafter, enemy patrols drove them into the mountainous interior. Food was scarce; they ate frogs, pythons and rats. But de Bruijn's spies continued to prowl the Japanese camps and bring back news of troop movements, which he radioed to Melbourne.

In April 1944, de Bruijn was told to meet a seaplane that would evacuate radioman Gout, who was suffering from ulcers. The rendezvous point was only 35 miles from his campsite. But to reach there, he and his men spent 95 days hacking a path through the jungle, dodging enemy patrols all the way. En route, de Bruijn received a radio message ordering the entire group to leave; their job was done. With help from their intelligence reports, MacArthur's forces had taken Hollandia on April 22, a key victory in his reconquest of New Guinea.

few small groups of Australian and Dutch and colonial troops managed to escape to the east and join the 2nd/2nd. Timor had passed into Japanese hands, a fact that the conquerors quickly broadcast to the rest of the world. At the ABDA Command in Darwin, the news was taken to mean that the 2nd/2nd had been destroyed.

The ensuing weeks were a hectic time for the erstwhile defenders of the Dili area. The men of the 2nd/2nd abandoned their bases at Three Spurs and Railaco, destroying whatever they could not carry, and fought their way past Japanese patrols to Villa Maria, a settlement 20 miles inland from Dili. Meanwhile, the Dutch troops at Dili scattered inland, hoping to find their way through the interior to their own territory to the west.

The men of the 2nd/2nd were now virtually alone, although they did not realize it. Since their short-range radios could not reach Kupang, they knew nothing of the surrender or of the fate of their parent organization. They knew only that they had to keep moving deeper into the interior. The Japanese were relentless pursuers; already the Aussies' rear guard had engaged and wiped out two enemy patrols on the way to Villa Maria.

Major Spence intended to take refuge in the mountains 15 miles from Dili, beyond a deep valley that was spanned by a concrete bridge. The trek was a hard one, and the Aussies would never have made it without the help of friendly tribesmen who, along with their ponies, carried tons of supplies, including 160,000 rounds for the Australian Bren guns, submachine guns and rifles. Once everyone had crossed the bridge, engineers blew it up. In the mountains on the far side, the Aussies split up their ammunition and supplies and made caches in several villages.

Spence continued his work as political liaison officer for the 2nd/2nd, negotiating with the Portuguese district chiefs in the area. Callinan, who was left in charge as field commander, decided that if the outfit was to survive, it would have to take the offensive—constantly patrolling to get up-to-date knowledge of the enemy and ambushing any Japanese they encountered.

Each of the 2nd/2nd's three platoon captains assigned his three section lieutenants an area of responsibility where concealed bases would be set up for patrols and harassing missions against the enemy. Local headmen helped to pre-pare and provision the bases, and each soldier soon acquired a servant who followed him everywhere, carrying his extra clothing and food, ready to dive into the underbrush at the first alarm and to return with kit intact after the shooting was over. This arrangement made the Australians far more mobile than the overburdened Japanese, whose brutality to the local people won them few supporters.

Callinan set off on March 1 from Hato-Lia, a village about three miles from Villa Maria, to make contact with Kupang in Dutch Timor and presumably put the 2nd/2nd again under the command of Sparrow Force. With him were two Australian enlisted men and two Dutch colonial soldiers, who also had escaped from Dili. Over the next two days, Callinan heard rumor after rumor about a great Japanese victory as he passed through a series of villages. He assumed that most of the rumors were incorrect, products of vivid imaginations and untrained eyes. Finally, just inside Dutch Timor, he found the mission church at Laharoes, run by Dutch priests and nuns of the Order of the Divine Word.

Callinan, himself a devout Catholic, knelt through the comforting service of vespers before seeking out the two priests in charge. Only after they had given him and his weary companions some hot soup and sandwiches to eat did the priests tell Callinan that Kupang had fallen before the onslaught of Japanese shock troops. Most of Sparrow Force had been taken prisoner.

On March 13, British Consul David Ross, who had been captured by the Japanese and had been forced into the role of an intermediary, made his way up into the hills under a flag of truce. He brought confirmation from Dili of the island's incorporation into the Japanese Empire and also a message from the Japanese garrison commander demanding that the men of the 2nd/2nd surrender or face execution as bandits. The Australians sent Ross back with a stiff reply, which castigated the Japanese for executing prisoners and informed them that the 2nd Independent Company would fight on as a regular armed component of the Australian Army. From now on it would be war to the hilt.

Armed by Ross with blank letters of credit on the British and Australian governments, Spence purchased enough food in the unoccupied interior villages to make the company truly independent. At the same time Callinan swept

*Accompanied by local bearers, Australian infantrymen of the 2nd/2nd Independent Company make their way along a streambed in Japanese-held Timor en route to an evacuation point in December of 1942. The Aussies avoided detection by a patrol of 200 Japanese who passed so close, reported a scout, he could have reached out and touched them.*

the countryside for abandoned Dutch weapons and ammunition to add to their already impressive caches. From that point on, the men of the 2nd/2nd were able to range far and wide without running out of food and ammunition. The Japanese, however, hesitated to move in force beyond their fortified positions on the coasts.

In early April, when the Australians broke up into several patrols, Callinan set out toward Dili with three Aussies and 60 tribesmen. For a week the detachment played havoc with a force of 150 heavily armed Japanese that was probing up the Glano River, just above the spot where the Australians had blown the bridge as they retreated. Snipers picked off Japanese at long range while the frustrated enemy peppered the ridgelines with mortar shells. "The Japanese flattered us by shelling various prominent features from which they thought we might be observing their movements," said Callinan. "Their shelling was remarkably accurate and very methodical; always four shells were fired before they moved on to the next target." The mortar crews failed to damage anything but local flora and fauna, for the

men of the patrol were dispersed in twos and threes, sometimes within yards of the Japanese mortar positions. On one occasion, another patrol was forced to lie motionless for 12 hours just downhill from a Japanese position.

Rarely were the Australians in one spot that long. Typically, they would do their killing and then retreat. They moved about like jack rabbits, leaping from spur to spur, burrowing into the bush when pursued, eluding bullets and mortar shells. At the end of the week, the Japanese withdrew, having lost 30 to 40 men killed and more troops wounded. The unscratched victors received the blessing of the local priest and the cheers of local spectators.

The Aussies' successes mounted. Japanese patrols persistently moved through the jungles by truck and on foot, and were as regularly forced back by snipers and submachine gunners, who appeared from nowhere, sprayed bullets and then vanished. Callinan did not engage the Japanese in major fire fights. "We were in no hurry to kill them," he wrote later. "This was a private war, and there was no time factor. We considered it much better to kill five or ten Japanese and

suffer no casualties ourselves than to attempt to kill more and suffer casualties. A wounded man was a serious burden to us; he was to the Japanese also, but they solved the problem in their own way. They shot their wounded.''

Eventually, the Japanese got tired of dying in driblets. By the middle of April, they had built up their strength at Ermera—18 miles southwest of Dili—to 1,200 men and had pushed up a nearby valley in force. The handful of Australians in that sector were well prepared, and they retired in front of the enemy, often letting a Japanese patrol walk through one of their outposts so as to catch it in a cross fire between stronger positions up ahead. The fast-moving Aussies had, Callinan noted, convinced the Japanese that they were facing a force of at least 200 men in the area, when, in fact, no more than 23 Aussies opposed them at any one time.

Of a typical harassing action Callinan wrote: ''Corporal Taylor took a patrol of four down to a position above the Three Spurs camp and there ambushed a convoy of trucks. The occupants of the first truck were almost entirely wiped out in the first bursts from the Bren gun, Tommy gun and two rifles at close range, and then fire was switched to the second truck. But these Japanese were good troops. Those in the rear trucks were already dismounting, and there was no confusion; while some were setting up their machine guns the others attacked straight at the ambush position. Taylor had to withdraw his men hurriedly, and they came under fire from the machine guns as soon as they moved. The Bren gunner was in a particularly bad way climbing up the steep hillside: the enemy had seen him and were closing in when two natives appeared from nowhere, whipped the gun off his shoulder and tore off up the hill. When the natives had led him to safety they put down the gun before

him. Against such support from the natives the enemy had little chance of success.''

Meanwhile, Major Spence had set up a headquarters on the other side of the mountains, and on April 22 he relayed a coded message to Callinan. It said that an Australian signalman, combining junked radios and the generator from an old car, had built a transmitter—christened ''Winnie the War Winner''—that had gotten through to Darwin. Headquarters at Melbourne had been notified via Darwin that the 2nd/2nd was alive and kicking, not ''missing presumed dead.'' Soon food and supplies would be arriving at a remote spot on the southern coast of the island—160 miles from Kupang and the Japanese—aboard a tiny coastal freighter and in airdrops.

Callinan and the others now fully expected that plans for an Allied invasion of the island would soon be forthcoming. The Japanese shock troops had departed to new ventures farther east in Rabaul, and there were not more than a few thousand marines and infantrymen remaining. While the 2nd/2nd sent back a stream of intelligence assessments and operational proposals to Darwin, Callinan organized an attack on the Dili garrison, a move that would force the Japanese to bring troops back in from the countryside to protect the main base.

On the night of May 15, Captain Geoffrey Laidlaw led 20 men, their faces blackened with grease and soot, from the village of Remexio, six miles southeast of Dili, in a classic commando attack. They crept down the drainage ditches flanking Dili's main street, past lamplit barracks and houses, to the large enemy machine-gun post in the main square. Laidlaw opened the proceedings, killing a hapless Japanese soldier at point-blank range.

There was a tremendous racket as each Aussie tossed ex-

*Sefanaia Sukanaivalu, shown in 1942, was a fisherman in civilian life.*

## THE FIJIAN HERO OF BOUGAINVILLE

In October 1944, Allied soldiers on Bougainville found the remains of Corporal Sefanaia Sukanaivalu, a guerrilla fighter from the Fiji Islands. They buried him with full military honors, for Sukanaivalu had died with uncommon valor.

In June, his Company E of the 3rd Fiji Battalion had penetrated deep into the jungle behind enemy lines. The jungle was home for these New Zealand-trained fighters, and their exploits in the wilds of the Solomons had already won them recognition as superb guerrillas.

But on the 23rd of June, the tide of combat turned against Company E. As the Fijis snaked through a patch of high grass, a

plosives through the nearest window or doorway. Then the submachine guns clattered, pouring fire into every barracks building as the raiders withdrew up the street at an unhurried pace. Japanese soldiers tumbled in panic from their bunks and raced through the shattered doorways—into a cross fire from a small covering force concealed on the beach. The Aussie tracers coming from the beach persuaded the Japanese that a full-scale invasion was under way, and long after the Australians had retired inland for the night, a torrent of Japanese shells and bullets rained seaward to repel the phantom invaders.

From accounts later given him by friendly locals, Callinan pieced together the Japanese reaction to the raid. "The next day," he noted, "every house in Dili was searched thoroughly, as the Japanese were convinced that the Australians could not have escaped. The few Portuguese still in residence there were subject to fresh indignities whilst Japanese searched cupboards and wardrobes for the terrible Australians. To restore their pride, the Japanese collected their dead and made two piles and burnt them with great gusto, at the same time displaying near each a pile of Australian boots, socks, trousers and shirts which they had acquired, telling everybody that they had captured all the Australians involved in the raid. The natives thought this very funny, and were not at all taken in by the subterfuge."

The Japanese were so chagrined by the raid that they spent a week building up Dili's defenses. Only then did they feel confident enough to venture forth in force, sending more than 400 troops with artillery support to attack Remexio. The troops performed faultlessly in taking Remexio, but came away empty-handed; no one was there. Four days after they had captured the town, the Japanese returned to Dili, followed closely by the will-o'-the-wisp guerrillas.

By July, the 2nd/2nd was receiving a steady stream of supplies dropped by Hudson bombers of the Royal Australian Air Force. Furthermore, the Hudsons were bombing Dili and other Japanese-held towns. The Japanese had no choice but to dig in around Dili, leaving 300 or so Australians in effective control of the rest of Portuguese Timor.

At this high point in the island war, the Aussies received a second message from the Japanese commander in Dili, relayed as before by British Consul Ross, traveling under a white flag. Colonel Sadahichi Doi complimented the Australians on the effective campaign they had fought and offered them a written guarantee, countersigned by the Japanese consul, of all rights and privileges as prisoners of war if they would surrender. There were other options, said the commander: The Australians could come down into Dili and fight it out man to man or he would hunt them down to the last man in the mountains. When Ross had commented to the colonel that there were not enough Japanese soldiers to accomplish the latter, Doi had surprised him by agreeing. Doi confided that he had studied British and South African tactics in the Boer War, and he knew that he would have to field 10 Japanese for every Australian. But, he concluded, "I will get what is required."

Colonel Doi was as good as his word. By August he had built up to his 10-to-1 ratio of Japanese troops, and had also coerced some of the local population into working against the Portuguese, Dutch and Australians. In the fall came additional reinforcements, 15,000 troops of the crack 48th Division, while an equal number of 5th Division veterans of the Malaya campaign went to Ambon and western New Guinea to guard against an expected Allied counterattack through Timor to recapture the Dutch East Indies.

hidden Japanese machine gun opened fire, wounding several men and pinning down the rest. Sukanaivalu twice crawled forward and rescued two fallen comrades. On the third trip, he too was hit and lay wounded in the grass.

Repeatedly Sukanaivalu's men tried to save him, but each time they were driven back by a hail of bullets. In vain, Sukanaivalu called out for them to abandon him. Finally, to prevent certain casualties on further rescue attempts, Sukanaivalu deliberately rose up and was riddled by gunfire. For his sacrifice, he was posthumously awarded the first Victoria Cross to be given to a colonial soldier in World War II.

*Passing an Allied honor guard, Fijis carry Sukanaivalu to the military cemetery on Bougainville.*

The Allies, still fighting against powerful thrusts at Port Moresby and Guadalcanal, actually could do no more on Timor than sneak in a second commando unit, the 2nd/4th Independent Company, in mid-September, while allocating a few medium bombers, fighter planes and U.S. submarines to strike at the Japanese troop concentrations and their supply lines. By December, the Japanese advantage over the Australians on the ground was at least 25 to 1. Australian headquarters in Melbourne was now convinced that the doughty commando force, as well as some Dutch troops and Portuguese civilians, had to be evacuated.

A rescue program began on December 1, 1942, when an Australian launch evacuated 70 Portuguese women and children from an inlet on the island's southern coast. On January 9, 1943, the last men of the 2nd/2nd and most of the men of the 2nd/4th were picked up by an Australian destroyer at Quicras, also on the southern coast. A month later, 21 Australian commandos who had stayed behind to cover the evacuation slipped out of Timor aboard the U.S. submarine *Gudgeon*.

For nearly a year, a force that never exceeded 600 men, many of whom suffered from recurrent malaria, had been the only Allied ground troops between India and New Guinea, and they had fought the enemy to a standstill. The Australians lost 40 men while killing at least 1,500 Japanese and pinning down thousands of troops who might have been more useful elsewhere.

While the Japanese Army was winning a hollow victory on Timor, it was suffering devastating defeats in New Guinea and the Solomon Islands. Throughout the last five months of 1942 and well into 1943, under the most appalling combat conditions of the War, Australians and Americans fought back from within an eyelash of defeat to end the Japanese threat to Australia and to a vital American life line to the far Pacific. A few tireless airmen swung the balance in New Guinea, keeping the Allies supplied with food and medical necessities, while the Japanese were starving and dying of virulent jungle diseases.

In the Solomon Islands, a handful of men belonging to the Royal Australian Navy's coastwatching service—a disparate group of a few hundred Australian, New Zealand, American and Dutch volunteers—ran an intelligence network that proved invaluable to the troops who fought for Guadalcanal into February of 1943 and then battled their way across other islands of the Solomons chain.

The coastwatchers also saved the lives of countless fighting men and civilians caught behind Japanese lines—sheltering, feeding and nursing their guests until a submarine or Catalina flying boat could rescue them. In addition, many of the coastwatchers fought their own vicious little wars against the Japanese occupiers.

One of the most unusual of these anonymous warriors was Father Emery de Klerk, a pint-sized Dutch Catholic missionary who clung to his parish of Tangarare on Guadalcanal's south coast and organized the area's inhabitants into an efficient guerrilla band.

At first, the Japanese thought they had a willing collaborator in the cleric with the beaming smile and bland manner. But it was all a ruse. Behind the invaders' backs, Klerk ministered to downed and injured Allied airmen, while his parishioners spied on the Japanese and bushwhacked their patrols whenever the opportunity arose.

Eventually the Japanese suspected that European missionaries were behind their misfortunes, and began hunting down priests and nuns. When news of this development reached Klerk's superiors, he was ordered to evacuate by both his church and the Allied command. Klerk and his band helped others escape, but the missionary defied the orders himself, choosing to remain behind to carry on the fight. Dropping all pretext of collaboration, he now took to carrying a rifle and openly leading his flock in increasingly bold assaults against Japanese patrols and outposts. All the while he sent a steady stream of information to Allied forces fighting for the island.

Try as they might, the Japanese were never able to catch up with Klerk. And soon after the Japanese evacuated Guadalcanal in February of 1943, Major General Alexander M. Patch, commander of the XIV Corps, personally pinned a U.S. lieutenant's bars on the khaki uniform that Father de Klerk had been given by a departing Marine.

Another prominent coastwatcher in the Solomons was Geoffrey Kuper, the son of a German planter and a local woman. Kuper was recruited and trained by Captain Donald G. Kennedy, a New Zealand coastwatcher at Segi Point on the island of New Georgia, and then sent off to the village of Tatamba on Santa Isabel in the central Solomons, with a radio, a scavenged motor cruiser and the wife he had married a few weeks earlier. In time, Kuper and his local agents rescued 28 Allied airmen and mounted hit-and-run raids against nearby enemy camps and patrols. In one of Kuper's boldest attacks he and his men surprised and killed 26 Japanese soldiers at their outpost on a nearby island.

Perhaps the most successful of the coastwatchers was an Australian named Paul Mason, who was the manager of a plantation at Kieta on the east coast of occupied Bougainville. Mason was a small, middle-aged, mild-mannered man who peered nearsightedly through thick glasses. But he was superbly equipped for the work of a coastwatcher. His strength and stamina made him more than a match for younger, bigger men; he had been living on the island since 1915 and knew it thoroughly. Mason was, moreover, an expert at repairing radios.

Mason sent his first important message in August 1942, when he spotted 27 Japanese bombers en route from New Britain to Guadalcanal in reaction to the American landings there. His radioed warning gave the U.S. invasion fleet an hour's time in which to prepare for the bombing raids. Later warnings from Mason made his call letters, STO, familiar to every radioman in the invasion fleet; his messages accounted for dozens of Japanese bombers and saved the lives of countless Americans.

Like most of the coastwatchers, Mason was known to the enemy; he had been betrayed by a tribesman in the pay of the Japanese. By Christmas time in 1942 the local Japanese political agent, a man named Tashira who had spent many prewar years on the island, was closing in on Mason and his small group of guerrillas in the mountains of southern Bougainville. Tashira cockily sent a runner to a suspected hideout of Mason's with a message reading, "Come in and spend Christmas dinner with us. If you don't we'll shoot you on sight." Soon afterward a Japanese patrol nearly caught Mason and an elderly planter friend huddled over their cold Christmas fare. Mason escaped, losing his radios and most of his supplies in his hurried getaway. The planter, who was too infirm to accompany Mason on his arduous, mountain-scaling escape route, was taken prisoner and soon died at the hands of his captors.

Mason and his men spent the next month trekking north to make contact with Jack Read, a coastwatcher who headed a small guerrilla band on the northern end of the island. The two groups joined ranks and for three months conducted ambushes and generally did all they could to torment the Japanese. By May, Mason had new radios and equipment, delivered by a U.S. submarine, and he headed back toward his own territory.

As Mason made his way south, the Japanese, exasperated by the guerrilla attacks, mounted a drive to wipe out both Read and Mason. Mason lost one man to a Japanese ambush. Read fared much worse, losing some rescued airmen in addition to a number of ragtag irregulars in a series of stiff skirmishes. Word of the antiguerrilla campaign prompted the coastwatcher headquarters in Australia to evacuate as many of the coastwatchers as possible. In July two U.S. submarines put in at prearranged sites, and Read, Mason and the 60-odd locals, Australians and Chinese whom Mason had picked up in his wanderings were shoehorned aboard.

*Charles Vyner Brooke, a descendant of merchant rulers of Sarawak, and his wife greet two chiefs of the Dayak tribe upon returning to Borneo in April 1946. Brooke, who had lived in Australia during the Japanese occupation, found his private domain so devastated by war that reconstruction was impossible without massive foreign aid. To get the aid, he stepped down as ruler—in spite of his people's protests—and ceded Sarawak to Great Britain.*

Mason had thought he would be returned to Bougainville after a short rest-and-recreation visit to Australia. But his stay in Australia stretched out for more than a year. In his absence, a large force of U.S. Marines and Army units invaded Bougainville on November 1, 1943. The Americans had a tough fight on their hands; it was not until April of 1944, after they had killed 7,000 Japanese troops, that the island was declared secure. Even then the invasion commanders, eager to move on, were satisfied to control a base area around Empress Augusta Bay; several thousand Japanese soldiers were still roaming the interior in small units.

The Japanese stragglers were very much on the mind of Paul Mason when he was finally returned to Bougainville in November 1944. His assignment was to gather intelligence and rescue European and Chinese internees. But he had elaborate plans to attack the Japanese. From a base in the mountains a few miles from his plantation, he launched an unrelenting campaign at the head of a growing band of locals. He tracked down or ambushed groups of Japanese stragglers, attacking first with spears and arrows and later with captured rifles and grenades. By the end of May 1945, when he was finally relieved (he was getting on in years), he and his men had killed several hundred enemy troops.

The task of mopping up the Japanese on bypassed islands was rarely left to irregulars like Mason's men. While the main forces of General Douglas MacArthur in the southwest Pacific and Admiral Chester Nimitz in the central Pacific were converging on the Philippines, troops of the Australian Army were assigned to contain and eliminate enemy garrisons in the wake of the Allied advance. This dirty job was a matter of honor to the Australian government, to the Aussies and especially to General Sir Thomas Blamey, their commander in chief; all agreed that Australia's wards in New Guinea and the Solomons had to be freed from Japanese rule as quickly as possible. When Blamey called his commanders and staff together in August 1944, he told them that the Army was now to undertake its "maximum effort during the War."

And so from late 1944 until the end of the War, Australian troops—by now among the ablest and most experienced jungle fighters in the world—scoured New Guinea, New Britain and the Solomons to rid the islands of bypassed Japanese. More than 1,000 Australian lives were lost in the course of these unpopular backwater offensives, which drew frequent criticism from the politicians and the press at home. The fighting men themselves knew that "the operations were mopping up and that they were *not* vital to the winning of the War," one of their commanders wrote. "So they ignored the Australian papers, their relatives' letters advising caution, and got on with the job in hand, fighting and dying as if it was the battle for final victory."

The Australians' last and biggest mopping-up assignment was to recapture Borneo, long the untended orphan of the Allied drive toward Japan. The world's third-largest island (after Greenland and New Guinea), Japanese-occupied Borneo was tantalizingly close to Australia, but it could not be taken without committing major forces. So the island waited until the Allies had troops to spare.

The prewar political organization of Borneo had had cer-

*General Douglas MacArthur inspects the ruins of Balikpapan on Borneo after the rout of the Japanese in July 1945. The preinvasion bombardment lasted nearly three weeks and involved the expenditure of more than 38,000 shells from U.S. warships offshore and 56,000 additional naval and artillery rounds in support of the attacking Australian troops.*

tain comic-opera aspects. In the island's oil-rich northern region, British colonial enterprises had carved out four enclaves: the Malay sultanate of Brunei; the much larger sultanate of Sarawak, run under British protection by hereditary "white rajas" descended from James Brooke, a 19th Century soldier of fortune; the tiny crown colony of Labuan in Brunei Bay; and North Borneo, the island's blunt northeastern tip, run under private charter by a London corporation. The broad southern end of the island was held by the Dutch, who maintained administrative and trading posts all along the coast and ran major oil pumping or refining centers along the east coast at Balikpapan and Tarakan Island *(pages 186-201)*. The vast interior of the island, ribbed with spiny mountain ranges, gouged by foaming watercourses and buried in dense primeval jungle, belonged to no one but the aboriginal tribes.

By 1940, Japan's designs on Borneo had become an open secret. The island contained oil desperately needed by the expanding Japanese war machine; moreover, air bases on Borneo would interdict Allied shipping to and from Java, Sumatra and the Malay Peninsula. If they captured the island, the Japanese could guard the flank of any invasion of Malaya and gain an excellent staging area for other campaigns in the area.

Expecting a Japanese invasion, the British had made plans by December 1940 to destroy their oil fields at Miri, near the northern boundary of Sarawak, and at Seria in Brunei. British sappers were sent in with a company of the 15th Punjabi Regiment; they laid demolition charges at the oil fields and at a refinery at Lutong, three miles from Miri. The British also decided that no attempt would be made to hold Brunei, Labuan or North Borneo. Instead, they elected to defend the airfield at Kuching, the capital of Sarawak, for if the airfield fell to the Japanese, it would put the enemy within 60 miles of a larger field at Singkawang II in Dutch Borneo, which in turn was only 350 miles from Singapore. In May of 1941, the British sent the remainder of the Punjabi company to Kuching under Lieut. Colonel C. M. Lane, who also took charge of local militia forces there.

On December 8, as Japanese bombers struck at the Philippines and Hong Kong, British orders reached Borneo calling for the demolition of the oil wells at Miri and the refinery

at Lutong. Five days later, with the installations and an airfield at Miri in ruins, the British sappers and the detachment of Punjabis left for Kuching—at the same time that a sizable Japanese task force, including troop transports, was steaming out of Camranh Bay in Indochina. The ships crossed the South China Sea and anchored off Miri just before midnight on December 15. By dawn, the Japanese were in control of the sabotaged oil field and air base.

Not until 9 o'clock that night did news of the landing reach Far East Headquarters in Singapore. For the next three days Dutch aircraft from Singkawang II bombed the task force, managing to sink a destroyer and a few landing craft.

On December 22, with the airfield at Miri once again operational, the Japanese reembarked most of their troops and headed for Kuching, 310 miles distant, leaving one battalion to hold British Borneo. A Dutch submarine attacked the task force, sinking two transports. But at dawn on the day before Christmas, most of the Japanese landing force was ashore at Kuching. Its main opposition had come from a Punjabi gun and mortar platoon that sank several landing craft before being wiped out to the last man.

By Christmas Eve the Japanese were in control of Kuching and had begun to flank Lieut. Colonel Lane's position at the airfield south of the town. While most of the force withdrew into Dutch Borneo, two companies of Punjabis fought a valiant rearguard action all Christmas Day and into the night. When the order came for them to pull out, only one platoon was able to fight its way westward and rejoin the main body. The remaining 230 men, led by four British officers, fought until their ammunition was exhausted and all were either killed or captured.

Another detachment of 180 Punjabis held a river crossing at the village of Batu until the main column—which was shepherding women, children and armed civilian volunteers—had crossed and continued westward toward Singkawang II. The Punjabis then eluded their Japanese pursuers by turning south into the jungle. Four days and 60 miles later, with little food or water, they reached the Singkawang II air base. By now Japanese landing craft were leapfrogging down the coast, and the civilian volunteers, sent ahead with the women and children, barely escaped to Java by boat ahead of Japanese troops.

The Punjabi force, much reduced and stripped of its auxiliaries, now joined with 750 Dutch colonial troops to defend the airfield and the surrounding territory. On January 26, they attacked five companies of Japanese troops approaching from the direction of Kuching. But that night a Japanese counterattack turned their flank and threatened the entire position. By the time the Dutch commander had ordered a withdrawal the next morning, it was too late: Two of the Punjabi platoons found themselves surrounded. They fought through the heat of the day, inflicting 400 to 500 casualties, and after they had fired their last rounds, they laid down their arms.

Between January 27 and early March, the remaining Punjabis retreated toward the south coast of Borneo, hoping to find ships that would evacuate them to Java, 290 miles distant. They reached the coast and found, instead of ships, Japanese waiting for them. They considered fleeing into the mountains of central Borneo for a guerrilla-style campaign, but the men were too weary and demoralized. Finally, 10 weeks and 800 miles after they had fought clear of Kuching, the last Punjabi defenders surrendered.

For the next three years Borneo served Japan as a major source of fuel for the Japanese Navy and as a concentration center for Allied prisoners. To the Allies, Borneo was a noxious blot on the charts between Singapore and the southern Philippines. Allied commanders were anxious to retake the island and deny its oil to the Japanese. The British wanted to reconquer their oil-rich colonies. The Australians believed that thousands of their troops captured at Singapore were imprisoned there. The Dutch and everyone else were worried about the fate of hundreds of stranded civilian administrators, oil-company families and missionaries.

Borneo lay too deep in Japanese territory to be assaulted until bases in the southern Philippines were available. Yet the achievement of that objective made the reconquest of Borneo unnecessary—at least from a strategic point of view. American forces in the Philippines now controlled the sea-lanes through the South China Sea, thus choking off the flow of oil for Japan's war machine. The huge island was isolated and could safely be left to wither on the vine. Besides, everyone—American, Australian, British—wanted to be in on the final drive against the home islands of Japan. No one wanted to be diverted into a costly sideshow when military glory and political benefit might be won farther north.

Nevertheless, General Douglas MacArthur, in his capacity as theater commander, ordered a full-scale Borneo campaign. The decision rested on a number of factors. MacArthur reasoned that Borneo would provide the Allies with new airfields covering Malaysia and Indochina. He also believed that Borneo would be an excellent base for Britain's Royal Navy, which was operating with increasing strength in the Pacific. And he remained concerned about the civilian internees and the Allied troops held prisoner in Japanese camps on Borneo.

But the main reason for the action was a simple matter of military make-work. As sometimes happens in war, MacArthur at the moment enjoyed a surplus of forces. The veteran Australian 7th and 9th Infantry Divisions had no current assignment; they were at rest and in the general's view they were losing their fighting edge. To keep them busy, he assigned these two outfits to sweep the Japanese from Borneo. And in spite of all protests, MacArthur had his way.

The Aussies proceeded with caution, choosing first to land teams of special agents on the island to gather intelligence for American-suported landings by the Australian 9th Division. These cloak-and-dagger teams were also to locate any prisoners of war and civilian internees.

*A Japanese antitank ditch, filled with crude oil and overhung with booby-trapped wires, guards a beach on Tarakan Island, off the northeast coast of Borneo. The Japanese garrison there intended to ignite the oil to impede an Allied invasion, but the Australians who stormed ashore in May 1945 drove the defenders inland before they could light the fire.*

Such was the mission that on March 25, 1945, sent Major Tom Harrisson and his seven intelligence men parachuting from a B-24 over a plain in the unmapped uplands of Sarawak, halfway between Brunei on the north coast and Tarakan off the east coast. Harrisson had last visited northern Borneo in 1932 as a student with an Oxford expedition in anthropology. By the time the War broke out he was established as one of Britain's leading social anthropologists.

Now Tom Harrisson was 33 years old, hardened by commando training and thoroughly pleased to be returning to Borneo, where he hoped to do some field research and bird-watching on the side. The drop into the Borneo interior had been Harrisson's idea. Australia's unconventional-warfare establishment—the Services Reconnaissance Department (Z Special)—had originally intended to land his team on the coast, but Harrisson persuaded the planners to parachute him and his men into the mountainous interior of Sarawak. He was sure that he would be able to recruit the tribesmen in the area to work against the Japanese in preparation for an Allied landing on Borneo. If all went well, Harrisson's Semut team—so called after the Malay name for a fierce species of ant—would be followed by others.

By a great stroke of luck, Harrisson happened to land in a swampy area less than a mile from a village of the Kelabit tribe, a proud and warlike people who had no love for the invading Japanese. The Kelabit headman was named Lawai Bisarai, and he was one of the few people in upland Borneo who could speak a little Malay, the lingua franca of the Borneo coast and much of the Dutch East Indies. Lawai welcomed Harrisson, his deputy, Captain Eric Edmeades, and the other six men. By nightfall they had rounded up their air-dropped gear and had crowded with 500 tribespeople into the village long house—the huge communal home in which all members of a village lived—for a ceremonial drinking session in which each had several cups of *borak,* the potent local beverage made from fermented rice.

Thanks to the major's crown on his cap, his team's seemingly miraculous descent and their treasures of arms and gold sovereigns—which the Kelabits coveted as tooth caps rather than currency—Harrisson was hailed as the "Raja from Above," instantly acquiring all the fealty normally accorded the absent Sultan of Sarawak.

One of Harrisson's first tasks was to reconnoiter Brunei

Bay on the northwest coast of the islands; the place was likely to be one of the primary landing sites in the Allied invasion, and the planners badly needed information on the Japanese defenses.

News of Harrisson's team quickly passed by word of mouth from tribe to tribe all the way to the coast—though not to the Japanese. Soon emissaries from many of the tribes of northern Borneo were arriving, swearing fealty and clamoring for something to do against the hated Japanese occupiers. "By the end of the third week," recalled Harrisson, "something like 100,000 people had voluntarily become involved in following, to some extent, Semut."

Harrisson quickly put them to work gathering intelligence and harassing Japanese patrols and outposts. The major's reports of his success fetched two more Semut teams. Soon, Z Special decided to enlarge the eight-man teams, using Australian Army commandos. As each newcomer parachuted in, he began Harrisson's graduate course—which began with a thorough grounding in local tribal customs and at least a nodding acquaintance with a tribal language. Then he would be sent off with 15 to 25 local men to test his skills on a grueling two- to four-week walkabout in the mountains, after which Harrisson would shake his hand and dispatch him to command an area of 100 or so square miles.

*Guerrilla fighter Negri Besar, a ranking member of the Kelabit tribe on Borneo, proudly displays his army shoes beside his sarong-clad Australian commander, Major Tom Harrisson. Like everyone else in the jungle interior of the island, Negri had gone about barefooted until Australian supply planes dropped 1,000 size-10 shoes on the guerrilla camp.*

The leaders of the Semut teams were, like Harrisson, hand-picked men with civilian or military experience in the southwest Pacific, trained in behind-the-lines intelligence and guerrilla operations by the Special Operations Executive (SOE), Britain's cloak-and-dagger branch of the services. Eric Edmeades, Harrisson's second-in-command, was typical of these resolute individualists. Harrisson later wrote of him: "He believed in toughness for its own sake; he took risks for fun; he looked nice, blond, clear-eyed, strong chinned, fine shouldered, most athletic; he was not primarily interested in ideas or principles, yet had a firm moral base from missionary parents in India." A New Zealander, Edmeades was a senior instructor in the tough Australian Parachute School and had made more jumps than anyone else in the country. "He literally did not accept the word impossible. Whatever he did, he did twice as fast and well as could be expected."

Major William Sochon, who headed Semut III, had been a police officer in the government of Sarawak before the War. Middle-aged and overweight, he nevertheless survived his jump into Borneo and went on to command a band of piratical Dayaks, a tribe whose fierceness gave rise to the term "wild men of Borneo," and to win a Distinguished Service Order.

New Zealander Toby Carter, head of Semut II, also had firsthand knowledge of Borneo: Carter had been an oil-company surveyor there before the War and quickly proved invaluable, guarding Harrisson's western flank and organizing the tough Kenyah tribe against the Japanese.

As other Semut teams arrived, an intelligence and subversion net was formed that stretched for hundreds of miles in all directions. Besides gathering information the teams rescued a number of downed Allied airmen. Some of the fliers had had a rough time. Four were survivors of an eight-man U.S. bomber crew shot down over the northwest coast in November 1944, five months earlier; the men managed to struggle eastward into friendly Kelabit country, where Harrisson's men had finally gathered them in. It was later learned that the other four crewmen, who had made for the north coast because it was nearer the Philippines, had been betrayed by a local tribe and executed by the Japanese.

Another airman was the sole survivor of a bomber that had caught fire after attacking the Japanese naval base at Labuan. After parachuting into the jungle, he lived on roots, grubs and mice until he was taken in by villagers 20 miles from Harrisson's camp in Bawang territory. When found, he was "a morass of ulcers and fantasies," said Harrisson, but in time he was nursed back to health. Soon Harrisson was caring for 13 American airmen.

In April, Harrisson put his Bawangs to work clearing an airstrip 200 miles from the coast as an emergency landing field for planes that might be forced down during bombing missions or when flying cover for the invasions scheduled to begin in May. It was slow, grueling labor; the Bawangs broke the ground with sticks, then trampled the earth with their feet to level it. To speed the work, Harrisson called in a special U.S. airdrop. "Within 48 hours," he related, "one of the long houses on the plain had been heartily dive-bombed. By good fortune nothing more than a goat was killed by the avalanche of spades, mattocks, pickaxes, hoes, rakes, graders and other things."

The Bawangs, who had been frightened by the airdrop, refused to use any of the equipment and went about finishing the airstrip without the benefit of modern technology.

It was completed just in time. On May 1 the Australian 26th Brigade stormed ashore on Tarakan Island off the northeast coast to seize the airfield there; it was supposed to serve as a base for planes that would fly cover for more important landings at Brunei Bay and Labuan in the north and Balikpapan in the south. But the airstrip had been too heavily damaged by the U.S. Navy's preliminary bombardment to be a base for bombers or fighters; Australian engineers managed to bulldoze a strip barely wide enough to handle Auster reconnaissance aircraft, which could land in 50 yards at 35 miles per hour. These nimble little planes were soon making regular runs to Harrisson's airstrip. More important, Harrisson's strip served for a while as the only landing field in Borneo available to Allied combat aircraft.

With Tarakan in Australian hands, Harrisson's men escalated their intelligence-gathering mission into subversion, sabotage and interdiction of the 3,000-man Japanese garrison forces at Labuan and Brunei Bay—target of the next landing. Surprisingly, the Japanese were still ignorant of Harrisson's force, and it was important that they remain ignorant until the very moment of the landings. Still, the Japanese could not help but be aware that the tribes around their perimeter were increasingly restive and that the flow of buffaloes, rice, tobacco, salt and laborers from the deeper interior had all but dried up.

The local procurement officer for the Japanese, a Dayak named Bigar anak Debois, coolly informed them that the supplies had been held up by floods, droughts, plagues of rats and birds, and pressing tribal ceremonials. Bigar, who happened to be Harrisson's principal supplier and contact with the coast, was quite convincing. All the same, the Japanese suspected that something was wrong and so they sent a strong force of Japanese soldiers and Javanese conscripts inland to see what they could find.

The Japanese, wearing heavy boots and loaded down with survival equipment, toiled upward over jungle tracks and pebbled streambeds, trailed constantly by Bigar's barefoot scouts of the Murut tribe, and then by Harrisson's own Kelabits. Seven days from the coast, at the steepest point of their climb, the Japanese and Javanese force was tumbled into a ravine by a volley from 300 British rifles. Not one Japanese soldier survived. The Javanese who did survive, 20 in all, eagerly joined Harrisson's band.

There were more and more recruits. A Chinese medical practitioner from Sarawak joined up, and brought 14 members of his family with him into the hills; they ran the hospital and the officers' mess at Harrisson's Bawang camp. A Dayak policeman arrived from Kuching and undertook to instruct the tribal recruits in riflery. A black-bearded, six-foot Sikh abandoned the cloth trade on the coast to indulge his passions for brandy and killing Japanese. By the summer of 1945, Harrisson's private army numbered in the thousands, and its operations were disastrous for the Japanese.

On the 10th of June, 14,000 troops of the Australian 9th Division landed on Labuan island and near Brunei town. When the 3,000 Japanese occupying the Brunei Bay area retreated into the jungle under a fierce bombardment, they found a shambles where once an efficient rear services administration had reigned. Radio operators, supply sergeants and district officers lay dead in their offices and gardens—speared, strangled or shot by Harrisson's Semuts and their fierce cohorts.

On July 1, after an enormous naval bombardment, the 21,000 men of the Australian 7th Division took the last Japanese stronghold: the town of Balikpapan on Borneo's southeastern coast.

Then came the mopping-up operations. Throughout July and August, Harrisson's men and Australian regulars pursued fugitive Japanese units through the interior. Many Japanese soldiers, overwhelmed by privation and terrorized by unseen pursuers, hanged themselves by their belts from the jungle branches. Others managed to surrender to the Australians. On September 10, almost a month after Japan's surrender, the Japanese commander on Borneo, Lieut. General Masao Baba, came out of the jungle and surrendered.

Late in October, Harrisson set out on his final official mission: to track down the last organized Japanese unit still operating in Borneo. With him was Major Rex Blow, one of the few Australian officers ever to escape a Japanese prison camp, and an assortment of Kelabits, Muruts and Dayaks. They took a week to locate the Japanese—several hundred men under the command of a captain named Fujino.

The two forces collided just as the Japanese emerged on an upland plain in Sarawak, and for two days a deadly scrimmage rolled over the plain and its jungle fringes. Finally Fujino assembled his battered unit at the center of the plain. At Harrisson's side, a captive Japanese officer wigwagged a request for a parley. The firing ceased and the interpreter went forward under a huge bed-sheet flag. In an hour, the last formal surrender on Borneo had taken place. It was October 29, 1945.

昭和二十年六月三十日

宮地隊、據点に向つて湿地を前進す。

（於「タラカン」島）

# LAST STAND ON TARAKAN

*Fleeing Australian invaders in June 1945, Japanese troops on Tarakan Island, just off Borneo, retreat into the jungle interior in this watercolor by a defender.*

# THE ISLAND OF THE DOOMED

A map drawn by Lieutenant Takashi Miyachi shows the natural and man-made features of Tarakan. Roads are represented with black lines, oil fields with triangles and the island's airstrip with a rectangular box. Purple ovals, some of them numbered, locate Japanese base camps, while the island's high points are marked in meters with black numerals. Pink arrows indicate the offshore positions of the Allied invasion fleet; the one at left shows the May 1, 1945, landing site of the Australian troops.

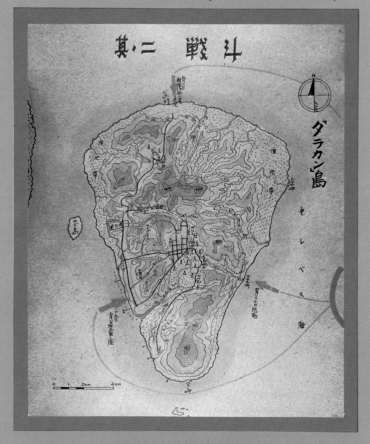

On the morning of January 1, 1945, members of the Japanese defense force stationed on Tarakan Island, just off the northeast coast of Borneo, assembled at a small shrine to celebrate their biggest national holiday. After a few minutes, the gathering was interrupted by the wail of warning sirens and the drone of enemy bombers. "An air raid on New Year's Day was not a good omen," wrote Lieutenant Takashi Miyachi. The 33-year-old communications officer, who later painted the watercolor scenes shown on these pages, added: "I wondered under what circumstances I would be celebrating the next New Year's Day. Would I be around to celebrate it at all?"

There seemed to be no hope for Tarakan's 2,173 defenders. They were virtually cut off from the homeland by the Allies' mastery of the air and sea. Yet the island, which Japan had seized from the Dutch in 1942, was so rich in oil that it could not be abandoned, as lesser conquests had been. Miyachi and the others were somehow expected to hold Tarakan against Allied attack.

The Japanese worked on, preparing for a showdown. They seeded the most likely invasion beach, Lingkas on the west coast, with mines and explosive charges. They prepared fallback bases deep in the jungle and tucked gun pits into craggy hillsides.

All this hard labor went to waste. Month after month, Allied planes bombed the little island at will, destroying defenses and oil tanks. At last, an Allied naval force gathered offshore, and on May 1 a brigade of the Australian 9th Division stormed ashore at Lingkas in the van of a 17,000-man invasion force.

The defenders were doomed from the start by the enemy's overwhelming strength and their own insurmountable shortages of artillery, ammunition and food. Within a week they had fought for—and lost—the airstrip, Tarakan's only town and a good portion of the precious oil fields. Those troops who survived continued the fight as jungle guerrillas with only one hope: to die honorably in battle as every Japanese soldier should.

昭和十九年十二月九日夜明
「タラカン」島は眼前にあり

Under a spreading pall of smoke, vessels bearing Lieutenant Miyachi's
unit approach Tarakan in December 1944. The smoke is rising from one of
the island's oil fields; the damage was inflicted by Allied bombing,
a constant fact of life for the Japanese in the latter months of the War.

昭和二十年一月元旦
大隊長タラカン神社に参拝す

Greeting a peaceful dawn a few months before
the Allied invasion, Lieutenant Miyachi
(left) and his superior, Major Tadao Tokoi,
pay their respects at a Shinto shrine.

Major Tokoi climbs into his staff car to
supervise the construction of the island's
defenses. Because Tarakan had no refinery and
there was not much gasoline available,
Tokoi used his automobile only as a symbol
of authority: He motored grandly among
the workers—and walked everywhere else.

昭和二十年三月
大隊長築城視察に出發す

The modest timber homes of oil-field
workers and merchants nestle in the island's
central river valley. Most of the workers
were Malayans who had been hired by Dutch
petroleum companies before the War.

A Malayan family strolls down a street in the
oil-field workers' village. The narrow trench
running the length of the street and spanned
by a footbridge is an open drainage ditch.

Japanese defenders duck artillery fire behind their palm-shrouded bunker during the Allied assault on Lingkas beach. The large square object at right is a monument to Japanese soldiers killed in the 1942 seizure of Tarakan; the elongated brownish objects near the shoreline are oil-storage tanks.

## "THE HONORABLE ENEMY IS HERE"

On the 27th of April a message was passed along from one Japanese unit to the next: "Finally *teki-san*"—the honorable enemy —"is here." Lookouts had counted some 150 Allied warships and landing craft closing in on Tarakan.

The heavy Allied aerial attacks of the past months paled in comparison with the thunderous preinvasion bombardment. Allied artillery emplaced on a tiny island just to the west blasted away at the Japanese positions; American and Australian cruisers and destroyers lobbed thousands of shells ashore. An endless chain of explosions "shook the core of the earth," Miyachi said, "showered us with blinding dust and changed the shape of the land."

Australian sappers led the way ashore, clearing mines from the beach; then came infantry units and dozens of tanks that provided covering fire. Swarms of planes swooped down to strafe and bomb Japanese units occupying prepared positions in the nearby hills.

The defenders fought with almost suicidal courage. "Our grenades were used up in no time," Miyachi wrote, "so we picked up grenades the enemy tossed and threw them back just before they exploded."

But the struggle decimated the Japanese. On June 13 their headquarters dispatched a terse cable to the high command: "The defending force no longer has ammunition, medicine or food. We are moving out of our besieged base and will engage in guerrilla war."

Japanese troops destroy the island's oil rigs rather than lose them intact to the Australians. Tarakan's oil fields had been seeded with demolition charges before the invasion began.

Smoke and flame billow up from a Japanese recreation building in the center of the island as low-flying B-24 bombers pass overhead. Senior Naval officers lived in the building at left.

## MAKESHIFTS TO MEET WORSENING SHORTAGES

Before the Allied invasion, the Japanese had bemoaned their shortages of material and their dwindling food supply. They had not seen a supply ship since December 1944; by the spring of 1945, they had been reduced to living off the land and building their defenses with odds and ends. Just as they had concluded that their plight could not be worse, the Australians came ashore, muscled them into the jungle interior and made the critical shortages even more desperate.

The survivors, scattered in small bands throughout the jungle, faced famine. If they were fortunate enough, they might spot their day's meal skittering across the ground in front of them. Miyachi and his group ate roasted snakes, rats and monkeys with gusto. Certain varieties of lizard tasted something like chicken.

Hunger drove the jungle fighters to risk their lives. They sneaked into Australian-held areas to retrieve underground caches of rice—only to find that the warm, wet soil had rotted the grain, turning it into powder. "When it was mixed with water, flattened into pancakes and cooked," Miyachi wrote, "it was sufficient to satisfy our empty stomachs."

Malnutrition took a heavy toll. More and more of the men succumbed to beriberi and dysentery. "Some men were losing their hearing," wrote Miyachi, "and some couldn't lift their feet. Our skin was turning the color of earth."

*Returning from a successful supply raid on enemy-held territory, Japanese soldiers tote sacks of rice back to their jungle encampment. Their unit leader, enfeebled by weeks of privation, uses a walking stick for support.*

昭
和
二
十
年
三
月
中
旬

マ
ル
海
岸
に
於
け
る
札
本
隊
の
地
曳
網

*Stripped to loincloths in the oppressive heat, soldiers haul in a fish net fashioned from hemp growing wild on the island. Fishing, Miyachi recalled, "provided us with a few enjoyable moments in an otherwise cheerless life."*

*A Japanese soldier cuts down a palm to get its edible heart. Miyachi reported that each tree provided just one day's food for one man.*

昭和二十年五月
擔架隊重傷者を後廊病舍に後送す

A Japanese soldier wounded by a mortar shell is carried to refuge in the Tarakan jungle. Battle casualties received only solace and shelter; medical supplies were unobtainable.

昭和二十年七月末
宮地隊藤泉宿舍

A crude lean-to—branches lashed with vines and covered with palm fronds—serves as shelter for Miyachi's five-man squad. At night, by the glow of improvised oil lamps, the men forgot their hardships by playing cards.

Japanese troops and civilian oil drillers
dig a shoulder-deep tank trap to block one of
Tarakan's few roads. The workers, idled
by Allied bombing raids on the oil fields, were
enlisted to help the shorthanded defenders.

Inching cautiously across a bridge of logs,
two Japanese soldiers transport a bulky aerial
bomb suspended from a carrying pole. All
remaining bombs and artillery shells
were parceled out and planted as mines.

Crouching in a hilltop gun pit, a Japanese gun crew fires at B-25 bombers. As the enemy closed in, aircraft gunners were told to abandon their positions. Then, Miyachi wrote, ''enemy planes had our sky to themselves.''

The island's airfield, seized by Australian troops in early May, is rocked by artillery shells in a daring Japanese night raid. Lacking guns to fire the rounds, the raiders modified the fuses, lighted them with matches and—after slipping past enemy sentries— heaved the shells onto the field by hand.

A Naval officer leads his men, armed only with swords, a rifle and a machine gun, in an attack on Allied tanks. About 10 of the Japanese lost their lives in this futile action.

A 350-pound aerial bomb, buried as a mine by the Japanese, wrecks an Australian tank (and, in a realistic touch by Miyachi, shakes the leaves off a tree). This was the only enemy armored vehicle destroyed by the defenders.

昭和二十年六月四日
タラカン島、一〇二高地附近ノ戦斗
敵火焔放射器ヲ以テ我攻撃ス。

*In one of the last actions of the fighting
on Tarakan, Hill 102 is set ablaze by enemy
flamethrowers. The Allies struck the area
after hearing of a Japanese encampment there.*

昭和二十年六月下旬
筏を組んで島外に脱出する者あり

## A FORLORN END
## TO THE ORDEAL

In midsummer of 1945, while Miyachi and his men were encamped on a jungled hill above the island's little town, they learned that some sailors nearby were constructing rafts for an escape attempt. Their plan—tried by others before with unknown results—was to drift five miles west to a part of Borneo where they believed they would have a better chance for survival.

On the appointed night, the men stole down to a channel on the island's west coast. They boarded rafts, rode the tide out to open water—and ran into an Australian patrol boat. Faced with certain capture, the men used their last hand grenades to blow themselves up. Only one survivor was picked up by the Australians.

Miyachi's ordeal soon ended. One day in mid-August he was puzzled to hear the sound of festive music and firecrackers drifting up from the town. Creeping down from his forest hide-out, he came upon a red-bordered notice of Japan's surrender, effective August 15. It was written in Japanese and bore the name of the local Australian commander. "In the last few days," read the note, "your fellow men, wearing Australian uniforms and white arm bands, have been looking for you."

Some of the soldiers suspected an enemy trick. But after examining the note, Miyachi decided that it was genuine and had not been written under duress. He assembled 10 men from his sector, led them into town and surrendered. Throughout the island, other groups of survivors were filtering in from the jungle. Eventually, 576 Japanese—less than 30 per cent of the original garrison—turned themselves over to the Australians.

Under cover of darkness, three raftloads of Japanese Navy men launch a bold attempt to flee to Borneo. For flotation, would-be escapees lashed empty oil drums to their craft.

# BIBLIOGRAPHY

Atwood, George H., *Along the Alcan.* Pageant Press, 1960.

Aye, Lillian, *Iran Caboose.* House-Warven, 1951.

Balchen, Bernt, et al., *War below Zero.* Houghton Mifflin, 1944.

Banani, Amin, *The Modernization of Iran, 1921-1941.* Stanford University Press, 1961.

*The Battle of Midway, including the Aleutian Phase, June 3 to June 14, 1942: Strategical and Tactical Analysis.* United States Naval War College, 1948.

Botting, Douglas, *Island of the Dragon's Blood.* Wilfred Funk, 1958.

Bowman, Waldo G., et al., *Bulldozers Come First: The Story of U.S. War Construction in Foreign Lands.* McGraw-Hill, 1944.

Broadfoot, Barry, *Six War Years, 1939-1945: Memories of Canadians at Home and Abroad.* Doubleday, 1974.

Buckley, Christopher, *The Second World War, 1939-1945, Five Ventures: Iraq-Syria-Persia-Madagascar-Dodecanese.* London: Her Majesty's Stationery Office, 1954.

Buggy, Hugh, *Pacific Victory.* North Melbourne: Issued by the Australian Minister for Information, the Hon. A. A. Calwell, M.H.R., no date.

Bykofsky, Joseph, and Harold Larson, *United States Army in World War II, The Technical Services, The Transportation Corps: Operations Overseas.* Office of the Chief of Military History, Department of the Army, 1957.

Callinan, Bernard J., *Independent Company—The 2/2 and 2/4 Australian Independent Companies in Portuguese Timor, 1941-1943.* London: William Heinemann, Ltd., 1953.

Calvocoressi, Peter, and Guy Wint, *Total War: The Story of World War II.* Pantheon Books, 1972.

Churchill, Winston S., *The Second World War:*
Vol. 2, *Their Finest Hour.* Houghton Mifflin, 1949.
Vol. 3, *The Grand Alliance.* Houghton Mifflin, 1950.
Vol. 4, *The Hinge of Fate.* Houghton Mifflin, 1950.

Churchill, Winston S., *Winston S. Churchill: His Complete Speeches, 1897-1963,* Vol. 6. Ed. by Robert Rhodes James. Chelsea House, 1974.

Conn, Stetson, and Byron Fairchild, *United States Army in World War II, The Western Hemisphere, The Framework of Hemisphere Defense.* Office of the Chief of Military History, Department of the Army, 1960.

Conn, Stetson, et al., *United States Army in World War II, The Western Hemisphere, Guarding the United States and Its Outposts.* Office of the Chief of Military History, Department of the Army, 1964.

Connell, John, *Wavell: Scholar and Soldier (To June 1941).* London: Collins, 1964.

Craven, Wesley Frank, and James Lea Cate, eds. *The Army Air Forces in World War II:*
Vol. 1, *Plans and Early Operations, January 1939 to August 1942.* University of Chicago Press, 1948.
Vol. 4, *The Pacific: Guadalcanal to Saipan, August 1942 to July 1944.* University of Chicago Press, 1953.
Vol. 7, *Services around the World.* University of Chicago Press, 1958.

Croft-Cooke, Rupert, *The Blood-Red Island.* Staples Press, 1953.

De Chair, Somerset, *The Golden Carpet.* Harcourt, Brace and Company, 1945.

De Gaulle, Charles, *The Complete War Memoirs of Charles De Gaulle.* 3 vols. Simon and Schuster, 1972.

De Gaury, Gerald, *Three Kings in Baghdad, 1921-1958.* London: Hutchinson, 1961.

Dod, Karl C., *United States Army in World War II, The Technical Services, The Corps of Engineers: The War Against Japan.* Office of the Chief of Military History, United States Army, 1966.

Driscoll, Joseph, *War Discovers Alaska.* J. B. Lippincott, 1944.

Dudgeon, Peter, *The Defence of Habbaniya and the Subsequent Air Operations during the Iraqui Rebellion—May, 1941.* Document in the British Imperial War Museum, no date.

Feis, Herbert, *Churchill, Roosevelt, Stalin: The War They Waged and the Peace They Sought.* Princeton University Press, 1957.

Feldt, Eric A., *The Coastwatchers.* London: Oxford University Press, 1946.

Ford, Corey, *Short Cut to Tokyo: The Battle for the Aleutians.* Charles Scribner's Sons, 1943.

Gandar Dower, K. C., *Into Madagascar.* Penguin Books, 1943.

Garfield, Brian, *The Thousand-Mile War: World War II in Alaska and the Aleutians.* Ballantine Books, 1969.

Gilman, William, *Our Hidden Front.* Reynal & Hitchcock, 1944.

Glubb, Sir John Bagot:
*Britain and the Arabs: A Study of Fifty Years, 1908 to 1958.* London: Hodder and Stoughton, 1959.
*The Story of the Arab Legion.* Da Capo Press, 1976.

Goodhart, Philip, *Fifty Ships That Saved the World.* Doubleday, 1965.

Great Britain, Central Office of Information, *Paiforce: The Official Story of the Persia and Iraq Command, 1941-1946.* London: His Majesty's Stationery Office, 1948.

Handleman, Howard, *Bridge to Victory: The Story of the Reconquest of the Aleutians.* Random House, 1943.

Harrisson, Tom, *World Within: A Borneo Story.* London: Cresset Press, 1959.

Heseltine, Nigel, *Madagascar.* Praeger Publishers, 1971.

Hinsley, F. H., *British Intelligence in the Second World War: Its Influence on Strategy and Operations,* Vol. 1. London: Her Majesty's Stationery Office, 1979.

Horton, D. C., *Fire over the Islands: The Coast Watchers of the Solomons.* Sydney: A. H. & A. W. Reed, 1970.

Howarth, David, *The Sledge Patrol.* Macmillan, 1957.

Jones, Robert Huhn, *The Roads to Russia: United States Lend-Lease to the Soviet Union.* University of Oklahoma Press, 1969.

Karig, Walter, and Eric Purdon, *Battle Report, Pacific War: Middle Phase.* Rinehart and Company, 1947.

Khadduri, Majid, *Independent Iraq, 1932-1958.* London: Oxford University Press, 1960.

Kirby, S. Woodburn, *The War Against Japan:*
Vol. 1, *The Loss of Singapore.* London: Her Majesty's Stationery Office, 1957.
Vol. 2, *India's Most Dangerous Hour.* London: Her Majesty's Stationery Office, 1958.
Vol. 5, *The Surrender of Japan.* London: Her Majesty's Stationery Office, 1969.

La Farge, Oliver, *The Eagle in the Egg.* Houghton Mifflin, 1949.

Langer, William L., and S. Everett Gleason, *The Undeclared War, 1940-1941.* Peter Smith, 1968.

Lenczowski, George, *Russia and the West in Iran, 1918-1948.* Cornell University Press, 1949.

Lewin, Ronald, *Slim the Standardbearer.* London: Leo Cooper, 1976.

Lias, Godfrey, *Glubb's Legion.* London: Evans Brothers Ltd., 1956.

Liversidge, Douglas, *The Third Front: The Strange Story of the Secret War in the Arctic.* London: Souvenir Press Ltd., 1960.

Long, Gavin, *The Final Campaigns.* Canberra: Australian War Memorial, 1963.

Lord, Walter:
*Incredible Victory.* Harper & Row, 1967.
*Lonely Vigil: Coastwatchers of the Solomons.* Viking Press, 1977.

McCarthy, Dudley, *South-West Pacific Area—First Year: Kokoda to Wau.* Canberra: Australian War Memorial, 1959.

Matloff, Maurice, and Edwin M. Snell, *United States Army in World War II, The War Department: Strategic Planning for Coalition Warfare, 1941-1942.* Office of the Chief of Military History, Department of the Army, 1953.

Miyachi, Takashi, *Tarakanto Funsenki.* Tokyo: private printing, 1968.

Mockler, Anthony, *Our Enemies the French: Being an Account of the War Fought between the French and the British, Syria 1941.* London: Leo Cooper, 1976.

Moorehead, Alan, *Mediterranean Front.* McGraw-Hill, 1942.

Morgan, Murray, *Bridge to Russia: Those Amazing Aleutians.* E. P. Dutton, 1947.

Morison, Samuel Eliot, *History of United States Naval Operations in World War II:*
Vol. 4, *Coral Sea, Midway and Submarine Actions, May 1942—August 1942.* Little, Brown, 1949.
Vol. 7, *Aleutians, Gilberts and Marshalls, June 1942—April 1944.* Little, Brown, 1951.
Vol. 8, *New Guinea and the Marianas, March 1944—August 1944.* Little, Brown, 1953.

Motter, T. H. Vail, *United States Army in World War II, The Middle East Theater, The Persian Corridor and Aid to Russia.* Office of the Chief of Military History, Department of the Army, 1952.

Moyse-Bartlett, Hubert, *The King's African Rifles: A Study in the Military History of East and Central Africa, 1890-1945.* Aldershot, Northeast Hampshire, England: Gale & Polden, 1956.

Penrose, Edith and E. F., *Iraq: International Relations and National Development.* Westview Press, 1978.

Piekalkiewicz, Janusz, *Secret Agents, Spies and Saboteurs.* William Morrow & Company, 1969.

Playfair, I. S. O., *History of the Second World War, The Mediterranean and Middle East,* Vol. 2. London: Her Majesty's Stationery Office, 1956.

Remley, David A., *Crooked Road: The Story of the Alaska Highway.* McGraw-Hill, 1976.

Roskill, S. W., *The War at Sea, 1939-1945:*
Vol. 1, *The Defensive.* London: Her Majesty's Stationery Office, 1954.
Vol. 2, *The Period of Balance.* London: Her Majesty's Stationery Office, 1956.

Runciman, Steven, *The White Rajahs: A History of Sarawak from 1841 to 1946.* Cambridge at the University Press, 1960.

Saville, Allison W., "German Submarines in the Far East." *Proceedings,* U.S. Naval Institute, August, 1961.

Sayre, Joel, *Persian Gulf Command.* Random House, 1945.

Slim, Sir William, *Unofficial History.* London: Cassell, 1959.

Stettinius, Edward R., Jr., *Lend-Lease: Weapon for Victory.* Macmillan, 1944.

Stratton, Arthur, *The Great Red Island.* Charles Scribner's Sons, 1964.

Thomas, Charles W., *Ice Is Where You Find It.* Bobbs-Merrill, 1951.

Turner, L. C. F., et al., *War in the Southern Oceans, 1939-45.* London: Oxford University Press, 1961.

United States Army, Medical Department, *Neuropsychiatry in World War II,* Vol. 2, *Overseas Theaters.* Office of the Surgeon General, Department of the Army, 1973.

United States Coast Guard, Historical Section, *The U.S. Coast Guard at War: Greenland Patrol.* U.S. Coast Guard Headquarters, 1945.

United States Navy:
*The Aleutians Campaign, June 1942—August 1943.* Publications Branch, Office of Naval Intelligence, 1945.
*Building the Navy's Bases in World War II,* Vol. 2. Government Printing Office, 1947.

Vatikiotis, P. J., *Politics and the Military in Jordan: A Study of the Arab Legion, 1921-1957.* Frederick A. Praeger, 1967.

*The War Department, The Capture of Attu (As Told by the Men Who Fought There).* The Infantry Journal, no date.

Warner, Geoffrey, *Iraq and Syria, 1941.* London: Davis-Poynter, 1974.

Wheeler, Keith, *The Pacific Is My Beat.* E. P. Dutton, 1943.

Wigmore, Lionel, *The Japanese Thrust.* Canberra: Australian War Memorial, 1947.

*Yank—The Army Weekly, 1942-1945.* Arno Press, 1967.

Ziel, Ron, *Steel Rails to Victory.* Hawthorn Books, 1970.

# ACKNOWLEDGMENTS

For help given in the preparation of this book, the editors wish to express their gratitude to E.C.P. Armées, Paris; Association Rhin-Danube, Paris; Lieut. Colonel A. J. Barker, Cape Town, Republic of South Africa; John D. Barnett, Assistant Curator, Navy Combat Art Collection, Washington Navy Yard, Washington, D. C.; Dr. Fred Beck, Deputy Chief, Corps of Engineers, Historical Division, Washington, D.C.; Dana Bell, Archives Technician, U.S. Air Force Still Photo Depository, Arlington, Va.; Douglas Botting, London; Carole Boutté, Senior Researcher, U.S. Army Audio-Visual Activity, The Pentagon, Arlington, Va.; Colonel Sir Bernard Callinan, Melbourne, Australia; Professor A. E. Campbell, The University of Birmingham, Warwickshire, England; Contessa Maria-Fede Caproni, Museo Aeronautico Caproni di Taliedo, Rome; Lew Casey, Chevy Chase, Md.; Bernard Cavalcante, Operational Archives Branch, Naval Historical Center, Washington Navy Yard, Washington, D.C.; Huguette Chalufour, Archives Jules Tallandier, Paris; Terence Charman, Imperial War Museum, London; Susan L. Cooper, Washington, D.C.; Chris Cooze, Librarian, Australian Embassy, Washington, D.C.; Geertje de Bruijn, Botma, Driebergen, The Netherlands; F. de Rochemont, Indonesian Department, Netherlands State Institute for War Documentation, Amsterdam; V. M. Destefano, Chief of Reference Library, U.S. Army Audio-Visual Activity, The Pentagon, Arlington, Va.; David Dexter, Canberra, Australia; Calvin Douglas, Photo Services Coordinator, Photo Service Division, The Pentagon, Arlington, Va.; Jack Dyer, Curator of Art, Marine Corps Historical Center, Washington Navy Yard, Washington, D.C.; Hans Ebbesen, Arktisk Institut, Charlottenlund, Denmark; Florence Edgington, Picture Resources Specialist, U.S. Army Audio-Visual Activity, The Pentagon, Arlington, Va.; Jack Elliot, Contract Administrator, The Smithsonian Institution, Washington, D.C.; Cesare Falessi, Rome; Fototeca Stato Maggiore Aeronautica, Rome; Valerie France, Imperial War Museum, London; Marylou Gjernes, U.S. Army Center of Military History, Washington, D.C.; Gerard E. Hasselwander, Historian, Albert F. Simpson Historical Research Center, USAF, Maxwell Air Force Base, Montgomery, Ala.; Charles Hendricks, Historian, U.S. Army Center of Military History, Washington, D.C.; E. C. Hine, Imperial War Museum, London; Professor Robert Huhn Jones, Chairman, Department of History, The University of Akron, Akron, Ohio; Mauritz C. Kokkelink, Lelydorp, Surinam; Richard D. Kovar, Reston, Va.; Jerzy Kucharski, New York, N.Y.; William M. Mack, Information Officer, State of Alaska, Department of Military Affairs, Anchorage, Alaska; Marian McNaughton, U.S. Army Center of Military History, Washington, D.C.; Marie-Antoinette Menier, Archives de la France d'Outre-Mer, Paris; Serge Michel, Association La Rahala, Paris; J. G. Millman, Brede, Near Rye, Sussex, England; Takashi Miyachi, Musashino-shi, Tokyo; Jules Muracciole, Secrétaire Général de l'Ordre de la Libération, Musée de la Libération, Paris; Shinkichi Natori, Ebisu, Tokyo; Maurizio Pagliano, Milan; J. W. Pavey, Imperial War Museum, London; Yves Perret-Gentil, Institut d'Histoire du Temps Présent, Paris; Janusz Piekalkiewicz, Rösrath-Hoffnungsthal, Germany; Jozef Pilsudski Institute of America, New York, N.Y.; C. G. Tudor Pole, Minehead, Somerset, England; Major Ib Poulsen, Holte, Denmark; David Pryce-Jones, London; Michel Rauzier, Institut d'Histoire du Temps Présent, Paris; Sarawak Museum, Sarawak, Malaysia; Dr. Robert Scheina, Historian, U.S. Coast Guard, Washington, D.C.; Paul Scheips, U.S. Center of Military History, Washington, D.C.; Amy K. Schmidt, Alexandria, Va.; Ada Scott, Photographic Research Technician, U.S. Air Force Still Photo Depository, 1361st Audio-Visual Squadron, Arlington, Va.; L. G. P. Shiers, London; Marilyn Murphy Terrell, Alexandria, Va.; James H. Trimble, Archivist, National Archives, Still Photo Branch, Washington, D.C.; Anthony van Kampen, Bergen, The Netherlands; Professor Geoffrey Warner, The University, Leicester, England; Dr. George Watson, Ornithology, Natural History Museum, The Smithsonian Institution, Washington, D.C.; D. L. White, Bromley, Kent, England; Paul White, National Archives and Records Service, Audio-Visual Division, Washington, D.C.; Colonel Paul Willing, Curator, Musée de l'Armée, Paris; M. J. Willis, Imperial War Museum, London; Hannah Zeidlik, Office of the Chief of Military History, U.S. Army Center of Military History, Washington, D.C. The editors especially wish to acknowledge the contribution of Douglas Liversidge's *The Third Front: The Strange Story of the Secret War in the Arctic* to the preparation of this volume.

The index for this book was prepared by Nicholas J. Anthony.

Printed in U.S.A.